Schall on Chesterton

James V. Schall

Schall on Chesterton

Timely Essays on Timeless Paradoxes

The Catholic University of America Press
Washington, D.C.

The paper used in this publication meets the mini-
mum requirements of American National Standards
for Information Science—Permanence of
Paper for Printed Library materials, ANSI Z39.48-
1984.

∞

Library of Congress Cataloging-in-Publication Data

Schall, James V.

   Schall on Chesterton : timely essays on timeless
paradoxes / James V. Schall.

   p.   cm.

   Includes bibliographical references.

   1. Chesterton, G. K. (Gilbert Keith), 1874–
1936—Criticism and interpretation. 1. Title.

PR4453.C4Z76 2000

828´.91209—dc21

99-42430

   ISBN 0-8132-0963-3 (pbk. : alk. paper)

Contents

Preface

When I was in my twenties, I first encountered the writings of G. K. Chesterton. I have often been struck, on almost constant reading of him since, by the extraordinary fertility and, yes, delight of his thought and expression. Not only was he himself prolific—our library here at Georgetown lists over 700 books under his name in its files—but almost every little essay he wrote, often just any paragraph of his off-handed remarks, was somehow insightful and fruitful when I thought about it, tried to reflect on what he might have meant, even when it was obvious what he meant. Paradoxically, if I dare use that word so often used to describe Chesterton's own style, it was when Chesterton was most clear and most obvious, which he was most of the time, that he caused the most further thought and refection. Chesterton remains, even some decades after his death in 1936, one of the most quoted writers in the English language. He is always memorable, worth quoting.

Chesterton in fact possessed a singular intelligence in which everything, even the smallest remark, seemed to be related to Wisdom. He could not see something without seeing everything, yet he really saw the something, the particular, the variable, the unique. Chesterton's name is nobly and unavoidably associated with the *paradox*—"a statement or proposition seemingly self-contradictory or absurd but in reality expressing a possible truth," as my dictionary defines it. His style is "paradoxical" because it somehow contained this relationship of one thing to all things. Thus, Chesterton's philosophy, his paradoxes, were both timely—what he said could be applied almost every day—and timeless—he constantly touched the permanent things we all seek.

On the surface, this book is a book of essays each occasioned by something I read in Chesterton. Thus, it is not a biography, or specialized tract about some side or other of his thought or experience. Rather these are original essays prompted by a man who wrote in the early years of the twentieth century. Chesterton was a man whose own thought provokes, challenges ever anew because it somehow originated in that place where things themselves seem to originate. Chesterton considered himself to be, as I indicate in the longer introductory chapter, a journalist. Almost all of his work was occasioned by some deadline or some particular incident that caught his fancy, something he read or some argument or debate he was involved in. His books are mostly collections of his essays, even when they really are, like *Orthodoxy,* books.

I have heard a couple of tapes of Chesterton's voice from the Canadian Broadcasting Company in the 1930s. His voice was rather high pitched. He obviously enjoyed speaking and was fascinating to listen to. He often debated in public fora with various men of his time. His most famous debates were with George Bernard Shaw.[1] I have even heard staged debates between Chesterton and his adversaries put on as dramas. For an evening of wit and profundity, nothing quite matches Chesterton and his friend Hilaire Belloc laughing, arguing, singing, proposing, or concluding. Belloc once quipped that "he who has the faith has the fun" and there is no doubt that these two men had both the faith and the fun, even though each lived rather poignant lives—something we all expect if the faith be true.[2]

The immediate occasion that began the writing of these short essays on Chesterton was provided by John Peterson and *The Midwest Chesterton News.* The Midwest Chesterton Society has an annual conference in Milwaukee to which I was once invited. At that time, Peterson was just beginning his very lively *Newsletter.* I proposed to Peterson to write a monthly column, something that would give me a chance regularly to reflect in print on Chesterton. Denise Bartlett, who had helped so much with a couple of Chesterton conferences that we ran here at Georgetown in conjunction with George Marlin, the general editor of Ignatius Press's *Collected Works,* further suggested that I keep in mind a book on Chesterton that would contain these essays.

The title of the column and of this book, *Schall on Chesterton,* was designed to state directly what I was doing. I was not merely repeating or reprinting or paraphrasing Chesterton, nor was I simply offering my own random thoughts. Rather, I was reflecting "on Chesterton," to allow Chesterton to let me think, because I always find in him an extraordinary richness and fertility of ideas that need or rather kindle further thought, provoke the wonder about truth and about how this man who was Chesterton was so remarkably fruitful in his thought, so remarkably true in his insights. Even though he wrote some six to eight decades before I did, what he said illuminates my time and my thoughts about my era, because Chesterton understood both our times and the reality itself of any time. He remains something of a mystery to me, because he has taught me, has been one of my principal teachers, even though I never met him and was only a boy of eight when he died.[3]

My point of view here, and what is perhaps unique about this book, following Chesterton and Belloc themselves, appears through the brief essay. I have argued, in my *Idylls and Rambles,* that the short, often lightsome essay, is one of the greatest of literary and philosophical tools or intellectual products of our kind.[4] The essay is, no doubt, what Chesterton wrote most and loved best. His books are usually collections of his essays; yet one finds that his books are likewise sustained arguments. His great works, *Heretics, Orthodoxy, What's Wrong with the World,* and *Everlasting Man,* even his biographies of Dickens, Stevenson, Shaw, or Chaucer, are largely composed of shorter essays that can be easily detached and read independently of the whole, yet are at the same time intrinsic to the whole. Everything fits tightly together.

Chesterton's books, when they are not in fact collections of essays, always remain coherent wholes. Every Chesterton essay, in fact, fits into the comprehensive intellectual unity that was his life. In some sense, Chesterton stands for the intelligible unity of all things. He sees the parts in the whole and the whole in the parts. His essays and his books, his plays and his poems, are all manifestations of this unity found in the immense diversity of things. This striking coherence lies behind the surprise and astonishment we always discover when reading Chesterton. Chesterton loved reality in all its particularity almost as if he saw it coming fresh from the hands of the Creator on the First Day.

I propose these essays, moreover, as teaching tools, if that is not too pedestrian a phrase for what I mean. That is to say, reading Chesterton, reflecting on his thought, is itself a most profound experience whereby we can reach the truth, the being, the order of things. There is, in my experience, something rather uncanny about Chesterton. As I point out often, he could foresee early in the twentieth century what would in all likelihood happen later, at its end and into the twenty-first century, because he understood what ideas meant and where they would in all probability take us when followed, both for good and for ill. For any one seriously concerned with the truth, *Orthodoxy,* written in 1908, is still the best and most profound book of the twentieth century, a remarkable preparation for the twenty-first century.

Each of these essays contains its own internal order, an order that has its origin in Chesterton himself when he made his own argument. Often an essay is based on a chapter in one of Chesterton's books, or on one or two of his essays in the *Illustrated London News,* something I would chance upon. Sometimes they are occasioned by something I read about Chesterton, or about some phrases that others cited from him. In all cases, there is an argument and unity that is mine and not Chesterton's. Figuring out for myself what he said, based on my experience, on what I know, in my time and place, led me to see more profoundly what he meant, what could be seen in the far reaches of his insight. I have been puzzled about the order in which to present these essays. I was tempted simply to imitate the Ignatius Press *Illustrated London News* collections of Chesterton's own essays and follow the chronological order in which these essays appeared. There is good reason for this procedure, because succeeding essays often relate to one another.

The choice of essays here is designed to show how I have learned to read Chesterton and to reflect on him. However, in the end, this collection contains essays that I have liked, that I thought fit together, that cover the variety of thought, mood, and inspiration to which the reading of Gilbert Chesterton has led me. If nothing else, I think, they simply reveal the fertility of Chesterton, of reading Chesterton, who remains both a delight and a teacher of truth. This book is first itself, my reasoned consideration of what Chesterton has taught me and, secondly, a reminder to the reader that Chesterton is too good to miss, which is, indeed, his paradox about life itself.

Some decade after I began these essays, however, I realize that there is no limit to the wisdom found in Chesterton, to the wisdom or to the delight. I often stress delight in reading Chesterton. Yet, there is an underlying seriousness to him. He was evidently a man of immense courtesy. He seems to have been loved by everyone who knew him, even those who most clearly disagreed with him. He must have been formidable to debate and to confront intellectually, as he saw so quickly where one's argument went and what it meant. I have often suspected that those who disagreed with him on fundamental things never really grasped how thoroughly he reduced their arguments to principle and found their error and what it meant. He had the extraordinary capacity to show how Christianity in particular made sense and how it was anything but grounded in irrationalism.

Stanley Jaki has written a useful book pointing out how clearly Chesterton understood the issues of modern science and its aberrations.[5] Etienne Gilson confessed that he was astonished that Chesterton could have written such an extraordinarily good book on Thomas Aquinas. Few have written better on Dickens than Chesterton. One of my students, to whom I had suggested reading Chesterton's book on Francis of Assisi, told me that a professor would not allow the book to be used in a paper. I asked him if he had read the book himself. He said he had. I asked him if he thought it a good book. He did. I told him that now he knew why he had to take what his professors told him very critically. In the end, I told him, "Let Chesterton, not your professor, be your teacher." Students, I have found, are simply taken aback, then charmed by Chesterton. No one tells them the things Chesterton does, certainly no one tells them in the way he does. Chesterton, I think, gives all modernity a bad conscience, because it is clear he knew what it was about and why many of its basic propositions did not hold. He knew such things in his own gentle, bemused way, a way that left no alternative to his logic but to refuse to think at all. Chesterton was not a mere lover of the past. He was a democrat and thought we all should own our own home and property.

So these are my essays on Chesterton, *Schall on Chesterton*. Somewhere, in *Orthodoxy*, I think, Chesterton has a quip about a gentleman who wrote a book called "Grant Allen on God." Chesterton remarked that he would be much more interested in a book called "God on Grant Allen." On the basis of this analogy, I would not be at all displeased if someone went to Chesterton himself rather than to Schall on Chesterton. I know that from Chesterton one gets to about everything important and unimportant. This reminds me of Chesterton's comment in his book

St. Thomas Aquinas, a truly amazing book, as Gilson said, that St. Thomas was interested in the multiplicity and particularity of things, tiny things and big things, things that were not God, but things that did not explain themselves either. If I can get someone to Chesterton, Chesterton will get him to everything else.

On the other hand, it is not my intention here merely to write a guide book to Chesterton. Each of these essays will reflect on a topic that a human being ought to think about, ought to have considered in one way or another. That Chesterton is my guide, let there be no doubt. But Chesterton himself, like the great thinkers he is so much like (I mean Aristotle and Aquinas and Samuel Johnson), does not lead the reader to himself. He leads him to the truth, to *what is.* This is what I seek to show in each of these particular essays, no matter what era of Chesterton's thought they might have come from. I found Chesterton as sane in 1905 when he first began to publish as in 1935, just before he died. I confess that I see little evolution of doctrine in Chesterton. Even though he came into the Church in the 1920s, one is hard pressed to know why he was not in it in 1908 when he wrote *Orthodoxy.* This is not to say that he did not learn anything as he grew older, but what he learned was information, not principle.

Let me say one final thing about these essays. I almost never knew, when I sat down to write them, what I was going to write about. They usually arose from something that I just picked up and began thumbing through. I began to realize that Chesterton was simply alive with thought, that he was amazingly coherent. Once I had begun on a line of thought that he had somehow suggested to me, it was impossible not to continue, to complete the thought in my own fashion. These essays are, in this sense, my essays, not Chesterton's. All good teachers, even ones that we have never met, lead us not to themselves but to the truth, to *what is.* Chesterton never failed to do this. I realize, now that I am older, that I shall simply never have the time to read and fathom all that is in Plato, Aristotle, Augustine, Aquinas, Johnson, or Chesterton. It cannot be done. And yet, one has the uncanny impression with all of these writers, Chesterton included, that everything that they knew and wanted us to know was somehow contained in a mere fragment of their work. Almost any essay in Chesterton's early 1905 book *The Defendant* contains everything he stood for.

The "outline of sanity," to quote the title of one of Chesterton's later books, was already there in all its glory in all he did and wrote. The words sanity and common sense are often applied to Aristotle, Aquinas, Johnson, and Chesterton. They are the right words. This sense of enormous sanity, of enormous common sense, was always found in Chesterton. I do not know, in conclusion, whether Aristotle was a very huge man, but evidently Aquinas, Johnson, and Chesterton were, almost as if they had to be huge men to contain their huge sanity.

Acknowledgments

The essays in this book were originally published in the *Midwest Chesterton News.* I wish to thank Mr. John Peterson, editor of the *Midwest Chesterton News,* for permission to collect them here in this volume. The Introduction, "G. K. Chesterton, Journalist," originally appeared in a shortened form in the *The Chesterton Review* XX (February 1994), 55–64. I wish to thank Father Ian Boyd, C.S.B., editor of *The Chesterton Review*, for permission to use this article. The Epilogue, "On the Enemies of the Man Who Had No Enemies," was published in *Vital Speeches* LXIV (July 15, 1998), 590–95, for the use of which I wish to thank the publisher, Mrs. Genevieve T. Daly.

Schall on Chesterton

Introduction

G. K. Chesterton, Journalist

And among many more abject reasons for not being able to be a novelist, is the
fact that I always have been and presumably always shall be a journalist.

G. K. Chesterton, *The Autobiography*.[1]

I

Peter Milward, in an essay in *The Chesterton Review,* has speculated on the problem that an unsuspecting cataloguer at some famous library might have in first confronting the works of Chesterton. How would they be identified? Works in literature? in
theology? in philosophy? in poetry? in detective stories? in humor? in science? in literary criticism? in politics? in English literature? in apologetics? in economics? in history? in biography? in
travel?[2] Yet, we know that Chesterton, when it came to identify-
ing what he thought himself to be, called himself simply a "journalist." Needless to say, we would be more than a little surprised
to find *Orthodoxy* or *The Man Who Was Thursday* or *What's Wrong*
with the World listed under "journalism" in any library. And we
would expect *Heretics* to be listed under, well what? Almost anything but theology!

At the same time, of course, we would be even more than
amused to discover that this Englishman who identified himself
as simply a journalist did not think that we could find much
truth in a newspaper, or that the "daily" papers had anything
much to do with what was actually going on that day. "The plain
truth is that, from official journalism, we cannot get the plain
truth," Chesterton quipped on May 16, 1914. "The daily paper is
a rich and suggestive document: personally, I love reading the day

before yesterday's daily paper. Some of the finest fun and wisdom in the world can be found buried in the files of old newspapers. But the daily paper is never daily. The daily paper is never up-to-date."[3] The minds of those who owned and wrote in the papers were conditioned by an earlier era and could never quite distinguish what was really going on.

In his *Autobiography,* Chesterton admitted that "the profound problem of how I ever managed to fall on my feet in Fleet Street is a mystery; at least it is still a mystery to me."[4] This "mystery," as he called it, however, did not prevent Chesterton from explaining his success as a journalist on this same Fleet Street. He continued: "I think I owed my success (as the millionaires say) to having listened respectfully and rather bashfully to the very best advice, given by all the best journalists who had achieved the best sort of success in journalism; and then going away and doing the exact opposite."[5] In pursuing this contrary approach, he continued, "I think I became a sort of comic success by contrast." There is, I think, in Chesterton's journalism a kind of metaphysical humor, yes a kind of divine comedy that explains the abiding attraction of his "comic success."

The "advice" that Chesterton would give to budding journalists, moreover, was that they should write two articles, one for the *Sporting Times* and one for the *Church Times,* and then proceed to put them in the "wrong envelopes." Subsequently, if these articles were reasonably intelligent and finally accepted, the sporting men would go about happily calling to each other across the greens or courts, "'Great mistake to suppose there isn't a good case for us; really brainy fellows say so.'" And likewise the clergymen would go about congratulating each other, "'Rattling good writing on some of our religious papers; very witty fellow.'"[6] Chesterton realized that the truth ever lies in something more than mere specialization, including theological specialization.

Chesterton, of course, was amused enough to call this unique hypothesis "a little faint and fantastic as a theory; but it is the only theory upon which I can explain my own undeserved survival in the journalistic squabble of the old Fleet Street."[7] As a result, Chesterton had the freedom to address various fora that had never heard of what he was talking about. In the old Nonconformist *Daily News,* for which he wrote a column from January 6, 1901, to February 1, 1913, he could tell the readers all about "French cafés and Catholic cathedrals; and they loved it, because they had never heard of them before." "I wrote in a robust Labour organ like the old *Clarion,*" he continued, "and defended medieval theology and all the things their readers had never heard of; and their readers did not mind me a bit."[8] To the narrowness of any sect or school or philosophy, Chesterton opposed nothing less than the whole world itself, full of particular, unique, and tiny things and not a vague abstraction.

Chesterton could not help but be delighted by all of those ironical turns of events that prevented him from being an academic or an artist, let alone a real estate agent in a family enterprise, while enabling him at the same time to earn his living in journalism.

> The autumn of 1905 was to bring considerable relief to the Chestertons' financial worries. Sir Bruce Ingram offered Gilbert the well-known "Our Notebook" column in the *Illustrated London News* on the death of L. F. Austin. This column, which had achieved a worldwide reputation during the time it was written by George Sala, gave Chesterton a regular weekly income for life, since he wrote it with hardly any interruption for the next thirty-one years until he died. The editor suggested a payment of £350 a year, which virtually doubled his income.[9]

Yet, he reflected later on in his *Autobiography,* the dedication to journalism did not arise either from his financial situation or from his lighter side, however much he might have enjoyed it all. "But it was not the superficial or silly or jolly part of me that made me a journalist," Chesterton explained.

On the contrary, it is such part as I have in what is serious or even solemn. A taste for mere fun might have led me to a public-house, but hardly to a publishing-house. And if it led me to a publishing-house, for the publishing of mere nonsense-rhymes or fairy tales, it could never thus have led me to my deplorable course of endless articles and letters in the newspapers. In short, I could not be a novelist; because I really like to see ideas or notions wrestling naked, as it were, and not dressed up in a masquerade as men and women. But I could be a journalist because I could not help being a controversialist.[10]

This passage is most illuminating. It hints at the reason for Chesterton's evident kindness toward those with whom he debated and radically disagreed. Chesterton ever respected the man with whom he argued, but he insisted on dealing directly, even bluntly, with the man's idea as such. He was enormously charitable to individuals, but he was incisive, logical, and unrelenting about their ideas. Chesterton seems to have remained exceedingly well-liked even when he left his opponent with no intellectual leg on which to stand.

II

Chesterton thus realized that ideas had to be considered in themselves as real forces in the human city and in the human heart. In an almost prophetic column, entitled "Conversion without Creed" (March 30, 1912), Chesterton wrote of the missionary and China. "Unless the Chinaman is a republican, China is not a republic," he observed.[11] But he was defending the classical missionary who, Chesterton thought, had the right idea.

[The missionary] is the last representative left of the idea of changing a community from the inside: of changing it by changing the *minds* of its citizens. Or, rather (to preserve free will, the only basis of political freedom), to get the citizens themselves to change their minds. . . . Missionaries do try to alter society from the inside; while all statesmen and sociologists, reactionary and revolutionary, old-fashioned and new-fashioned, try to change it from the outside.[12]

Needless to say, the whole future controversy about liberation theology, if not the Chinese revolution itself, was anticipated in that brief passage. One could not ultimately start or end with institutions, but with ideas that support them. China, Chesterton thought, was conquered by arms; but as a nation of philosophers, it has never been converted to ideas that might support a republic.[13]

Chesterton understood that someone had to pay attention to ideas as such, for it was on the validity of these ideas that kingdoms and empires ultimately rose and fell, that men and women lived humanly happy lives or not. "The ideas of logical and dogmatic men (especially the skeptics, those very dogmatic men)," he mused, "are disputable; and I always wanted to dispute about them."[14] Chesterton realized that the university or the parliament or the church was most often too limited as an arena in which to confront the myriads of controversial ideas that actually surged forth from a people. These ideas had to be met on their own grounds, on the grounds in which they initially appeared, which was usually in the newspapers.

Opinion is the suspicion that one side of a contradictory proposition has more evidence for it than its opposite. But the evidence did not yet reach certitude, so that either side ultimately might be true. Opinion, *doxa,* not truth, is the condition of ordinary human life—opinion about war, peace, song, God, virtue, sex, sports, sin, angels, devils, business, property, poverty, socialism, wealth, foreigners, schools, the Irish, divorce, females, males, humor, punishment, parliament, poetry. This wealth of divergent views and judgments on *everything that is* constitutes the life of the people in the cave, in Plato's famous analogy, the life of any polity.

In Aristotle's *Rhetoric,* opinion is where we begin to know anything, where we begin to examine life.

> The "reputable opinions" (*endoxa*) on any particular subject are usually confused and even apparently contradictory, but Aristotle as-

sumes that in most cases they manifest at least a partial grasp of the truth, and, therefore, that any serious inquiry into moral or political subjects must start from them. . . . Rhetoric involves opinions in their original state without the refinements of philosophical examination.[15]

We may or may not succeed in rising above opinion to truth, though this effort is the natural function of the human intellect. But we cannot avoid beginning with opinion, for it already surrounds us wherever we may be.

Chesterton found this raw material, which he sought to engage in argument, in ordinary conversation but mainly in the press, in the daily and weekly newspaper. "There is no more strange and even amusing modern figure than the Foreign Correspondent of an English paper. I mean the man permanently placed at Paris or Rome or Constantinople, and sending a thin, continuous stream of information to London." Thus he began his column of April 2, 1910, "English Ideas about the French," a favorite theme of Chesterton.[16] Chesterton began in the familiar, in the ordinary, which everyone knew from the papers.

But Chesterton took what he read quite seriously, even when he found it amusing. He would begin an essay entitled "Carrie Nation and Teetotalism" (December 26, 1908), with utter delight: "I was inflamed with joy when I heard of the arrival on our shores of Mrs. Carrie Nation, the enthusiastic American lady who breaks other people's bottles with a large axe."[17] But he would proceed to discuss the serious aspects of drink and civil prohibition, a debate we are experiencing today under the heading of tobacco, not alcohol. Chesterton sought to give even the most absurd topic that he ran across in the press a refinement of philosophical examination that illuminated what we are about in our opinions, what it is we search for precisely because we have minds that we intend to use properly. There is hardly a column in the *Illustrated London News* that does not refer to something he had just read in the press that very morning. Chesterton never began far from where most people were.

We distinguish, furthermore, between common sense and learned opinion. Yet we do this recalling Aristotle's admonition about who is the best judge of a feast or the best judge of whether a shoe fits. There was a sense in which the wearer of the shoe, not the cobbler, was the best judge of the fit; the many were the best judge of the feast, a principle that grounded Chesterton's democratic instincts. But there was also a sense in which the finest cook was the best judge, a principle that grounded Chesterton's own philosophical stature. In fact, however, we could not escape the beginnings in opinion, nor the need to refine opinion to see what truth was found in it. The chaos of opinion was not to be allowed to remain simply chaos.

Chesterton's preference for journalism then was, if you will, both a political and a metaphysical preference. He was really concerned that the common man could come to the truth within the myriad of swirling theoretical views that engulfed him. This concrete situation was why, in his view, it was more worthwhile to write weekly columns than metaphysical books. Indeed, Chesterton did both, but the latter, the metaphysics, proceeded from the former, from the context of daily opinion.

III

What I propose to do by way of introduction is to follow Chesterton's way of journalism. I will use substantially his *Illustrated London News* columns from 1905 to 1913, for no worse reason than that they are delightful, recently republished, and I have been reading them.[18] The first thing that any reader of Chesterton will notice about these generally brief, four- to six-page articles, published in a widely read weekly paper in London, is the recurrence of familiar themes found in *Orthodoxy,* in *Heretics,* in

What's Wrong with the World, in his collections of essays, which themselves are often no more than selections or refinements of essays from these or other journals for which he habitually wrote.

Admirers of Chesterton like W. H. Auden did not appreciate his lifelong devotion to journalism. Auden wrote:

> Chesterton's insistence upon the treadmill of weekly journalism after it ceased to be financially necessary seems to have puzzled his friends as much as it puzzles me. . . . Whatever Chesterton's reasons and motives for his choice, I am quite certain it was a mistake. . . . His best thinking and best writing are to be found, not in his short weekly essays, but in his full length books where he could take as much time and space as he pleased.[19]

Few will disagree that Chesterton wrote exceedingly well in his longer works. Yet, on reading and re-reading his weekly columns, it becomes clear that he hammered out most of his ideas originally in some controversy or column hastily composed for a deadline. And even his early columns that have two or three different topics, oftentimes not apparently related (i.e., May 12, 1906, "St. George and the English; Women, Worrying, and the Higher Culture"; December 9, 1905, "Public Houses; Christianity and Christian Science; Noses and Compliments") make very good reading for the newspaper audience, who might not have realized what he was about but who came to understand Chesterton's sudden and profound insights.

One of the most memorable chapters in *Orthodoxy,* for instance, was that entitled "The Ethics of Elfland." Anyone who remembers this extraordinary chapter will not be surprised to find a column in the *London Illustrated News* for December 2, 1905, three years before *Orthodoxy,* entitled "Education and Fairy Tales," while his column for February 29, 1908, was called "The Ethics of Fairy Tales." Chesterton had a lifelong aversion for the word "education," which, as he insisted, was not a "subject" of knowledge, but merely a description of how knowledge was passed on. Nevertheless, "without education we are in a horrible and deadly danger of taking educated people seriously," he mused in the first essay.[20]

What had occasioned this column, however, was naturally an incident in the morning paper. The Duchess of Somerset had been going about to school boards to inform them that the teaching of fairy tales was "nonsense," that the children should be taught about "Julius Caesar and 'other great men.'" Needless to say, Chesterton could hardly resist challenging this preposterous, but popular, proposal. "Civilisation changes," he pointed out, "but fairy tales never change." Chesterton went on to illuminate the philosophic point: "Fiction and modern fantasy and all that wild world in which the Duchess of Somerset lives can be described in one phrase. Their philosophy means ordinary things as seen by extraordinary people. The fairy tale means extraordinary things as seen by ordinary people."[21] This was the theme fully developed in *Orthodoxy*. The fairy tale was much more educative in the true sense than even Julius Caesar, let alone the Duchess of Somerset.

And in the second essay, Chesterton was even so brash as to compare elves and fairies with journalists. In this, he brought out a second great theme of his, that behind the whole of human creation lies a veto which alone can make life dramatic.

> Fairies and journalists have an apparent gaiety and delusive beauty. Fairies and journalists seem to be lovely and lawless; they seem to be both of them too exquisite to descend to the ugliness of every day duty. But it is an illusion created by the sudden sweetness of their presence. Journalists live under law; and so in fact does fairyland.[22]

And of course, this law under which even journalists and fairies live is an ancient one, and it is the only one that gives life an absolute meaning. Here is how Chesterton, on an ordinary morning, explained this ultimate truth:

> A girl is given a box on the condition she does not open it; she opens it, and all the evils of this world rush out at her. A man and a woman are put in a garden on the condition that they do not eat

one fruit: they eat it, and lose their joy in the fruits of the earth. This great idea, then, is the backbone of all folk-lore—the idea that all happiness hangs on one thin veto; all positive joy depends on one negative.[23]

Clearly, Chesterton had this uncanny knack of seeing where the ordinary but strange ideas of the Duchess of Somerset might lead. That is, he saw ultimate truths in the daily paper. Perhaps this is why, in a way, he was really the ultimate journalist, the man who took the "daily bread" of ordinary life and saw how it necessarily rose to the everlasting nourishment of the mind. This is the highest dignity, really, toward which journalism, let alone education, can strive.

IV

We cannot but be aware that, in these weekly essays, a very active mind is thinking its way through idea after idea, fad after fad, principle after principle, philosophy after philosophy, thinker after thinker. Yet all of this is while he is discoursing on favorite themes like Christmas, or fairy tales, or progress, or censorship, or beer, or witches, or why Shakespeare could not have been Bacon. We cannot be but struck by Chesterton's awareness of underlying philosophical and religious themes, even when the context in which they were argued may be unfamiliar to us. This context was familiar to everyone who read him at the time, which familiarity is, after all, what a daily or weekly newspaper is about.

Chesterton wrote, moreover, of the deaths of Edward VII, George Wyndham, Ibsen, Swinburne, Andrew Lang, and George Meredith. He wrote on "The Silliness of Educated People" (April 27, 1912), on "The Payment of Politicians" (October 23, 1910), on "Books on How to Succeed" (November 2, 1907), and on "The Naming of Children" (April 29, 1911). Chesterton talked about progress, the Suffragettes, Christian Science, Mormonism, Montessori, prisons, the Welsh, Jekyll and Hyde, the Jesuits, faith healing, South America, ghosts, the theatre, Tolstoy, pageants, punishments, and vegetarianism. Yet what he had to say was never merely ephemeral. Chesterton, as I have suggested, always saw some universal principle or import in everything he reflected on. Chesterton saw, in other words, how all things are connected, and he insisted further that even ordinary people could and should see this connection.

We read along, for instance, in the essay "The Character of King Edward" (June 4, 1910), expecting to find I know not what and suddenly we are stopped cold by the following utterly lovely reflection: "There is the tragedy that is founded on the worthlessness of life; and there is the deeper tragedy that is founded on the worth of it. The one sort of sadness says that life is so short that it can hardly matter; the other that life is so short that it will matter for ever."[24] Chesterton was quite right. The purpose of his sort of journalism was to state clearly what no one else was saying. Chesterton was not afraid of ordinary erroneous ideas that fill the daily papers, because he could see that, when properly analyzed, even these ideas contained some glimpse of truth. The catching of this glimpse was the very purpose of a real journalist, which Chesterton considered himself to be first of all.

The first thing that strikes the reader in these some three hundred and fifty essays is, as I have suggested, that they almost always contain something Chesterton had just read in the newspaper or in a book or perhaps some popular idea he ran across in a Fleet Street pub. That is, he always began with common opinion, something that was being bandied about in the public. There are two things one could do with such chaotic opinion. One could simply ignore it as unworthy of consideration. Or one could do what Chesterton in fact did—consider it, argue with it, see where it went.

His column for March 31, 1906, for example, began this way: "I do not know why it is that some paragraphs in newspapers are very funny."[25] Of course, this column was entitled "Pouring Boiling Water on Snails." The column of July 27, 1907, "Jingoism and Sports," began, "I notice that some papers, especially papers that call themselves patriotic, have fallen into quite a panic over the fact that we have been twice beaten in the world of sport, that a Frenchman has beaten us at golf, and a Belgian has beaten us at rowing."[26] Few can resist sports, snails, and humor.

Or else Chesterton began with some rather provocative view that he had just been thinking or talking about. "It is sometimes said that our age is too fond of amusements: but there are further facts to be remembered. One of them is this: that it so often happens that the amusing entertainments are the only places where the serious truth is told." So he began a column, "Wisdom in Comic Songs," on July 10, 1909.[27] Actually in this essay on comic song, he treated capital punishment and how it was that "only the poor get hanged." But he concluded, "One of the few gifts that can really increase with old age is a sense of humour." His application of this latter principle, however, was utterly remarkable: "That is the whole fun of belonging to an ancient civilisation, like our own great civilisation of Europe."[28] There was in Chesterton's journalism that relentless effort to see the truth in even the most ephemeral, humorous, or insignificant incident that he happened to run across. Who else but Chesterton could have suspected that perhaps humor was greater in a civilization that actually had a longer time to laugh about itself?

v

Chesterton wrote rather often about journalism as a profession and how it was perceived. He is actually one of journalism's most ardent defenders and most incisive critics. He held, to be sure, that no one could really find the truth in newspapers. Indeed, what one should be reading in a newspaper was not the meaty articles or sober editorials, but the "snippets" and mistakes that appeared in it. He held that the most interesting and truthful aspect of journalism was probably the obituaries that could finally tell the truth about someone. "It is by this time practically impossible to get the truth out of any newspaper, even the honest newspapers," he wrote on January 23, 1909. What is interesting about this remark and instructive about what Chesterton thought he was doing in journalism was the reason for this difficulty in finding truth in any newspaper: "I mean the kind of truth that a man can feel an intelligent curiosity about—moral truth, truth that is disputed, truth that is in action and really affecting things."[29]

The point Chesterton was making was of some importance in understanding his particular genius in journalism. "One can find the fact that a man is hanged, but not the truth about his trial; one can believe the journalist when he says that war has broken out, but not when he says that war was inevitable."[30] The statement that "war is inevitable," of course, is a philosophic statement that strictly speaking makes journalism, if not life itself, impossible. But if this determinism is the operative thesis of the journalist, then there is nothing of interest in the fact that a man was hanged, for it had to happen also. And it is precisely the reason why he was hanged, not the fact that he was hanged, on which all true human curiosity lies. "About the real struggles of the modern world the newspapers are practically silent—until the struggles are over."[31]

It is in this context that Chesterton's statement of why he became a journalist is of some interest. We have seen his explanation for his selection of this profession in his *Autobiography,* that it was something of a happy "mystery." On August 21, 1909, Chesterton wrote a column entitled "Succeeding in Journalism."

Every journalist, even unsuccessful ones, he remarked, is asked "how to succeed in journalism." With some delight, he responded that the only advice is the ordinary advice we give to anyone—that is, not to get drunk, but to prefer "even drunkenness to drinking," not to be insolent, not to be servile, "to write in a legible hand, and to take notes of everything which one cannot remember."[32] Chesterton's own memory seems to have been such that he could recall endless reams of conversation and reading. One wonders what he would have made of the tape recorder.

In any case, Chesterton did not advocate writing about what a paper thinks it might want.

> My own effect, such as it is, is entirely due to this simple process. I began by reviewing books, about printing, and sculpture. Into these I introduced disquisitions on theology or folklore, disquisitions which would have seemed quite ordinary in the *Hibbert Journal,* but which attracted attention when abruptly introduced apropos of Etruscan Pottery, or "The Treatment of Poplars by Corot." Very often, while the journalist is doing his best to imitate the tone of the paper, the editor (torn with despair) is trying in vain to find someone who will alter the tone of the paper.[33]

If Chesterton was a popular journalist, which he was and still is, it is because of these theological or philosophical disquisitions he introduced into his essays.

But of course, it was not just that Chesterton was both witty and philosophical. He combatted precisely the content of the philosophies he disagreed with. He was not a skeptic or a relativist and made it very difficult for his readers to be either. In a column he did on the two hundreth anniversary of the death of Henry Fielding (May 11, 1907), Chesterton brought up the question of what was a good book. He saw a change in the definition of this proposition, for the worse. Fielding's *Tom Jones,* he noted, was called a "bad" book because Jones did a goodly number of bad things. But Chesterton did not see this narrative as at all immoral. Fielding never called these bad things good. "The modern instinct is that if the heart of man is evil, there is nothing that remains good. But the older feeling was that if the heart of man was everso evil, there was something that remained good—goodness remained good."[34] Writing books merely about nice people is not serving morality. "Telling the truth about the terrible struggle in the human soul is surely a very elementary part of the ethics of honesty. If the characters are not wicked, the book is."[35]

Again, such a disquisition reveals the marvel of Chesterton's capacity to draw forth first principles in the most normal of topics, that of literature itself. Right existed outside of human error and weakness. This understanding was in Fielding, and it was in Shakespeare (whom Chesterton unaccountably sometimes, as in this case, spells Shakspere). "Whenever [Shakespeare] alludes to right and wrong it is always with this old implication. Right is right, even if nobody does it. Wrong is wrong even if everybody is wrong about it."[36] This was the sort of truth that Chesterton was able to place in the oddest of places, in the morning press. And he thought this well worth doing.

Chesterton, indeed, did not think that newspapers really were able to see important contemporary events. In a thoroughly delightful column entitled "What the Newspapers Don't See" (September 30, 1911), Chesterton pointed out that the press was too much devoted to speed and the swirl of events ever to have noticed the important things as they actually happened. Had Roman dailies appeared after Caesar was killed, Chesterton speculated, they would indeed have had an account of the murder, interviews with Anthony and Cassius. "But the papers would display no notion of what was really happening. The editors would never have noticed that Caesar crossed the Rubicon. They certainly would not know that when that little river was crossed the Roman Empire was founded."[37] Rather the papers would mostly have dealt that morning with Lucullus's dinner, the divorce court for Caesar's wife, Clodius's bankruptcy, in short, "gladiators and the money market." And when a small sect appeared in Rome, many of its members would dramatically be thrown to lions before the papers took up the subject as anything different from anyone else being thrown to the lions. "Newspapers pay the penalty of the blind idolatry of speed. They go so fast that they never notice anything; and they have to make up their minds so quickly that they never make them up at all."[38]

VI

Chesterton is sometimes said to be too pleasant, too prone to wit to be taken seriously. Allan Massie wrote:

> Both [Samuel Johnson and Chesterton] were professional writers who knew that they must please the reader if they were to influence him (only solemn and tenured blockheads can afford not to do so). Both were moralists. Chesterton was proud to be a journalist, if only because he knew that more people read newspapers than books. His preferred form was the essay because it is by nature delightful and didactic.[39]

The accusation of over-jocularity was something that particularly annoyed Chesterton.

Part of this annoyance, no doubt, was due to the fact that Chesterton thought life itself was mostly more amusing than he was. In a very profound essay entitled "Incompatibility in Marriage," a theme that appears full blown in *What's Wrong with the World,* Chesterton recounted with utter delight an explanation of one Ferdinand Earle about his divorce in America. Here is what Chesterton read:

> My first wife and I were extremely happy, and our happiness increased when we came to live at Monroe by the birth of our son. But soon things began to arise between us—call it what you will: Incompatibility of temper, conflict of ideas. We did not explain, but I,

who am an artist, and have the artistic temperament, sailed for Europe. On the voyage I met a woman, who, I found, was, like myself, a Socialist. We quickly realised that our marriage was foreordained before our births.[40]

Chesterton did not make up this passage. He found it in a newspaper. Of this extraordinarily absurd narrative, he simply said (one can just see him throwing up his hands in laughter): "It is impossible to parody that passage." Like Malcolm Muggeridge, he would have agreed that the life of a humorist is difficult because life itself is more amusing.

Chesterton himself addressed the topic of his own delight in humor in a column on May 21, 1910, "Jokes and Good Sense." Chesterton's column appeared in the very beginning of the *Illustrated London News*. He mused, "I introduce myself on this page every week with all the feelings of the stage villain when he exclaims, 'At last, now I am alone.'"[41] Chesterton explained that people do not read magazines beginning with page one. "A magazine is a thing one opens anywhere but at the beginning."

Noting this aloneness of page one, Chesterton decided to address in it the complaint about the wit found in his writing. Most people were sometimes telling jokes and at other times they were serious. However, "when I tell the dull truth about anything, it is said to be a showy paradox; when I lighten or brighten it with any common jest, it is supposed to be my solid and absurd opinion."[42] Chesterton told of a controversy with some writers in a local journal, who maintained that the doctrine of miracles is not the truth, but merely "symbolic" of the truth. To this, Chesterton responded, "What is the truth of which it is a symbol."[43] To this response, which Chesterton thought "courteous, relevant, and reasonable," the journal's reaction was to "cast up its eyes and clasp its hands, and ask distractedly how it could be expected to argue with such a wild, elusive, ever-changing, fantastical, and irresponsible jester as myself."[44] That is to say, that Chesterton's humor and amusement were directed at the truth. His amusement did not in the least deflect him from that truth in the very act of delightful joking at the expense of some more sober or solemn adversary. He did not see why he could not be witty and profound at the same time, since everyone else was. He demanded, as it were, equal rights.

VII

How does one conclude, sum up Chesterton, the journalist? When we finally ask what was Chesterton, we are not wrong to reply as he did. He was a journalist. The very word means that he was concerned with the events of the day on which he wrote. Chesterton's columns began with common opinion, with, as it were, the news of the day. "I have been to a large number of dinners, and heard a large number of successful and unsuccessful Parliamentary candidates make long speeches, occasions which, of course, were very delightful when they were not a little too long."[45] So began a column entitled magnificently "On Long Speeches and Truth, Ceremonies, Celebrations, and Solemnities" for February 23, 1906. Here he was concerned with the phenomenon of hearing a thing, even truth, so much that it loses its novelty. "But the truth is sacred; and if you tell the truth too often nobody will believe it."[46] That is, of course, the plot of a famous fairy tale.

But where does Chesterton go with this idea? He immediately pointed out that just because a speech is long does not mean that it is "unworthy of attention." As an example of this, he cited Thomas Carlyle, who, when asked to say grace at meals, "had a cheery way of reading to the company the whole of the Book of Job," no small feat. Chesterton immediately pointed out that the Book of Job contained some truths that the modern agnostic and even the modern Christian may have never really heard. "From it [the Book of Job] the modern Agnostic may for the first time learn Agnosticism: a sane and a sacred and manly ignorance. From it the modern Christian may with astonishment learn Christianity; learn, that is, that the mystery of suffering may be a strange honour and not a vulgar punishment."[47] Chesterton, in other words, used journalism to teach agnostics agnosticism, Christians Christianity.

We might even go further and suggest that Chesterton used his column in an ordinary journal to teach human beings the uniqueness of their lives. His column for March 16, 1912, "Free Will in Life and in the Drama," began: "What fun it would be if good actors suddenly acted like real people!" His column had the most serious of purposes. He pointed out that the actors already know the end of the drama they are engaged in. The difference [between drama and life] is that all events in genuine art are decided: all events in genuine life (in anything worth calling life) are undecided."[48] All plays are either tragedies or comedies, but we do not, because of free will, know what real life will be. From this Chesterton concluded:

> Every human life begins in tragedy, for it begins in travail. But every human life may end in comedy—even in divine comedy. It may end in a joy beyond all our jokes; in that cry across the chasm, "Fear not, I have conquered the world." Real human life differs from all imitations of it in the fact that it can perpetually alter itself as it goes along.[49]

It is in this sense that comedy is more profound than tragedy. But Chesterton concludes by also claiming tragedy itself.

Political philosophy and tragedy were founded in that city, Athens, that asked the question about who is the best man. Chesterton has seen that the best man might suffer, that he might stand for joy. And in seeing this, in the human condition, we can see the dimensions of the opposite: "I think 'MacBeth' is the one supreme drama because it is the one Christian drama; and I will accept the accusation of prejudice. But I mean by Christian (in this matter) the strong sense of spiritual liberty and of sin; the idea that the best man can be as bad as he chooses."[50] All of this, I say, was written by a journalist on March 16, 1912, by a journalist who did not hesitate to take his readers seriously, who did not hesitate at the same time to tell them that sins and jokes belong to the same philosophy.

Chesterton knew, of course, that his readers would probably be surprised at that thesis, because such things were not the common fare of their daily or weekly journals. He had, again, as it were, put the right article in the wrong envelope and sent it to the wrong journal, which accepted it. The delight of G. K. Chesterton's philosophy itself remains: the unexpected surprise and gift that this truth exists at all midst the confused gyrations of daily opinion so often based on the "heretics" of other ages apart from the common sense of our kind.

Chesterton's gift to journalism was simply that he took the time to think things out clearly. "There is a kind of work which any man can do, but from which many men shrink," he wrote during the Great War, "generally because it is very hard work, sometimes because they fear it will lead them whither they do not wish to go. It is called thinking."[51] The mystery of G. K. Chesterton's success in journalism, the thinking from which he did not shrink, the intellectual paths on which he did not fear to tread, is simply that he perceived that the truth about which he wrote existed there before everyone's eyes. And he found it, as did his loyal readers, even those of us who still find him in "the day before yesterday's daily paper," to be both up to date and delightful.

The Natural Home of the Human Spirit

In 1927, Chesterton's book *The Catholic Church and Conversion* was published. Belloc did the "Foreword" and Chesterton himself wrote his own "Introduction," which he called, not without some amusement, "A New Religion." Both short essays remain of considerable and refreshing interest. Belloc was the "born-Catholic" of the two, so, as he remarks, "it is with diffidence that anyone born into the Faith can approach the tremendous subject of Conversion." The convert always has the aura of choice; the born-Catholic of tradition, of not having had to change anything, only fulfill the promise already his.

As I was born the year following the publication of this book, also a "born-Catholic," I find both of these essays, that of the born-Catholic and that of the convert, to be of considerable interest. I have always considered Belloc's remark in *The Path to Rome*, I think, that "it is a good thing never to have lost the Faith," to be a comforting one. Both to have the faith and not to have lost it, to be sure, are graces. We should not be so foolish as to attribute too much to our own powers. And yet, there can be no doubt that being born into the faith enables us to live in a much more ordered and, yes, delightful universe than we might otherwise have known. Born-Catholics, to be sure, often do not show that angst or earnestness about what they hold to be true as do converts. But this calmness is only because born-Catholics are more aware of and comfortable with the fact that things really do fit together, that ultimate quests are not merely prodding our souls but that these very quests are not in vain. There is an end to the journey that can be reached.

Belloc did, to be sure, speculate on an experience that was no doubt his, about how "born-Catholics" frequently do go through an analogous conversion experience. We are all aware, of course, that a gift given must sooner or later be a gift consciously accepted or else it is not a gift. And in the matter of faith, this acceptance will relate to the depths at which we choose to allow the faith, in its intelligibility, to speak to us.

Belloc continued:

> Those born into the Faith often, I say, go through an experience of skepticism as the years proceed, and it is still a common phenomenon . . . for men of the Catholic culture, acquainted with the Church from childhood, to leave it in early manhood and never to return. But it is nowadays a still more frequent phenomenon—and it is to this that I allude—for those to whom scepticism so strongly appealed in youth to discover, by an experience of men and of reality in all its various forms, that the transcendental truths they had been taught in childhood have the highest claims upon their matured reason.[1]

The second "conversion" in Belloc's sense, thus, had to do with the sudden realization that the skeptical alternatives did not in fact make as much sense as what had been taught in youth, had we but been willing to learn and live it.

Belloc's approach was to remark on the many different sorts of men and women who came into the Church as converts from all sorts of backgrounds. We find the cynic and the sentimentalist, the fool and the wise man, the doubter and the man who does not doubt enough. Moreover, we find people entering the Church from all sorts of experiences and nationalities. "You come across an entry into the Catholic Church undoubtedly due to the spectacle, admiration and imitation of some great character observed. Next day you come across an entry into the Catholic Church out of complete loneliness, and you are astonished to find the convert still ignorant of the great mass of the Catholic effect on character."[2]

Belloc remarked that "the Church is the natural home of the

Human Spirit."[3] This is a striking phrase, for the Church is not supposed to be the "natural" home of anything, unless, of course, our spirit is made for something that is not merely nature. Belloc found that these myriads of reasons for entering the Church converged because the reality to which they pointed was one. "It is in this convergence of witnesses that we have one of the innumerable proofs upon which the rational basis of our religion rests." The supernatural religion rests on a solid rational basis.

Chesterton, for his part, the convert, the man not born Catholic, found a paradox, that this ancient religion was really quite new. This amused him. "It would be very undesirable that modern men should accept Catholicism merely as a novelty; but it is a novelty." Today, in a way, the public world has so deviated from Catholicism that Catholicism is a "revolt," something quite different from anything about us, something quite novel, quite new, quite unfamiliar. Chesterton, as I said, called his essay "A New Religion." Needless to say, when Chesterton calls something as old as Catholicism "new," he is probably saying something quite unexpectedly true. "There is something almost legendary about the religion that is two thousand years old now appearing as a rival of the new religions."[4]

During the last decade or so, under John Paul II, the Catholic Church has in many ways recovered itself. It has reformed or better, re-presented its canon law, both Western and Eastern, its social teachings, its moral philosophy and theology. The new *General Catechism* is no doubt the most complete, systematic, and coherent presentation of the whole faith ever composed. Where does this old institution get the vitality to be the newest religion on the block? Indeed, most Catholics do not even know this newness themselves. Most are in great need of a Belloc-type conversion. "The mark of the faith," Chesterton said, "is not tradition (however good that is) but conversion." The Spirit breathes where it wills, but the Church is not an abstraction. It is here to challenge souls, either to accept or to reject. The Church as "the natural home of the Human Spirit" is also witness to the sign of contradiction.

What both Chesterton and Belloc were sure of, however, was that the Church was the home of reason. The modern world will never be humble enough to admit its own skepticism. But Chesterton had it right early in the twentieth century, I think. He already saw in the first quarter of this century most of the dire things that would occur at its ending.

> [The Church] is already beginning to appear as the only champion of reason in the twentieth century, as it was the only champion of tradition in the nineteenth. We know that the higher mathematics is trying to deny that two and two make four and the higher mysticism to imagine something that is beyond good and evil. Amid all these anti-rational philosophies, ours will remain the only rational philosophy.[5]

At the end of the twentieth century, at the beginning of the third millennium, a convert, I suspect, could with cold intelligence still make the same claim. *Veritatis Splendor,* John Paul II's great study of truth, is written directly against that now more developed "higher mysticism" that imagines that something can be "beyond good and evil," a phrase Chesterton recalled from Nietzsche, who died, ironically, precisely in 1900. In this light, it should come as no great surprise that Nietzsche and Heidegger are the popular philosophers at the end of the twentieth century. Nor should it be any surprise that it was the pope-philosopher who wrote *Fides et Ratio* near the century's conclusion.

What needs to be put together, I think, from these two insightful essays on conversion by Belloc and Chesterton is the relationship between "the only rational philosophy" and "the natural home of the Human Spirit." Modernity and post-modernity have been built on the premise that these two things cannot belong together in the same community, that faith and reason are completely alien to each other. What Chesterton called "a new religion," however, turned out to be the very old faith no longer recognized or intellectually confronted. "Amid all these anti-rational philosophies" it remains "the only rational philosophy." What Belloc called the transcendent truths of our childhood ironically do have "the highest claims on our matured reason." The Human Spirit precisely does have a "home" because all things converge as "innumerable proofs upon which the rational basis of our religion reposes."

On the Nature of "Yes" in the State of Maine

Chesterton is often called amusing, mostly because he is. In a column on March 21, 1914, he mentioned that he was also called an "Apostle of Unreason." Needless to say, Chesterton never thought of himself as merely a humorist, a sort of Art Buchwald of his times. But he did enjoy a good laugh even when occasioned by a philosopher. Yet he was astonished to find himself called an Apostle of Unreason. Chesterton chronicled practically the whole of modernity from Bergson to James and Nietzsche. Every one of these philosophers advocated one or another form of unreason. Since Chesterton adamantly opposed them, how could anyone reasonably associate him with unreason?

Was it his religion? he wondered. "We may really say that nearly all the people who consider themselves specially progressive, advanced, up-to-date, modernist, or futurist, are avowedly Apostles of Unreason. Practically, it comes to this, that the people who are now opposed to reason are practically all the people who are also opposed to religion." This conclusion touched upon a disturbing theme that Chesterton was later to work out in his books on St. Francis and St. Thomas, namely, that when man sets out to be merely reasonable, he ends up in unreason; somehow it requires the openness of faith to keep our reason.

Chesterton even noted that Pius X's encyclical *Pascendi Dominci Gregis*, at that time recently published (September 8, 1907), was itself a list of these same apostles of unreason. "Nearly all the Modernists who were condemned in the Pope's Encyclical were condemned for being Pragmatists and Apostles of Unreason. Anyone who will read the Encyclical will see that I state the essential fact." In these days when a spaceship can pass Jupiter and

Neptune, we find Chesterton noticing that George Brandes had "set the fashion of being the Apostle of Unreason" by asking, "Who knows that two and two do not make five in the planet Jupiter?" To this question, Chesterton simply but firmly in the name of common humanity responded, "I do." It is not enough to say that the spacecraft that flew by Jupiter depended upon Chesterton's affirmation, depended on the addition of two and two. What is important is that Chesterton saw that it was the function of the ordinary man to say that he did know certain things.

Chesterton went on—how could he resist?—"The question seems to me quite as senseless as saying, 'Who knows that "yes" is not the same as "no" in the State of Maine?'"[1] Chesterton affirmed that "thank God" he had "never even been to the State of Maine," but "I know that 'yes' is not the same as 'no' anywhere." Again, who knows this? Chesterton's answer still rings in the name of common humanity—"I do."

The gentleman who had charged Chesterton with being an apostle of unreason, Mr. William Archer, had apparently based his position on an incident at Cambridge. Chesterton was both amused and a little put out at this accusation: "Well, I pass over what I cannot help calling the rather cheap part of the argument, which seems to consist in chaffing me with the little-known and carefully concealed fact that I cannot work miracles. Nevertheless, as Mr. Archer gloomily notes, I said at Cambridge that I thought it probable that some other people could." Evidently, this latter remark was the origin of Chesterton's being called an "Apostle of Unreason."

With amusing reference to his own considerable girth, Chesterton admitted that he himself could not "work miracles." "I cannot move the Albert Hall from London to Paris; and levitation in my own case would probably be as difficult as in the case of the parallel structure of the Albert Hall." And with this sally,

Chesterton concluded the philosophic point, that the fact that one or another person could not work miracles did not mean that no one could. And even Christ, who could, refused to do so on the Cross when called to perform one.

If Archer was a monist in philosophical theory, Chesterton suggested, then no miracle was possible. But if he was a realist, which he wasn't, then he might consult the evidence to see if miracles ever happened. "A miracle is, by definition, a marvel. That is to say, it is a very rare and very unexpected thing. If it could be done by anybody at any minute, it is surely as plain as a pikestaff that it could not fulfill the function, true or false, which its supporters suppose it to fulfill." And characteristically Chesterton concluded this reflection with a reference to, of all things, witchcraft in his defense of miracles.

Chesterton thus wanted to know if the vast history of witchcraft had no theoretic basis. His conclusion again reveals the depths of his reason, because he could see what was really at stake in the question of miracles:

> Nobody can begin to understand the theoretic defense of the miraculous who does not understand the idea of a positive fight against positive evil. We should be right in thinking it silly for the good angels to interfere if none of us believed in bad angels. A miracle, if you like, proclaims martial law in the universe. But it is not unreasonable; for it may be the only way of reconciling reason with liberty.[2]

Again in this brief snippet, we realize Chesterton's capacity to proclaim that "yes" is "yes" even in the State of Maine and that miracles might just be tinged with intelligence and freedom.

The Philosopher with Two Thoughts

Several years ago, a friend of mine who was living in England at the time found an 1888 edition of Thomas Babbington (Lord) Macaulay's *Essays*, a volume reprinted from *The Edinburgh Review*. This was a handsome old tome, published by Longmans, and printed by Spottiswoode on New-Street Square in London. This book is a kind of gift that can just sit there on your shelves for no reason except that it is a nice book. You do not have to read it right away, but every once in a while you will pick it up. I have, because of my friend's interest, read with particular attention the wonderful essay on Fanny Burney ("Madame D'Arblay"), especially because of her relation to Samuel Johnson. Recently, I happened to pick up Chesterton's *Victorian Age in English Literature*. On some earlier reading, I had underlined Chesterton's remark on Newman about dogma—"For dogma means the serious satisfaction of the mind. Dogma does not mean the absence of thought, but the end of thought."[1] I liked that, "the serious satisfaction of the mind," precisely what a relativist age and metaphysic does not know about its own mind. I began to read backwards in the book. I noticed that before Newman, Chesterton treated Mill; and before Mill, he discussed Macaulay.

So I took another look at Macaulay's book. The Preface began modestly: "The author of these essays is so sensible of their defects that he has repeatedly refused to let them appear in a form which might seem to indicate that he thought them worthy of a permanent place in English literature." It seems that he decided to publish these essays in England only because the American edition was at the time being imported into England. Hence he thought it was unfair to his English publisher not to be able to compete with the American edition. Macaulay allowed that he permitted in the English edition only those corrections that had to do with dates or places. He wanted the essays to appear substantially, with all their faults, as they had stood in the *Review*. Thus, he did not perhaps think them "worthy of a permanent place in English literature," but he did not want the Americans to be reaping profits when they could just as well go to the English.

Chesterton suspected that there were, indeed, "two Macaulay's"—"a rational Macaulay who was generally wrong, and a romantic Macaulay who was almost invariably right."[2] In examining the rational Macaulay, Chesterton remarked: "As a philosopher he had only two thoughts; and neither of them is true."[3] The first of these ideas was the idea of progress, the idea that "politics, as an experimental science, must go on improving, along with clocks, pistols or penknives, by the mere accumulation of experiment and variety." Chesterton recognized that Macaulay was not really a modern man who believed that the soul could change. Macaulay thought indeed that religion could not get any better and that poetry was getting worse.

Yet, Chesterton argued, Macaulay did not see the flaw in his own theory that political things were getting better. The flaw was this: "Unless the soul improves with time there is no guarantee that the accumulations of experience will be adequately used." All science and experiment depend on man doing something about what he knows, and he may quite well decide not to do anything. "If the soul of man is subject to other laws, is liable to sin, to sleep, to anarchism or to suicide, then all sciences including politics may fall as sterile and lie as fallow as before man's reason was made."[4] So behind science lies human will. Nothing happens without our choosing it to happen. Macaulay, however, "seemed sometimes to talk as if clocks produced clocks, or guns had families of little pistols, or a penknife littered like a pig." The soul of man, as Chesterton held, is indeed "subject to other laws."

The second error, Chesterton thought, was Macaulay's "utilitarian theory of toleration." This thesis, so apparently plausible, seemed to hold that if, for instance, we wanted a good butcher, we should ignore the butcher's theology, whether he be "a Baptist or a Muggletonian," and get the best one in his craft. What bothered Chesterton about this theory, however, was that Macaulay did not carry the principle far enough to see its implications. For example, few Englishmen of whatever traditional English religion would have scruples about butchering. Nonetheless, "a good butcher might be a Baptist; he is not very likely to be a Buddhist. A good soldier might be a Wesleyan; he would hardly be a Quaker." That is to say, if our theology does not allow us to take life at all, or to fight at all, then we could not really "tolerate" someone who held exactly the opposite dogmas. Toleration is not superior to dogma unless it itself becomes the only doctrine, intolerant to all others.

Chesterton, in other words, thought that it made a considerable difference what we held to be true. Indeed, this seeking of what was true, to articulate it in propositions, was the very end of the human mind, its purpose. Macaulay himself in his Preface had decided, though "strongly urged to insert them," not to reprint three essays he had written critical of John Stuart Mill. Even though Macaulay did not do "justice" to Mill in them, he did not intend to "retract a single doctrine which they contain." Chesterton, I think, would have found this affirmation, if he read it, as he might have, to be philosophically admirable. If as a philosopher Macaulay had only had two thoughts, neither of which was true, still he was not disposed to retract "a single doctrine" he thought was true, even though, as Chesterton quipped, he seemed to talk as if "guns had families of little pistols" and Buddhists would make good butchers.

Equal with the Souls of Hildebrand
and Shakespeare

In our childhood home in Iowa, we had two rather special books, as I recall it now, books my father often used to talk about with some earnestness, books I remember reading with distinct awe as quite a young boy. They were by an English priest by the name of Owen Francis Dudley. One book was called *The Shadow on the Earth* and the other *Will Men Be Like Gods?* Just what their plots were, I cannot now recall. But they had to do with themes that remain quite modern, the questions (a) of whether men by themselves can continue even to be men and (b) in what men's choice to substitute themselves for God might consist. I suppose when I read these books I had little idea what they were about, except I do recall being quite alarmed by their implications.

The Chesterton Review for August 1989, much to my astonishment, reproduced Chesterton's Introduction to the 1925 edition of *Will Men Be Like Gods?* It was with some interest that I read this unknown essay. I was so taken with it in fact that I immediately read it out loud to a friend. As I think of it now, Chesterton's Introduction seems quite the most extraordinary insight into the very question of our making ourselves to be like God, itself no doubt a theme from Genesis. Indeed, I had just finished talking about this issue in class, on Genesis' teaching that the location of evil is not to be found in a second god, or in nature, or in things, but in that aspect alone in creation that is good but which can be otherwise by its own power, in our will, that is.

Chesterton—I wonder if that Introduction was in the edition I read long ago?—merely wanted to comment on a couple of themes in Dudley's argument about the insufficiency of humanism. Dudley thought that contemporary humanitarianism was connected with hedonism, but he doubted whether this had "very much to do with happiness." Chesterton thus wondered, "Would the world even be happy if it gave up [as the humanist proposition argued] all that has been counted holy?"

At this point, Chesterton first queried whether the study of any merely humanist utopia, even though "interesting," could really be called "exhilarating? Does anyone feel those descriptions to glow in his memory like the real memories of human enjoyment?" Chesterton here touched on a theme that was often in his writings, namely, that the visions of a perfect world, such as humanisms propose, lack the real delight and wonder we find in the actual world about us. The atmosphere in Utopia, of whatever vintage, is in fact less fascinating than the atmosphere of any tavern in which we might find a Dickens character like Mr. Tony Weller. What is wrong with the manmade ideals of the utopias is that by hypothesis they are limited to merely human things, something even Aristotle warned us not to do.

If we take an irreligious mankind to be itself a utopia or a religion, if we eliminate, that is, what mankind has called "holy," we immediately leave out most of the things that have caused the most noble words and deeds of actual human beings. Is mankind enough for itself? In truth, actual "mankind has never felt it enough to be enough." If the theoretical limit of humanity is a manmade utopia, what is missing is what most of us really long for. "The spiritual hungers of man are never merely hungers for humanity." Thus, if we are left to ourselves as children, we long for something beyond ourselves, we long for "fairyland." Poets especially make bad agnostics because they will necessarily seek something beyond themselves, almost in spite of themselves.

The second point that Chesterton made concerning Dudley's thesis was that "it is more possible to love men indirectly than to love them directly." What Chesterton meant by this paradox was that we simply do not notice the ultimate reality of what an ordinary man or woman we meet is really like. "Few are fired with a direct individual affection for the five people sitting on the other side of a railway-carriage." These odd sorts will be doing all kinds of vulgar or pedestrian things—powdering a nose, smoking a "limp cigarette," snorting, sneering, vaguely looking out the window. However, "all these are sacred beings of equal value in the sight of God with the souls of Hildebrand and Shakespeare, but a man needs to be a little of a mystic to think so." We are hard pressed to see in normal humanity anything much, especially if we are agnostics. "That the halo will in any case shine out of the interior of the fat farmer, by itself, and be visible to anybody any- where, has never been scientifically demonstrated."

We feel somehow, then, that poetry or romance points to something beyond itself; and we have in us, in spite of human or- dinariness, this sense of our sacredness that implies something be- yond ourselves. The best way to see this transcendence is in someone beyond ourselves. It is difficult for ordinary people to see much loftiness in their neighbor, but we can all see that a St. Francis loved both saint and sinner. "And what is true of St. Fran- cis is more true of his Divine model; men can admire perfect charity before they practice even imperfect charity, and that is by far the most practical way of getting them to practice it." Charity does not exist in a humanist utopia.

So we cannot leave mere men standing around staring at each other as if that is all there were to them and to the world. They would merely grow "weary." Men need to look out on some- thing beyond themselves even to see themselves. The sun that "shines on the evil and the good" is seen by each of us looking out on what it is we have done and what it is we are for. What really "exhilarates" us is what possesses the vitality of the real that did not cause itself, and therefore it reaches through our very or- dinariness to our "Divine model." We human beings will be like Gods only if we choose not to be ourselves gods. Only in that way can we be free to love one another as we are, as ordinary folks, "sacred beings of equal value in the sight of God."

The Traditional Scene of the Nativity

Several years ago, I was given the collection of Chesterton poems and essays called *The Spirit of Christmas*.[1] In this little book, there is found an essay from *The New Witness* (December 8, 1922) entitled "The Heart of Bethlehem." In this essay, Chesterton brought up the curious fact that the Holy Family at the Birth of Christ has been painted as if they, its members, were to be found in almost any climate or architecture, in any economic, geographical, racial, or cultural setting.

Yet, we know that the whole romance of Christmas is that it happened but once, like all the times in which any of us live. Christ's birth did not happen just any place, but in some place, in Bethlehem, under the reign of Caesar Augustus, when the whole world was at peace. Reflecting on these infinite varieties of drawings and paintings of Christmas that depict Christ's birth happening just anywhere, Chesterton wrote:

> No man who understands Christianity will complain that [these pictures] are different from each other and different from the truth, or rather the fact. It is the whole point of the story that it happened in one particular human place that might have been any particular human place; a sunny colonnade in Italy or a snow-laden cottage in Sussex.[2]

Christ came in the fullness of time. Yet, we suspect that the omnipotent power of God that made it possible for Christ to come at all would not have prevented Him from being sent in any time or any place. And this was Chesterton's point. The sunny colonnades of Italy and the snow-laden cottages in Sussex are likewise human places under the same power of God that manifested itself in the stable at Bethlehem.

There is a phrase I have always loved in Chesterton. I came across it first in *Dickens*, but I find it here in this collection also, this time in a poem, "A Child of the Snows." The third stanzas is as follows:

> And at night we win to the ancient inn
> > Where the child in the frost is furled,
> We follow the feet where all souls meet
> > At the inn at the end of the world.[3]

That is the phrase I have loved so much since I first ran across it, perhaps not the phrase but its imagery—"the inn at the end of the world." The inn at the end of the world is the inn in which there is now room. The Child furled in swaddling clothes is the Son of God who was born homeless in this world.

Chesterton believed that Christmas was the feast of the home. "Now Christmas is built on a beautiful and intentional paradox: that the birth of the homeless should be celebrated in every home," Chesterton wrote in another essay.[4] We can ironically be really homesick only if we have a home. Unless we understand this longing that we are not where we want to be, even when we are where we want to be, we shall never understand why we are, in our very metaphysical condition, homesick at home, even in this world.

Inns, homes, stables that could be anywhere even when they were in fact somewhere leave one final point on which Chesterton insisted about Christmas. Christmas was a reality, not a "spirit." "The idea of embodying good will—that is, of putting it into a body—is the huge and primal idea of the Incarnation."[5] "The traditional scene of the Nativity," as Chesterton called it, was not a scene of abstract spirit, or of ideas, or of pure forms. It was literally an "incarnation." The stable in the cavern in Bethlehem, as there was no room in the inn, is the one path that can lead us who exist anywhere, be it in the sunny colonnades of Italy or the snow-laden cottages in Sussex, in any time, perhaps even in our own time, to the inn at the end of the world.

On the Qualified and Experienced

In the October *Midwest Chesterton News*, Christopher Derrick wrote a brief reply to Frances Farrell's earlier essay in which she questioned Derrick's use of the term "sado-masochism," which he had applied to Chesterton.[1]

I too was surprised and quite dubious about the wisdom and truth of this allegation when I had first seen it in Derrick. What concerns me here is merely the sort of tack that Derrick used to establish his view, a line that I consider very much against the spirit of common sense philosophy that Chesterton stood for. Of course, we might say that Derrick is not a common sense philosopher, so he is not bound by our rules. But the whole point of common sense philosophy is that everyone, even those who deny it, must be bound by it, for that is what philosophy ultimately is.

In this context, I was also struck by the related essay of Dean R. Rapp, "G. K. Chesterton's Criticism of Psychoanalysis," that appeared in the August 1989 *Chesterton Review*.[2] In view of the fact that there has been increasing discussion of the grounds of psychology and psychoanalysis coming from many intellectual sources, Chesterton's common sense concerns seem almost prophetic. Rapp wrote:

> But whatever their image of the unconscious, Chesterton believed that the Freudians' emphasis on it was misplaced, for conscious reason was the more important mental activity. As he once declared, the "thing I call myself is the thing that wills and reasons and chooses and salutes God; and not the thing that dreams, or snores, or walks in its sleep."[3]

Aristotle could not have said it better.

Moreover, the spirit of Chesterton's response here is pertinent to the kind of justification that Derrick offered for his own suggestion that Chesterton was somehow "sado-masochistic" because of certain drawings or references to gore in his novels.

To prove his point, Derrick suggested that, before we are qualified to speak to this issue, we must take the following three steps: We should all

> consult somebody who [a] is familiar with GKC's literary and graphic work, [b] reveres his genius and his colossal wisdom, but in no idolatrously uncritical spirit, and [c] is well qualified and experienced in the field of psychology.

Evidently, unless we have all three of these items in our *curriculum vitae*, we are excluded by that very fact from maintaining that Chesterton was a perfectly normal and rational man who, like Plato's philosophic man in his dreams, that is to say, like every human being who ever existed, sometimes had demons and terrors floating about in his imaginings.

Modern common sense philosophy, as it stems from Aristotle and Aquinas—I think of Henry Veatch or Leo Strauss—has tried to make sure that some form of "science" does not stand between ourselves and our understandings of the world and ourselves. If I read Derrick correctly, none of us can possibly understand what the real "us," be it ourselves or someone else, is like. We have to depend, for the understanding of Chesterton's own inner workings, on some scientific analysis of psychology to find out whether, say, sado-masochism is not a part of our very souls, whether we know it or not.

We all, consequently, will have to hide our drawings and our writings lest some scientist read between the lines to find out that what we are saying by our conscious and rational selves, that which is really us, to the best of our knowledge, is actually a little short of the Marquis de Sade, the Hunchback of Notre Dame, or Jack the Ripper.

We can all, indeed, be familiar with Chesterton's literary and graphic work, revere his genius not idolatrously, and still have never noticed what Derrick evidently has noticed. As far as I know, Derrick himself is not someone "well qualified and experienced in the field of psychology." Does that suggest that Derrick himself is dependent on someone else's theory and practice of it? And even if he is so qualified, are we to forget all we read in Chesterton and suspect that what was really going on in his soul was something quite deviant?

Chesterton said somewhere that we all should commit murders and such like—presumably all the capital sins—but not in our actual lives. We should do so in our novels. Again as in Plato's education, we should know evil through tales, literature, judgment, and experience gained by observing its happenings in others, not by our actually doing it.

Let me cite Rapp again:

> [Chesterton] had great fun mocking "those wonderful modern analyses of the meaning of dreams; in which digging up a cabbage and putting it in a hat-box is the spontaneous spiritual expression of a desire to murder your father." And of slips of the pen, he asked, "Is any man who hastily writes 'shooting peasants' when he means 'shooting pheasants' to be looked upon as a homicidal maniac?"
>
> He thought this no more nonsensical than an actual Freudian example which contended that in a note explaining the inability to keep an appointment, someone has mistakenly written "foreseen circumstances" instead of "unforeseen circumstances" because he unconsciously realized that the interview would be an unpleasant one. Chesterton thought that no such speculations were required since anyone with common sense could see that it was just a slip of the pen, nothing more. He could not believe that "the unconscious mind . . . leapt out of her abyss for one wild instant in order to omit the two letters "u n" [from "unforeseen"] and then sank again to her primeval repose." Such an interpretation was "a pedantic fancy," exhibiting "a lack of practical judgment."[4]

These comments seem to me to reach the heart of the matter at issue here. Was Chesterton what he thought himself to be in his general moral life, over which he had control with good will and common sense, or was he really concealing a hidden self that peeped through "literary and graphic work" to reveal a much less pleasant fellow, for the real knowledge of whom we are dependent on the obscure folks "qualified and experienced in the field of psychology"?

"The thing I call myself is the thing that wills and reasons and chooses and salutes God; and not the thing that dreams, or snores, or walks in its sleep." This is the great theory of common sense. This is the Chesterton who appears in his works and in the hearts of those who knew him. And no, I am not "well qualified and experienced in the field of psychology." I count my blessings if what it means so to be qualified is to conclude that Chesterton was someone else but the wonderful man whom we increasingly read, partly so that we will keep that sanity which preserves our capacity to will, reason, choose, and salute God. I am sure Christopher Derrick would be the first to want to do these things. I just wonder if his theory allows him to do so. For me, if there is a choice between his theory and Chesterton's common sense, I do not need an expert to tell me which way to decide.

On Staring at the Picture of "Tuesday"

In the collection of stories and fables by Chesterton entitled *Daylight and Nightmare*, there appears a four-page story called "A Picture of Tuesday." This story originally was published in something called *The Quarto*, in 1896, that is, when Chesterton was twenty-two years old. At that time, Chesterton was working for Fisher Unwin Publishers, reading hundreds of novels.

This particular story puzzled me on first reading it because I was not quite sure what it was about. I read it again and began to sketch out the characters and what was said about each of them. The story is ostensibly about a small sketching club that always met on Tuesday. In the story, there are four members of the club who appear—Oscar Plumtree, Noel Starwood, Patrick Staunton, and a man by the name of Middleton. The club evidently did a theme painting assigned in rotation for a given week. Whoever wanted to present a painting on the theme selected would show his painting or sketch with the others who decided to pursue the same topic that week.

The main figure in the tale is Plumtree, who is described as a "rising artist" and "decorative." Starwood is a symbolist and a visionary, while Staunton is a realist. Middleton seems to paint jolly monks and have a good business at it. When the question of the topic of the week's painting came up, Plumtree protested that he did not believe in such exercises or definite themes. Pictures were just pictures, he thought. They did not need specific subjects. However, as it was Plumtree's turn to designate the title for that particular week's exercise, he in some flippancy decided to have everyone paint on the subject of "Tuesday."

Of course, we all, on seeing this title, are aware of *The Man*

Who Was Thursday, which was to come a decade later in Chesterton's life (1908). Plumtree's work is described by Starwood as having "arbitrary color." Then Starwood added, "but, like all the works of God, you have to see him twenty times before you see him for the first time." The works of God, in other words, can be seen but not seen. What does it take to see these works that are not seen the first nineteen times we see them?

Staunton, the realist, was young, "but not quite young enough to have grown weary of the world." That is to say, that only the very young can be really weary of the world, for they have not yet seen the works of God twenty times. Staunton is said to have the two good qualities of a young man—"a sense of humor and an aversion to egoists." This is why Staunton did not much like Plumtree. Starwood, on the other hand, did not dislike Plumtree. Indeed, he said "that it was the great test and trial of true Christian philosophy not to dislike Plumtree." That is, there is something divine even in an egoist.

Plumtree, in Staunton's view, however, was going to the devil, but that only made him pity the devil. "But the joke of the thing is that Plumtree is for ever telling us that the artistic mind cares no more for the subject of a picture, than for the weight in avoirdupois." Plumtree thinks that just any subject will do, or better that no subject is possible. Starwood, the visionary, sees that just anything symbolizes "the everlasting Yea" of things that are out of nothingness. Yet, Starwood continues, "it is but a superficial philosophy which is founded on the existence of everything. The deeper philosophy is founded on the existence of anything."[1] Why is this thing this thing and not that thing? Why does this thing exist at all?

Plumtree's topic for the weekly sketch—"Tuesday"—brought forth the four entries. The first was Middleton's drawing of the jolly friars, who were tossing pancakes at each other to evoke the image of "Shrove Tuesday." Plumtree's own painting was something like a "gaslight in early morning" but it might just as well be Tuesday morning as any other morning. Staunton's painting was of his own mother's at-home day, which was a Tuesday, "in which he introduced all his uncles who told him things for his own good."

The surprise painting, which filled the whole room, was that of Starwood. Plumtree stared at this strange painting for he was "far too good an artist to let cynicism rob him of the gift of wonder." Starwood's painting was a huge human figure with its back to the viewer. The figure seemed to be parting the waters with his legs planted in the sea. "It was a dark picture, but when grasped, it blinded like a sun." When it came to the title of this painting, it was again called "Tuesday." And underneath were written the words—"And God divided the waters that were under the firmament from the waters that were above the firmament and the evening and the morning were the second day."

Staunton wanted to know why Starwood had made this the second instead of the third day of the Jewish week? Starwood replied, "I had to reckon from my own seventh day: the day of praise, the day of saying 'It is good,' or I could not have felt it a reality." It seemed unbelievable that anyone could look on the days of the week in that way, as realities that count back from the day of praise. And Starwood cried, "The week is the colossal epic of creation."

In the meantime, Middleton thought all this a lot of religious nonsense. He asked the realist if he could think of a biblical text for his at-home day? Staunton suggested, "And Job lifted up his voice and cursed his day."

Then came the end of the story in a single sentence. This was the sentence: "But Plumtree was staring at the picture of Tuesday." Did he finally see the thing of God for the twentieth time so that he really saw it for the first time? Did he finally understand the deeper philosophy that "is founded on the existence of anything?" Did Plumtree see that days were not to be cursed, that wonder had finally saved him from cynicism?

Starwood had once painted a series called "The Seven Dreams of Adam before the Creation of Eve." Did Starwood's "Picture of Tuesday," of God dividing the waters under the firmament, teach him that all real subjects are particular, that the divine artistic mind does care for the subject of His unique creation? I think so. In staring at the "Picture of Tuesday," Plumtree, like Starwood, began to count backwards from "the day of praise," the day of saying "It is good." Only in praise can we really stare at, grasp the reality of *the things that are*, even if it takes us twenty times to see *what is* for the first time.

The Real End and Final Holiday
of Human Souls

An original mind, I think, is one that sees truth as it exists in things. To be sure, we must affirm what we see to make it ours and therefore fulfill in some sense the higher purpose of things that are not ourselves. But books and philosophies and discourses ought not to stand between ourselves and *what is*. We know too that most often what we come to understand depends on our ability to let ourselves see what is there, not what we want to be there, or what we intend to do with what is there. The disarming thing about Chesterton, I think, lies often not in his formal analyses but in his asides, his almost incidental and fanciful flashes of insight into truth that occur when he is really attending to something else.

What brings this sort of reflection to mind was a column I chanced on one Winter evening entitled variously "Oxford from Without" in *The Chesterton Anthology* of the Ignatius–Bodley Head edition (1985) or "Aristocracy at Our Universities" in the Ignatius Press (1986) *Collected Works* Edition (Vol. XXVII)—where it is dated August 17, 1907, because the American columns of Chesterton appeared two weeks after the English ones. Clear? Thus, this column originally appeared in the *Illustrated London News* for August 3, 1907.

In it, Chesterton was bemusedly commending the then Bishop of Birmingham for calling Oxford and Cambridge places where young aristocrats played. What concerns me here is not the class status of Oxford and Cambridge youth in the time of Chesterton, but what he made of the subject of play itself as a kind of background to his main concern in the column.

> The old English University is a playground for the governing class.
> That does not prove it is a bad thing; it might prove that it was a very
> good thing. Certainly if there is a governing class let there be a play-
> ground for the governing class. I would much rather be ruled by
> men who know how to play than by men who do not know how to
> play.[1]

Chesterton thought in fact that the English, "almost alone of all
the peoples of the world," had a "good natured aristocracy."

Before I cite Chesterton, to illustrate my point about his extraordinary "seeing" of things, however, let me recall Plato, a famous passage, also about play, in many ways one of the most
wonderful and profound passages in our philosophic literature.
The passage is one I often cite, from *The Laws* (803–5):

> I assert that what is serious should be treated seriously, and what is
> not serious should not, and that by nature God is worthy of a com-
> plete, blessed seriousness, but that what is human has been devised as
> a certain plaything of God, and that is really the best thing about it.
> Every man and woman should spend life in this way, playing at the
> noblest possible games. . . . Each person should spend the greatest
> and best part of his life in peace. What then is the correct way? One
> should live out one's days playing at certain games—sacrificing,
> singing and dancing.

This passage is the great prelude to the Christian notion that the
world that God made is not necessary to Him, that what goes on
in it is not analogous to work or duty or determinism, but to
freedom, delight, and play, to things that are beautiful but not
necessary, in the freedom of what need not exist but yet, when it
does exist, is joyful and delightful.

With such classical ideas in mind, let me return to the
Chesterton essay on play at Oxford. Again, this deeper level of
meaning, though never far from the surface of his thought, is not
at all what Chesterton was directly dealing with. While there
may thus be many a reason to "smash" present universities as insignificant, Chesterton suddenly wondered rather if it would not

be well to preserve them not as universities but as playgrounds— "places valued for their hours of leisure more than for their hours of work." Chesterton did not find this position so much "reasonable" as "attractive." He continued:

> It is not only possible to say a great deal in praise of play, it is really possible to say the highest things in praise of play. Earth is a task garden; heaven is a playground. To be at last in such secure innocence that one can juggle with the universe and the stars, to be so good that one can treat everything as a joke—that may be, perhaps, *the real end and final holiday of human souls.*[2]

In his own way, Chesterton has seen, almost as an aside, the very same thing that Plato saw in *The Laws* about the origin of what is serious and what we are in relation to what alone deserves our full attention.

And Chesterton, even in a way that is reminiscent of The Book of Wisdom about how Wisdom "played" before the Lord, went on to reflect:

> When we are really holy we may regard the Universe as a lark; so perhaps it is not essentially wrong to regard the University as a lark. But the plain and present fact is that our upper classes do regard the University as a lark, and do not regard it as a University. It also happens very often that through some oversight they neglect to provide themselves with that extreme degree of holiness which I have postulated as a necessary preliminary to such indulgence in the higher frivolity.[3]

We are almost—as in Plato's use of the word "plaything" to refer to ourselves in our highest state—prepared to say that Chesterton again is just jesting, all this larkness, this joking, this frivolity.

Yet Chesterton has intuited in reality the profound connection between the highest things and play, between the seriousness of God Whom we must approach in silent holiness and the fact that God's holiness is also our delight, to which we respond freely, happily, as Plato said, in "singing, sacrificing, and dancing," in liturgy, in praise. The real end and final holiday of human souls is to spend our lives at the most serious things. We are to play at the noblest games; the blessed seriousness of God is worthy, the singing, the dancing, the sacrificing. All of this depth of understanding the *things that are* is found in Chesterton simply explaining what ultimately is meant when we think of play, even of playing at Oxford.

A Definite, Defiant, and Quite Unmistakable Thing

Every so often, I receive a note from W. Shepherdson Abell in Chevy Chase, Maryland. Mr. Abell once made the mistake of asking me to recommend a number of books to read on the centrality of faith and truth. He may even have been the immediate catalyst that finally resulted in the lists of books in my *Another Sort of Learning*.[1]

In the mail the other day, Mr. Abell kindly sent me a copy of a book his father, William S. Abell, had recently published with Christian Classics (1991). *Laughter and the Love of Friends*, a book whose title sounds like Belloc, is rather a series of reminiscences of Father Martin C. D'Arcy, S.J., who was a good friend of the Abell family during the years Father D'Arcy was in Georgetown. As Father D'Arcy was a professor of mine while I was studying at Georgetown, these reflections seem especially familiar.

I recall that Father D'Arcy often used to confuse me. With respect to organization and confusion of purpose and content, his classes were among the worst I ever attended. However, once in a while he would give a lecture someplace in Washington that would be positively brilliant. Likewise, I would often find him sitting in the haustus room over a cup of tea and engage in most stimulating conversation with him.

Among Father D'Arcy's reflections are those on Belloc, Chesterton, and Baring. Of Chesterton, D'Arcy remarked:

> People are always comparing Belloc with Chesterton, you know, and it is a difficult comparison to make. I, for one, do not straightaway concede the higher niche to Chesterton. I often say of Chesterton that God must have been looking the other way when he was con-

ceived because you'd think the man didn't have original sin in him. He did talk about having dreadful evil images, but I fancy those were just childish. He didn't really know what evil was. Chesterton remained to his dying day a beloved genius still something of a child. There was always a certain innocence about him.[2]

D'Arcy was right, of course, that Belloc had his own genius and that the world is filled with more than one genius, thank goodness.

About the question of Chesterton's innocence, his wonderful goodness and good will, his not knowing what evil was, I think Father D'Arcy had it quite wrong. Clerics who think they know about the world are often no match for men of the world who do know about spiritual things. Chesterton was no great sinner, of course. The proper point of comparison on this question is St. Thomas, who is often judged in the same way Chesterton is.

I did a course on St. Thomas last semester and I am doing one on St. Augustine this semester. I often tell the class that when it comes to the knowledge of good and evil, there is no essential difference between St. Thomas and St. Augustine. The difference has to do with their actual lives. St. Augustine did most of the things that qualify as intellectual or moral evil or disorder. St. Thomas thought about them but did not do them. This is why *The Confessions* of St. Augustine are more fascinating than treatises in the *Summa Theologiae* on evil or sin, at least at first sight.

Nevertheless, I would be hard pressed to say of either St. Thomas or Chesterton that he "did not really know what evil was." Somehow the notion has gotten about that we need to "know" evil by doing it, lest we understand it not. I would not claim that anyone, even St. Thomas or Chesterton, or St. Augustine, for that matter, "knew" all there was to know about evil. All three thought that the more we knew about it the better off we were. But I would claim that an intellectual saint like St. Thomas and a philosophic essayist like Chesterton did "know" about evil.

Something about the human experience and intelligence can penetrate to the mystery of evil without going through the trouble of doing it, or of putting the actions in which it exists into the world through our disordered wills. This very issue may be, as both St. Thomas and Chesterton seemed to have understood, more of a problem with angelic than human intelligence, however much it also exists in human intelligence.

The Ignatius Press recently sent me a copy of Volume XXXIV of the *Collected Works of G. K. Chesterton*. These are the essays from the *Illustrated London News* from 1926–1928. I decided to take a look at what Chesterton was writing about the time I was born, so many eons ago. He had been doing a number of essays on Cromwell and the Puritans. About six days before I was born, a piece of additional good news I am sure neither of my dear parents realized at the time, Chesterton published in London an essay entitled "Criticism of the Creeds."

In this essay, Chesterton remarked that there is a considerable difference between technological instruments that do not work and social systems that do not work. If, for instance, you presume to make an air ship out of wood and paper and use salt water for fuel, under the present level of technology the darn thing won't fly. Even though some day we may well make a flying machine out of wood and paper and fuel it with salt water, at present this inability is a test of our idea. "The flying ship fails when it falls."[3] Social systems, on the other hand, may be different. "A bad social system may fail because it endures." And a "bad government may fail by governing." Just because we live in an existing society, it does not follow that we live in a good one.

That is to say, in order to know that something is failing, we have to know what the truth of the thing is. This truth may have to be derived from someplace other than from our failing system. This is particularly the case with human beings. Bad regimes may quite well be enduring or governing but the people in them may be unable or unwilling to see their own disorders. In this sense, we might say of both Chesterton and St. Thomas, that they could see the disorder of soul, could well know evil and feel its horror because they could understand where disorder really went. To express this incisive "seeing" was why Chesterton wrote novels and detective stories and why St. Thomas wrote *Summae*.

This clarification of what the real structure of reality is, is why, Chesterton thought, we have a Creed in the world, a defiant proclamation before the ages and before eternity of what we are and what we are not. "About Christian dogmas I am quite ready to dogmatise," Chesterton remarked. "There cannot be the slightest doubt that a definite, defiant, and quite unmistakable Thing had come into the world when the Creed was roared from a thousand throats in an ancient Council or in a modern cathedral." I suppose this challenge of the "thousand throats" is why I get so annoyed at those Sunday morning Masses in which, contrary to the guidance of the Church that they serve, priests drop reciting the Creed. We recite the Creed—"we believe"; "I believe"—because our minds need to formulate what it is we know on the basis of what it is we believe.

Whether we recite, sing, or, with Chesterton, "roar" the Creed, it is a reminder and a guide about what is to be held. Denials of the Creed are not merely pious aberrations or minor errors. In their logic, they lead to the Gates of Hell. If a man like St. Thomas or Chesterton could see this logic, as I think each did in his own way, it is not right to suggest that he is merely "innocent," as if he lacked that original sin that taints the rest of us in mankind.

I would think, however, that the opposite might be more the case. Precisely because they could see these consequences, St. Thomas and Chesterton were more aware of evil than were those who merely did evil things and only later reluctantly came around to suspect the depths of the mystery of evil in their very lives and in the lives of mankind. Compared to St. Thomas and Chesterton, who thought of evil, the doers of evil were relatively naive.

In one sense, I suppose, it is more consoling to read St. Augustine than to read St. Thomas or Chesterton. The former shows us, *ex post facto*, that our thoughts and deeds have gone wrong. The latter two seem to have had such a clear insight into the very aberrations possible to us that they tell us beforehand even when we do not want to know. In this sense, paradoxically, there is more genuine "innocence" in St. Augustine than in St. Thomas or Chesterton.

In words that could almost be directly applied to the seventy years of Marxism, if not even more so to our own culture, Chesterton wrote,

> It is by no means easy to settle exactly when a working system of human civilisation does not work. All such societies have something to be said for them and a great deal to be said against them. We can say we proceed by the process of trial, but we cannot always prove that it was a fair trial. We can say we approached truth by a process of error but we cannot always convince the persons who erred that it was an error.[4]

And yet, this endeavor to convince on the level of the knowledge of good and evil is where the real issue lies. The sin of the angels was not a material thing. St. Michael was not less aware of evil than Lucifer.

"A definite, defiant, and quite unmistakable Thing had come into the world" when the Creed was affirmed before the ages.[5] We may not convince those in error that they are in error. "A criticism that corrects itself is not the same as a criticism that contradicts itself," Chesterton remarked. "It is very nearly the contradictory of it. We correct a thing because we wish to keep it and improve it in some respects. We contradict a thing because we wish to sweep it away altogether."[6] The Creed tells us what

contradicts life and reality in order that we may keep and improve what it is we are. By seeing what contradicts, Chesterton
and St. Thomas knew evil in a way the rest of us poor sinners can
only derive from our experience. This is why, I think, Christianity is both a religion of forgiveness and a religion of intelligence,
the divine intelligence that is in the Creed addressed to our own
intellects.

On Looking Down at the Stars

I do not recall now when I first read Chesterton's *The Defendant*. It was one of his earliest books, from 1901, basically a revised series of essays from a journal called *The Speaker*. Until Christmas, I did not have a copy of this book, but John Peterson somehow dug up a copy—the 1914 Dent fourth edition. As ever, such thoughtful gifts are just that—thoughtful, things that make us think.

This particular book, I noticed, had three previous owner-markings on it. The first is a kind of sticker on the inside front cover on which there is an owl enclosed in a wreath. The shield is divided diagonally into a black and white sector; in the center of each division is a smaller owl, no doubt the symbol of wisdom. At the bottom, there is a Latin inscription that reads: "*Ratione Non Vi.*" Evidently, this phrase is intended to mean that we should proceed by reason and not by force. I could write a whole book on the qualifications and understandings that we ought to have before we accept this otherwise very Aristotelian position. Aristotle would have said that if we proceed by force, as we must sometimes do, we should do so with reason. He would also have maintained that the purpose of force, even of punishment, is to establish and protect reason.

The second marking is on the page opposite to the inside cover with the Three Owls. It says: "St. Vincent de Paul Missionary Cenacle, 900 North 17th Street, Harrisburg, Penna." As there is no Zip Code of any kind on this stamped identification, I will presume that this book was in this, I imagine, seminary library, before the invention of Zip Codes. Then on the Table of Contents page there is another stamped inscription: "Blessed Trinity Juniorate."

The books's number in this library was evidently "3164." On the inside of the back cover there is also one of those old library "Date Due" forms. What is of interest to those who see doom everywhere in seminaries is that this particular book was apparently never checked out, as there are no dates due on the slip.

Well, I want to talk here rather about one of the essays, that entitled "In Defense of Planets." It seems that the young Chesterton had come across a book of a man by the improbable name of Mr. D. Wardlaw Scott who claimed to have discovered that "the earth is not a planet." Chesterton could hardly contain himself about the man's logic—"This sort of thing reduces my mind to a pulp," he wrote of *'Terra Firma': The Earth Is Not a Planet.* But what interested Chesterton was not the science part of this strange theory but its poetic aspects. Men of science have claimed that the Bible is not based on any true theory of astronomy. But if it had been, Chesterton remarked, "it would never have convinced anybody."[1]

What bothered Chesterton was that if we take the theories of Copernicus or Newton seriously (and *a pari* almost any scientific theory) we would never write any poetry. Take for example, Chesterton reflected, the case of a thoroughly scientific man who had a proper picture of the twirling Earth. Suppose we have "an aggressive egoist" who is vigorously maintaining his philosophic position. All the while he is making such absolute claims, we see him with proper astronomical theory. In fact, he is "announcing the independence and divinity of man" while he is seen to be actually "hanging on to the planet by his boot soles."[2]

Chesterton had great fun with this imagery. In spite of everything, Chesterton thought that Mr. Wardlaw Scott would never teach us to speak romantically of "early earth-turn" instead of "early sunrise." And even more amusingly, the scientific poet will have really an awful time in "speaking indifferently of looking up at the daisies, or looking down on the stars." It took me a bit of time to catch the humor of this remark. If we recall the man hanging on to the planet with his boot soles, we will see that in truth, looking at us as we actually are, the man standing fixed to the Earth when he looks at the stars is looking down, not up, and when he looks at the daisies, he is looking up, not down. So from our point of view, the man opposite to us in, say, New Zealand, is upside down. From our point of view, he looks up to see the daisies and to see us, and, hanging by his boot soles, he looks down to see the stars. Chesterton remarked that if we really do learn to write poetry this way, we will have discovered a new planet.

The fact is that even though astronomy and the Bible seem to be in contradiction, what the spirit of the Bible suggests is the right scientific spirit. "The writers of the Book of Genesis had no theory of gravitation, which to the normal person will appear a fact of as much importance as that they had no umbrellas."[3] That remark is so delightful. But the theory of gravity does have something akin to "Hebrew sentiment." It has a sense of "dependence and certainty." Chesterton recalled a passage from the Book of Job, "Thou hast hanged the world upon nothing." And he added, "in that sentence [we find] the whole appalling poetry of modern astronomy." *Ex nihilo, nihil fit*, as the old Scholastics used to say, from nothing, nothing comes forth.

I happened to be reading also Josef Cardinal Ratzinger's little book *"In the Beginning . . .": A Catholic Understanding of the Story of Creation and the Fall*. Josef Ratzinger gave a series of homilies at the Liebfraukirche in Munich in 1981, while he was still Archbishop there. Chesterton remarked that "the old Jews," the Jews of the Old Testament, would have had no "objection to being as much upside down as right way up." And the reason for their feeling this way about up and down is that "they had no foolish ideas about the dignity of man."[4]

Of course, "the old Hebrews" had some ideas about the dignity of man, that he was made in the "image" of God or that he should observe the Commandments, for example. But they had no "foolish" ideas, like the theory that man evolved by chance from a cosmos that one morning came by itself prancing out of nothingness. Nor did it come from a world that always was.

Cardinal Ratzinger took up a similar point in dealing with the French atheist biologist Jacques Monod, for whom both the universe and human life are so scientifically improbable—which they are—as to be almost impossible. Yet, a believer in chance still has to maintain this infinitely rare coincidence in which both the cosmos and human life appeared by accident from nothing in the peculiar order that eventually produced our next door neighbor or Mr. D. Wardlaw Scott, who subsequently proved the world is not a planet. Ratzinger pointed out that this very improbability of existence is the same notion of "contingency" that we find in Christianity. We are in fact in existence in the most surprisingly improbable manner.

Yet, we exist and are created for a particular purpose. The purpose of the world depends on our purpose, not the other way around. The scientist on scientific grounds has to believe in the most extraordinary confluence of improbable probabilities even to maintain that his theory of chance is plausible. Taking the same scientific evidence, believers can see a purpose in creation. "God created the universe in order to enter into a history of love with humankind. He created it so that love could exist," Ratzinger wrote.

> Behind this [position] there lie words of Israel that lead directly to the New Testament. In Jewish literature it is said of Torah . . . that it was in the beginning, that it was with God, that by it was made all that was made, and that it was the light and the life of humankind. John only needed to take up these formulas and to apply them to him who is the living word of God. . . . God created the universe in order to be able to become a human being and pour out his love upon us and to invite us to love him in return.[5]

We can indeed imagine such a world once we believe it exists.

"If we once realize all this earth as it is, we should find ourselves in a land of miracles," Chesterton wrote. "We shall discover a new planet at the moment that we discover our own."[6] It is precisely this "new planet" that we need most to discover not merely in the poetry of the world as in the Old Testament, but in the science of today. As Cardinal Ratzinger pointed out, there does seem to be some scientific evidence of the intrinsic temporality of the world. Yet, with regard to ourselves and our pace in the world, Chesterton was right. "For with all the multiplicity of knowledge there is one thing happily that no man knows: whether the world is old or young."[7] We do not know the times or moments that God had chosen for His purposes with us. Chesterton is right to call this ignorance "happy."

"In his atheistic parlance Monod has expressed anew what faith over the centuries has referred to as the 'contingence' of the human person," Josef Ratzinger wrote.[8] From this faith we have this prayer—"I did not have to exist but I do exist, and you, O God, wanted me to exist." And Chesterton would add to this idea, that our dignity is such that we must scientifically imagine ourselves strapped to this Green Earth by our boot soles whirling about at "nineteen miles a second," all the while looking down at the stars and up at the daisies.

As I think of it now, I feel sorry for those seminarians who never checked *The Defendant* out from the "Blessed Trinity Juniorate" Library, who never wondered about the meaning of *Ratione Non Vi.* How they would have laughed to learn that the Book of Genesis had no theory of gravitation, to learn that to the ordinary man this odd fact had about as much significance as the fact that the Bible does not mention that the Hebrews had any umbrellas. Yes, it is worth looking down at the stars once in a while so that we might also look up at our boots and at the daisies. As Chesterton said of Mr. D. Wardlaw Scott after he proved with another argument that the world is not a planet, "This is altogether one of the quaintest arguments we have ever seen." In the end, it is worthwhile defending both "In the Beginning . . ." of Genesis and our Planet itself, whether new or old, on which we live out our days. "God created the universe in order to enter into a history of love with mankind. . . ."

The Most Inexhaustible of Human Books

John Peterson called my attention to an essay in a book I had never heard of, but which fortunately I found in the Georgetown Library, namely, *G.K.C. as M.C.*. This is a wonderful book published by Methuen in London in 1929, *Being a Collection of Thirty-Seven Introductions*, as its subtitle reads. The book was collected and edited by J. P. de Fonseka, a name I do not know. The book's frontispiece consists of a drawing by J. H. Dowd from May 1929, entitled "Bibliophilus Maximus," a drawing that shows a very portly Chesterton with slouchy hat, cape, moustache, umbrella, baggy pants, attentively standing at a newsstand reading a book with total absorption, a marvelous drawing really.

In this collection is an essay entitled "Dr. Johnson." Chesterton did a number of essays on Johnson and one on Boswell. I want to comment on "Dr. Johnson." Well, I love Johnson and read something of him almost every day. Whether I like him more than I like Chesterton I cannot say, because we do not have to choose between such wonderful things. In the end, I think, they are both given to us. But Chesterton does give us a good estimate of his own appreciation of Johnson, a man with whom Chesterton himself is often and rightly compared. I believe the other man with whom Chesterton is most often compared is Thomas Aquinas. One cannot, I think, be in better company.

The burden of Chesterton's essay is to point out the great difference between Johnson as he appears in Johnson's own writings, essentially his *London, The Vanity of Human Wishes, Rasselas, The Lives of the Poets*, and *Irene*, and the Johnson we find in Boswell. It is not Chesterton's thesis that we have some sort of split personality here or a kind of a "two-man" theory. Rather, it is how the two aspects belong to one man.

Th[...]   ve find
"John[...]   :ing all
alone,[...]   ation,"
with [...]   re find
accoun[...]   , with
Burke,[...]   ounts,
Cheste[...]   it "*the*
most in
Bos[...]   :s and
feasts c[...]   call it
"the m[...]   vine"
book, e[...]   vine"
in hum[...]   on in
the san[...]   him.
Johnson[...]   .vorld

[handwritten note:] this gigantic + detached good Sense is Johnson; it is T. Aqu. It is Aristotle; it is Gue himself

will always return to him, almost as it returns to Aristotle; because he also judged all things with a gigantic and detached good sense."³ This "gigantic and detached good sense" is Johnson; it is Thomas Aquinas; it is Aristotle; it is Chesterton himself.

Chesterton reflected on this contrast between the loneliness of Johnson in his own books and his wit in presence of others. The difference is that Boswell could record these freer conversations and so save them for us while Johnson could not have done this himself. Johnson was, moreover, aware of a basic trait in every "sane man," namely "that he knew the one or two points on which he was mad."⁴ That remark, in a way, recalls the chapter on the madman in *Orthodoxy*, about the man who has one idea completely right but does not know where it fits into the whole of things.

The "varied companionship" that we find in Boswell counteracted the soul of Johnson in solitude. "Standing by itself in the wilderness, [Johnson's] soul was reverent, reasonable, rather sad and extremely brave." It was not that such solitude was not part of the human condition. Indeed, the point here is not the dying by oneself, the ultimate solitude. "I will not say that [Johnson] died alone with God, for each of us will do that," Chesterton wrote. The point was rather that in solitude there was a temptation, the temptation to confuse our world with *the* world. Johnson, Chesterton thought, "did not wish his own soul to fill the whole sky."[5] What a wonderful sentence! Human companionship was that grace that kept us mindful of what we are. We are not sufficient by ourselves "to fill the whole sky." We want the sky to be filled by what is not ourselves because we know that at certain points we are mad; we know likewise that we are not God.

What Chesterton saw in Johnson was the "divine comedy" of things, if I might put it that way. We are indeed creatures of God, but we are *human* not divine. Johnson should have been put on the stage, Chesterton thought. "There was in his nature one of the unconscious and even agreeable contradictions loved by the true comedian."[6] Again we touch on that delight and humor that pervade our lot. We are to uphold the gigantic truths of creation but we mostly show in the very upholding of them our own fallibility. And this, in the best of what is us, makes us laugh. "I mean a strenuous and sincere belief in convention, combined with a huge natural inaptitude for observing it," was how Chesterton defined this trait he saw in Johnson and in ourselves.[7]

Chesterton thus imagined several scenes on the comic stage with a Johnson in the center. And these scenes or skits would portray inconsistencies that would reveal "a perfect unity in the character of Johnson." For example, we can easily imagine Johnson explaining that "a delicacy towards females is what chiefly separates us from barbarians."[8] However, on stage, we would see this eloquent and tender insight portrayed by a huge, ungainly, unhandsome man who in the very locution would have one foot on a lady's skirt and the other in her embroidery frame as she was trying to finish a scarf stretched on it.

Or we could imagine Johnson on Fleet Street announcing to everyone within hearing distance that "mutual concessions are the charm of city life," all the while he was standing in the middle of the street blocking traffic. All of this would demonstrate, Chesterton thought, that Johnson's "preaching was perfectly sincere and very largely right." The fact that it was carried out in a situation that contradicted the theory it espoused was not an argument against the theory but a reminder of what funny creatures we are. Johnson's practice was inconsistent "but it was not inconsistent with his soul, or with the truth of things."

Another thing that Chesterton admired in Johnson was not merely his considerateness and graciousness in listening and reflecting on almost any topic of human discourse, but that once he had taken up a topic he, to use Boswell's phrase, "talked for victory."[9] Johnson did not think human conversation was merely delightful, which it ought to be. Chesterton thought that Johnson only "talked for victory" at that moment when talk "became a fight," that is, at the moment when something serious about "the truth of things" was at issue.

Thus Chesterton added, in words of marvelous wisdom and insight about truth, "every man fights for victory. There is nothing else to fight for." Chesterton noted that often such earnest conversation ended in shouting, yelling, and "rude remarks." But again this result is merely the condition of men in similar situations. It only recalls "the vast number of the men, wise and foolish, who have argued with each other in taverns."[10]

Johnson was sometimes annoying to his listeners, Chesterton thought, because he got the victory he argued for. And yet, we should not think that when Johnson argued for victory, he was interested primarily in the victory. "If the idea is that [Johnson's] eye was first on victory and not on truth, I know no man in human history of whom this would be more untrue." What a fine insight and comment that is, that argument for victory is necessary that truth might appear. And we should positively enjoy the combat that it takes to find it, but still what we look for is not the victory but the truth.

Chesterton returned to Johnson's solitude, to Johnson as a writer, not to Johnson at the taverns in conversation. Johnson was "one of the bravest men ever born, he was nowhere more devoid of fear than when he confessed the fear of death." Here Johnson identified himself with "the mighty voice of all flesh." Chesterton said that Boswell did not include the "deathbed scene in the old bachelor house in Bolt Court in 1784," when Johnson himself died. This scene was not part of "the sociable and literary" Johnson but of the "solitary and immortal one."[11]

Johnson died in "a doubtful and changing world" and yet he managed to "detach himself from time . . . and saw the ages with an equal eye." With this death scene, Chesterton concluded his essay on Johnson. And Chesterton remarked with great profundity that Johnson "was not merely alone with God; he even shared the loneliness of God, which is love." One has to read such a sentence many times, I think, to fathom its import.

When I first read that final sentence, I copied it out and sent it to a friend, remarking "what do you think of this?" The very essence of God, of the Trinity, of course, is not to be lonely. The very heart of love is to find the good someone that is not ourselves. All of us die alone with God. The point is that Johnson saw the ages with an equal eye, "the loneliness of God which is love."

Perhaps this is why Chesterton called Johnson "one of the bravest men ever born," not because he confessed the fear of death but because this very confession showed that he was "devoid of fear." What did Chesterton mean by this remark? That experiencing the loneliness of God is prelude to the love that is God's companionship with us? The "rollicking sagacity" of Johnson's conversations that fill "the most inexhaustible of all human books" suggests that the love that "fills the whole sky" did not come from our "own souls."

On God's Making both Hell and Scotland

Let me continue the thought in the previous chapter on Dr. Johnson, by talking about the first essay in Chesterton's *G.K.C. as M.C.*, his essay "Boswell." Actually, this essay is not so much on Boswell as on Boswell's book on Samuel Johnson. I say this because I have read Boswell's journeys to the Continent and his *London Journal*, where we see a younger Boswell, a less edifying Boswell, yet still the Boswell who eventually encounters Johnson. Chesterton is quite aware that Boswell's *Life of Samuel Johnson* is the record not of one great man but "it is the record of two very great men," one of whom is Boswell himself.

There is ever something refreshing about Boswell. In Chesterton's essay, he remarks that Boswell "towers above the whole eighteenth century, as the one man who had discovered that it was not necessary to praise a man in order to admire him." Even more fundamentally, Boswell was the first to discover that "in biography the suppression of a man's faults did not merely wreck truth, but wrecked his virtues." What an extraordinary remark that is! The truth about it is that we have vices and without this truth about our vices, we cannot describe our virtues, our wholeness.

The occasion of Chesterton's essay on Boswell is the issuing in 1903 of an abridged edition of Boswell's *Life of Samuel Johnson*. Chesterton takes pains to explain why it is quite all right to abridge a great book. Most of the books we possess including the Bible and the Greek classics are but abridgments of the original whole. "If there is really no justification for dipping into a book, as is the habit of some of us," Chesterton remarks in a most self-revealing passage in defense of reading only selections from

Boswell, "it seems really doubtful whether there is any justification for dipping into existence, as all of us do. Whenever and wherever we are born, we are coming into the middle of something."[1]

That Chesterton would have liked Boswell in many ways can be ascertained from Chesterton's notion that real conversations about the highest things never really end, which is why we find earnest young men staying up most of the night arguing about God, sex, religion, the things that are most worth arguing about.

Take this passage from Boswell's *London Journal*, for St. Patrick's Day, 1763. Though the Scotsman Boswell does not note this Irish feast, he does note it is a Thursday. Boswell had made it a habit to dine in many different places in London—St. Clement's Chop House, the Chop House near New Church in the Strand, Dolly's Beef-steak House, Chapman's Eating-house on Oxford Road, Slaughter's Coffee House, Harris's Eating-house in Covent Garden, the great Piazza Coffee-house, Clifton's.

What does he do this March 17th? He breakfasts with "young Pitfour." Pitfour is good for "a very copious meal." This put Boswell in high humor because of Pitfour's "oddity." Boswell next dines at the Lord Advocate's, where there is a formal, mixed company. "I was but dull," Boswell confesses. Alexander Weddeburn was there, a man who later became Chief Justice and Lord Chancellor. He was "overbearing and flippant." From Glasgow, there was a lady by the name of Mrs. Miller. Her terrible accent "excruciated" him. Indeed, "I resolved never again to dine where a Scotchwoman from the west was allowed to feed with us."[2]

Boswell then goes to George Dempster's, a Member of Parliament living in St. James Street. There he meets his friend Andrew Erskine and has tea with the Dempsters. Boswell found the society most agreeable. What I want to emphasize about Boswell and why Chesterton liked him is what follows: "Time galloped along. We stayed and had a little supper, and then getting into a deep speculative conversation about the immortality of the soul, human nature, the pursuits of men, and happiness, we did not part till near three."[3] So Chesterton is prepared to admit that almost anything in Boswell is worth reading, even if we cannot read all of him. "I am prepared to maintain," Chesterton wrote in defense of his position, "that if one cannot have too much of a good thing one cannot have too little."[4] In one sentence, Chesterton turns a well-known saying upside down to affirm both the unlimitedness of the good and the truth that in the tiniest good we approach infinity.

Chesterton took great care to point out that Boswell did not "eaves-drop," that his life of Johnson contains nothing "about Johnson except what half a score of other people heard; he only describes him as he is on the surface, but he reads that surface like a man of genius."

The main issue that Chesterton wanted to make clear about Johnson was that his irresistible conversation and Boswell's "over-solemn treatment of the great Johnsonian debates" contains a certain danger. "The truth is that nothing is so delicate, so spiritual, so easy to lose and so difficult to regain as the humorous atmosphere of a social clique. Frivolity is, in a sense, far more sacred than seriousness."

What does Chesterton mean by this remarkable sentence—*"Frivolity is far more sacred than seriousness?"* As an example of what he means, he takes Johnson's continual chiding of the Scots. Many people, Chesterton observed, think Johnson is serious when he teases Boswell about his origin.

Take as background, the scene in the *London Journal* for May 16, 1763, when Boswell first meets Johnson. Boswell had been "drinking tea at Davies's in Russell Street, and about seven came in the great Mr. Samuel Johnson, whom I have so long wished to see."[5] Mr. Davies is about to introduce Boswell to Johnson, but Boswell in mock seriousness over Johnson's alleged antipathy to

the Scots, "cried to Davies, 'Don't tell where I come from.'" But
Davies tells Johnson anyhow that Boswell comes from Scotland.

Then follows one of the great repartee's in all of English literature. Boswell seeks to forestall Johnson, "Mr. Johnson," said I,
"indeed I come from Scotland, but I cannot help it." To which
Johnson immediately quips, "Sir, that, I find, is what a very great
many of your country-men cannot help."[6] Chesterton at this
point takes great care to make us realize that we must strive "to
realize to ourselves the peculiar uproar and frivolity of the table
at Johnson's Club." For Chesterton, it seemed "perfectly evident"
that Johnson did not hate the Scots. Many of his best friends
were from Scotland, including Boswell.

"It is perfectly evident that Johnson's hatred of Scotchmen,"
Chesterton observed, "was a standing joke in the circle, recognized as such by him as much as by every one else, and that,
whenever an opportunity offered he braced himself for an attack
on Scotland in the same way that a recognized humorist would
for a comic recitation."[7] To illustrate this point, Chesterton recalled the story of the Scotsman who once in a "waggish" tone
maintained that "after all God made Scotland." To this, Johnson
responded, "You must remember, that He made it for Scotchmen; comparisons are odious, but God made hell." Frivolity is
more sacred than seriousness. Chesterton concluded, "There do
positively exist in the world people who can read that conversation [about hell and Scotland] and think it was serious."

And what about the conversations that keep us up till three in
the morning, conversations about the immortality of the soul
(about which Socrates talked on his last day), about human nature (of which St. Thomas spoke), about the pursuits of men
(which Plutarch described so well), and about happiness (the first
theme of Aristotle in his *Ethics*)? Are these serious or are they
frivolous? Are they comparable in spirit to God's making both
Scotland and hell? Of course they are. Chesterton implies that in

this circle about Johnson as recorded by Boswell, that is, in the circle in which the deepest of human things are indeed talked about, we need the protection of the seriousness of frivolity if we are to glimpse the highest things.

"I am prepared to say that if one cannot have too much of a good thing one cannot have too little." And why is this? This is Chesterton's last word: "The truth about a man comes out much more truly when he is telling his dreams and standards, as Johnson does in the great conversations, than when he is scolding his cook or being scolded by his wife." It was Socrates who was scolded by his wife, as was Boswell, who recorded the conversations of Johnson. As to the cooks—Boswell also dined at the Mitre, at the Turk's Head Coffee-house, at the Queen's Head in Holborn, where "we had a bit of supper, and every man drank his bottle of Rhenish with sugar." This was July 8, 1763.

About a week later, on July 14, as it is recorded in Boswell, Johnson and Boswell are again at the Mitre. They are discussing how to study. "I myself," Johnson admitted to Boswell, "have never persisted in any plan [of study] for two days together. A man ought to read just as inclination leads him; for what he reads as a task will do him little good. A young man should read five hours in a day, and so may acquire a great deal of knowledge."[8]

In the frivolity we need to understand these things, we might conclude with Chesterton that whether we need to go to Hell or to Scotland, both of which God made, to learn these things, we can be content once we find them. "If one cannot have too much of a good thing, one cannot have too little." Whether at the Turk's Head or Clifton's, whether at the Mitre or at the Dempster's, such principles hold us together in the conversations that last till three in the morning, in conversations that last forever.

The Ten Thousand Reasons

The very first words in Chesterton's essay, "Why I Am a Catholic," are these: "The difficulty of explaining 'why I am a Catholic' is that there are ten thousand reasons all amounting to one reason: that Catholicism is true."[1] That this claim to be true is the real problem with Catholicism, I have no doubt. To the modern mind, any claim to truth, especially divine, revealed truth, is looked upon as arrogant, a denial of equality. The human intellect has gotten itself into such a bind that it can no longer recognize exactly what it is for, that is, an instrument of knowing the truth.

This particular essay I had never seen before. It is found in Volume III of the Ignatius Press *Collected Works*. It was originally a chapter in a 1926 book quaintly entitled *Twelve Modern Apostles and Their Creed*, a book I had never heard of. I am not sure if the original book is a Chesterton collection or one in which he merely contributed a chapter. I presume the latter.

A friend of mine in Rome recently wrote to me about the difference between American and Italian cultures. He remarked that on Easter Sunday, "*Il Messaggero* [a leading Roman paper] had a fabulous front-page, two column essay by Cardinal Ruini on the meaning of Easter." My friend continued, "Would any American prelate be able to write anything that intelligent on Jesus as the Risen Christ and would any U.S. secular newspaper dare to publish it?" Needless to say, he suspected not on both scores.

Chesterton, in his few succinct words, has in fact put his finger on the one thing about Catholicism that is most unacceptable to the modern world, namely, its claim to be precisely true. No doubt, if Catholicism is true, a remarkable number of theses are false, even though nothing is so false that it does not contain a glimmer of truth.

This short essay of Chesterton, however, spells out just why this claim to truth, the thousand reasons, is so controverted. First of all, Chesterton pointed out that the Church is always accused of never having anything "new" to say. The only trouble with this accusation, he quipped, is that the accusation is itself "not new." Chesterton continued that the Church did in fact have something quite new to say and it has kept saying it.

The stubbornness of the Church in maintaining the content of its own newness is not that something better has come along, but only that something incredibly new did once come along. Whether something is also "better" because it is "new" is the whole issue. Chesterton would argue not that nothing new has come along, but that what has come along lately is not nearly so interesting or true as what was once new, the "good news."

The fact is that what the Church maintains is remarkably new in every generation, so new that we are still not prepared to recognize how extraordinary it is. The Church acts as if it is "a real messenger refusing to tamper with a real message." This refusal, of course, constantly runs against the "new," that is, the latest ideas, that turn out to be, on examination, very old ideas that were once shown to be wrong. "Nine out of ten of what we call new ideas are simply old mistakes."[2] That these old mistakes keep coming back should surprise no one who is prepared to recognize that each generation, each person must think his way back into the newness of the faith.

Another of Chesterton's reasons for being a Catholic is that the Church is "the only large attempt to change the world from the inside; working through wills and not laws."[3] This remark is the essence of so much that is wrong with those "faith and justice" theories that try to affirm that man's interior life is primarily a question of the structures, usually political or economic structures, of the world. No one person is, in this latter view, responsible for himself. Others are. The Church, however, realizes that, whatever the importance of laws or regimes, man is changed from within, by wills and not by laws. Or to put it another way, we can change the laws and constitutions until doomsday but we will succeed in nothing if we do not change our wills.

What concerns Chesterton is the fact that our "worst foes" are in fact "old mistakes" that keep coming back in new forms. The very existence of the Church, in this sense, stands in the cause of truth and intelligence. "There is no other case," Chesterton remarked with great insight, "of one continuous intelligent institution that has been thinking about thinking for two thousand years."[4] Those who recall their Aristotle will remember that "thought thinking itself" was his definition of the First Mover, of God.

The argument for the Church as an institution is, in this context, that we need God even to think straight. The record of our not thinking straight is the history of ideas, the map that the Church has worked out while locating all the errors, why they are possible, where they fit into the scheme of things. The Church, then, definitely "does take the responsibility of marking certain roads as leading nowhere or leading to destruction, to a blank wall, or to a sheer precipice." The trouble with an institution like the Church is that it recognizes that truth has consequences. And if truth has consequences, so does error.

The world is in fact full of millions of institutions that are based on a single truth. But this truth is by itself. As Chesterton said elsewhere, the madman has one truth, but that is all he has. He does not have it balanced with other truths, does not have it in proportion to *all that is*. Thus another reason Chesterton is a Catholic is this very proportion.

> Now there is no other corporate mind in the world that is thus on the watch to prevent minds from going wrong. . . . All other sects and schools are inadequate for the purpose. This is not because each

of them may not contain a truth, but precisely because each of them does contain a truth; and is content to contain a truth.[5]

It is this "contentment" with but one truth that stands in the way of familiarity with all truth.

What is different about the Church is that it is not content with just one truth, but confronts and contains all truth. "The highest mind of man," Chesterton knew, needs to be "guided by God." This affirmation will seem to many to be anti-human, to imply the insufficiency of the human intellect to arrive at all truth by itself. The Catholic argument, of course, is not that the human intellect is not made to know the truth, even the truth of God, but that the empirical record of our mind gives us no confidence that it will do so by itself.

"There is no end to the dissolution of ideas," Chesterton continued, "the destruction of all tests of truth, that has become possible since men abandoned the attempt to keep a central and civilized Truth, to contain all truths and trace out and refute all the errors."[6]

This passage struck me as almost prophetic. "There is no end to the dissolution of ideas." There is no end to "the destruction of all tests of truth." These errors leading to further errors have become possible "when men abandoned the attempt to keep a central and civilized Truth." These positions, one might add, are those most established in contemporary academia, those that follow on "the destruction of all tests of truth."

Of course, in fact, "the tests of truth" are not destroyed. They are merely the victims of old mistakes that each generation, including our own, needs to think its way out of, even with the help of grace. The fact is, however, that if the world does not want or accept this help, it will in all probability remain locked in the old mistakes. It will continue to watch helplessly the "dissolution of ideas" that must result from ideas that are not founded in *what is*.

The mission of the Church to truth requires that it state what it holds and state clearly what is not in conformity with the message it is given. Over the centuries, this affirmation, this dogmatic obligation, if you will, requires many pronouncements about the same old mistakes that come back as if they were new, but that are in fact quite ancient. "Every moment increases for us the moral necessity for such an immortal mind."

One further, and for me, final reason that Chesterton gave for being a Catholic was that the Church was "the only thing that frees a man from the degrading slavery of being a child of his age." This freedom lies at the heart of the newness of Catholicism. The original newness remains, even through the obscurity of many contemporary theologians and philosophers who really doubt it, who really shroud it in old errors. The remarkable thing about Catholicism is not that it has nothing new to say, but that its startling newness is not seen in its really genuine radicalness.

"In so far as the ideas really are ideas, and in so far as any such ideas can be new, Catholics have continually suffered through supporting them when they were really new; when they were much too new to find any other support. The Catholic was not only the first in the field but alone in the field; and there was as yet nobody to understand what he had found there."[7]

"There is no end to the dissolution of ideas." There is no end to "the destruction of all tests of truth." We would be hard pressed to find a more accurate and even prophetic statement of our present predicament and its solution. What is different between now and Chesterton's time, I think, is that the clarity of the Church's doctrine is itself obscured by Catholics, particularly by intellectual Catholics.

The fact remains, however, that the Church "is the only thing that talks as if it were the truth; as if it were a real messenger refusing to tamper with a real message."[8] This refusal to tamper with the truth grounds the Church's intelligence. The history of dogma is a history of a thousand reasons why mistakes are mistakes and why truth is truth. The alternative to this truth, it seems, is not merely error. Rather it is the single error contentedly held in the limited truth that all error contains unaware, at the same time, of "the destruction of all tests of truth."

If then there are no tests of truth, we are, of course, "free," free to make our own world, our own truth, based on nothing other than the fact that we made it. The primary reason why Chesterton was a Catholic, then, when he thought about it, was that without this divine mind, there could be no truth at all. In the end, he did not see any objection to truth. God has guaranteed its abiding newness. The ten thousand reasons all amount to one reason, one staggering reason that is so new that, by denying it, we dissolve all the ideas. But by affirming it we keep the truth in the midst of the myriads of "old mistakes" that we persist in calling "new ideas."

Against Pride

Chesterton once tried to steal some of the thunder belonging to us clerics. In Robert Knille's collection, *As I Was Saying*, I found an essay entitled "If I Had Only One Sermon To Preach," an essay originally collected in *The Common Man*. It is not without revealing a very deep understanding of the modern mind that Chesterton proposed to give his sermon this title. "If I had only one sermon to preach, it would be a sermon *against pride*," he affirmed. At the end of his essay, he playfully doubted whether he would ever be invited to give another sermon, though I suspect he would have been invited back again and again. Such are the very sermons we long most to hear. We are ourselves, however, probably too full of this first vice of pride ever to subject ourselves to another such analysis. But Chesterton did not think that pride was the primary vice of most men, though it could be of some.

This proposed sermon against pride arose from Chesterton's reflections about what he had learned because he had become a Catholic. The main thing he learned, he thought, was a kind of "active humility." His concern about the devastating consequences of pride was "but one of the thousand things in which I have found the Catholic Church to be right when the whole world is perpetually tending to be wrong."[1] In its own way, this essay is a strikingly accurate analysis of the modern mind, of modernity, and why it is, at its theoretical depths, so disordered.

Chesterton began his essay by chiding the scientific method of social analysis. He suspected that the scientific inquirer with analytic notebook, asking presumably learned questions, never really noticed what is going on in the average pub or tube (that is, underground, that is, subway). "As he is a scientific enquirer with a notebook, it is very likely that he never saw any ordinary human beings before." But if we notice what goes on in an average pub, there is invariably one person who is distinctly disliked by everyone. He is not the habitual tippler, the lost soul, or even the thief, each of whom can be tolerated and excused in some way. Of the man whom everyone dislikes, some cockney remarks, "'E comes in 'ere and 'e thinks 'e's Gawd Almighty."[2]

Chesterton points out that in this instance, in theological terms, the ordinary man in the pub has given an accurate and even learned definition of Satan. "Will men be like Gods?" The trouble with pride, Chesterton thought, is that "it is a poison so very poisonous that it not only poisons the virtues; it even poisons the other vices." He meant that, while the other vices are bad enough in themselves, this is all they are. They bear only their own corruption. Pride corrupts the vices when it uses them for its own ends.

"The more I see of existence, and especially of modern practical and experimental existence, the more I am convinced of the reality of the old religious thesis; that all evil began with some attempt at superiority."[3] Chesterton explained in this outline of his "only one sermon" why the characteristic of modernity in particular was in fact related to pride, to an attempt at unwarranted superiority. But exactly in what this "attempt" consists needs again and again to be clarified, however much the ordinary man may recognize and dislike it in practice.

The classic religion, as we know, had as one of its primary tenets that pride was the worst vice. No one explained this vice more clearly than St. Augustine. Chesterton thought that most ordinary men in your average pub still understood this truth, though sometimes I wonder about his optimism. Just today a young friend of mine in law school told me that one of her burly classmates had somehow heard of *Veritatis Splendor*, John Paul II's analysis of truth. He wanted to know "just who this Pope thought he was, trying to tell him what to do?" This self-right-eous protest has the same roots as those of the man in the British pub whom everyone disliked because he thought he was "Gawd Almighty." The young law student whom no one could tell what to do, obviously deficient in both self-awareness and logic, al-ready affirmed that same prideful claim to superiority that con-fuses his own will with "Gawd Almighty."

To neglect the spiritual teaching about the danger of pride, Chesterton thought, is a formula for disaster, the one thing guar-anteed to make us unhappy, the one thing guaranteed to make us isolated. Pride is really spoken very little of in modern literature, not to mention in modern sermons or modern politics. This neglect may be one of the reasons why pride is so prevalent. Pride can be practical or theoretical, or, I suppose, both in some given person.

"The practical case against pride, as a mere source of social discomfort and discord, is if possible," Chesterton thought, "even more self-evident than the more mystical case against it. It is the setting up of the self against the soul of the world."[4] But if mod-ern theory encourages egoism, encourages the view that we make our own rules from only ourselves ("who does the Pope think he is telling me what to do?"), practice often retains more common sense. "Modern practice, being exactly like ancient practice, is still heartily discouraging it. The man with the strong magnetic personality is still the man whom those who know him best desire most warmly to kick out of the club."

The spiritual vice of pride consists in turning all our actions, including our vices, into aspects of self-admiration. Pride is that "condition in which the victim does a thousand varying things from one unvarying motive of a devouring vanity."[5] Modern psychology has, in Chesterton's view, really very little to say about this vice. The old maxim that "pride is from hell," howev-er, was closer to the truth.

In our days of trying politically to introduce prohibition for tobacco and for penalizing those who drink with insurance rates, it must come as a shock to hear Chesterton say that "the learned go wandering away into discourses about drink or tobacco, about the wickedness of wine glasses or the incredible character of public-houses. The wickedest work in the world is symbolized not by a wine glass but by a looking glass; and it is not done in public-houses, but in the most private of all private houses; which is a house of mirrors." We live in a world in which we successfully prohibit tobacco and promote abortion. Could Chesterton have been closer to the truth of what is at issue? We live in a world in which we want only to look at ourselves, and it is the loneliest world of all.

But the passage in this "sermon" that I found most fascinating was the one in which Chesterton, warning us against pride and realizing that his remarks might be misunderstood, told us that his sermon would begin by his telling people "not to enjoy themselves." Paradoxically, he pointed out, to take this phrase—"enjoy yourself"—literally is the very definition of pride. We cannot enjoy ourselves if we set out to enjoy ourselves. This is the truth of things. What would Chesterton have told the people to do if not to enjoy themselves?

> I should tell them to enjoy dances and theatres and joy-rides and champagne and oysters; to enjoy jazz and cocktails and night-clubs if they can enjoy nothing better; to enjoy bigamy and burglary and any crime in the calendar, in preference to this other alternative; but never to learn to enjoy themselves. Human beings are happy so long as they retain the receptive power and the power of reacting in surprise and gratitude to something outside. . . . The moment the self within is consciously felt as something superior to any of the gifts that can be brought to it, or any of the adventures that it may enjoy, there has appeared a sort of self-devouring fastidiousness and a disenchantment in advance, which fulfills all the Tartarean embers of thirst and despair.[6]

Chesterton went on to explain that when we use the mild phrase that a man is "proud of his wife" or of his winning the one hundred yard dash, we mean something the very opposite of pride. These very phrases imply that something outside of oneself is needed to give us our glory—it does not come from ourselves.

Chesterton's definition of pride is as good a definition as anyone ever comes up with—and we are not to forget that the original definition of pride is found in the first chapters of the Book of Genesis in which the superior being who first rejected God tempted our first parents precisely to be themselves the cause of the distinction of good and evil. Pride is when we make ourselves to "constitute the supreme standard of things." This is why there is always something of obedience in our love of God, for His ways are not our ways, without denying that we are to be in our lives the intelligent beings who seek to know His ways.

"Pride consists in a man making his personality the only test, instead of making the truth the test."[7] This is really as good a one-sentence summary of John Paul II's *Veritatis Splendor* as I could ever imagine. "It is not pride to wish to do well, or even to look well, according to a real test. It is pride to think that a thing looks ill, because it does not look like something characteristic of oneself." Somewhere else, I forget where, I think in *Orthodoxy*, Chesterton distinguished pride from vanity precisely on these grounds. Pride is personal, when we do not care what others think because we are making our own rules, whereas vanity, though something of a minor vice, still cares what others think. Indeed, this is vanity's essence. It is outside of ourselves in a way pride is not.

Chesterton was concerned that if we were not warned about pride, were not tought its depths, we would lead ourselves precisely to where we have in fact come. "Now in the general clouding of clear and abstract standards, there is a real tendency today for a young man to fall back on that personal test, simply for lack of any trustworthy impersonal test. No standard being sufficiently secure for the self to be molded to suit it, all standards are to be molded to suit the self."[8] This is a remarkable observation, no doubt more true today than when Chesterton wrote it.

Pride, we should not forget, is the sin of the intellectual, indeed, the sin of the angels who fell. It is the one vice that is not of the flesh and was possible even at the Gates of Heaven. We can look on our times perhaps as ordinary, in which there are demonstrable and frequent incidents of all the vices. Yet, there is a nagging worry that it is a time in which everything is molded around one vice. This is the vice that corrupts all the virtues and all the vices. It is the vice that justifies abortion on a theory of choice and divorce on a theory of freedom. It is the vice that maintains that no one is guilty. It is the vice that abolishes any distinction of good and evil. It is the vice that says that all is relative, that nothing is true. Its model remains "I shall not serve." Chesterton's one sermon *against pride* remains the one that we most need to hear in our days. This may be the reason why we are least likely to hear it. And this too is pride.

The Christian Ideal

Recently, Ignatius Press published a new paperback edition of Chesterton's 1910 book, *What's Wrong with the World*. Over the years, I have owned not the original but still several earlier editions of this wonderful book but somehow I have misplaced, lost, or given them away. I think my sister in Medford, Oregon, has one that is now hers by right of long possession. It is one of those seminal books that every man who seeks the truth should own and reread on a regular basis. It is almost the only book that explains what is ultimately at stake when we discover what we are, men, women, children of our peculiar kind. If this encomium sounds like another Schall enthusiasm, well, it is and, I think, justly so.

What's Wrong with the World was in Volume IV of Ignatius Press's *Collected Works*, along with Chesterton's books on eugenics and divorce. I wrote the Introduction to that Volume IV and have long considered Chesterton's insights into the family, marriage, the home, man, woman, and the child to be of extraordinary perception.

Not only did Chesterton understand the romance and the virtues of the family, he had an uncanny realization about those aberrant ideas and laws that would later appear in fact at end of the twentieth century, ideas and laws that would in effect undermine and destroy the family as it has been and should be known. He understood that some form of collective existence would come along and justify the taking of human lives first at their beginning, then at their end, and, in all cases, for any "public" purpose deemed necessary. "In resisting this horrible theory of the Soul of the Hive," Chesterton wrote, "we of Christendom stand not for ourselves, but for all humanity; for the essential and distinctive human idea that one good and happy man is an end in himself, that a soul is worth saving."[1]

I have often remarked that Chesterton is enormously difficult to deal with when it comes to citing his works because he is easy to remember but difficult to place. Some of his most memorable passages are in the most unlikely of places so there is no easy "logic" that would help someone to find where he said something.

Fortunately, when I myself am at a loss to find where Chesterton said something, John Peterson, that most helpful editor of *The Midwest Chesterton Review,* can usually come up with what I want. Recently, for instance, pertinent to this essay, though I did not know it at the time, Mr. Peterson told me where Chesterton mentioned Nietzsche. Recently too, I had recalled, or thought I did, that Chesterton had said something somewhere on Benjamin Franklin, which if he did, I would like to see. So Mr. Peterson has received a note about Franklin. I await the results.

Why bring all this up? Partly because *What's Wrong with the World* is so full of brief passages that I often cite but never realize that they are in this particular book. Take for example the following two sentences, which may have parallels in *Orthodoxy* and elsewhere—Chesterton is happily capable of repeating himself like any good teacher: "The Christian ideal has not been tried and found wanting. It has been found difficult; and left untried."[2] Surely no two sentences better display simultaneously Chesterton's style, wit, and insight.

What immediately comes to mind in reading Chesterton's two sentences is the famous passage from, I think, Nietzsche to the effect that "the last Christian died on the Cross." The question is, are these passages from Nietzsche and Chesterton substantially the same statements? Is Chesterton, who often commented on Nietzsche, a covert Nietzschean? Of course, Nietzsche's problem was not with the Last Christian but with all lesser Christians who, he thought, too much imitated Christ and therefore left us politically and militarily weak because we turned too many other cheeks.

One of the main purposes of *What's Wrong with the World* is to show that a principle or ideal is not refuted if it is defeated or not practiced. If the Last Christian did die on the Cross, it would not necessarily mean that His life was useless or a failure. It just may mean that the rest of us are not Christ, which is good Christian dogma and the reason why He came in the first place, to do something we ourselves could not do.

The winning sides, moreover, are not always or even mostly the right sides. Chesterton observed to this point: "The task of modern idealists indeed is made much too easy for them by the fact that they are always taught that if a thing has been defeated it has been disproved. Logically, the case is quite clearly the other way. The lost causes are exactly those which might have saved the world."[3] If the Last Christian died on the Cross, if Christianity has been found difficult and therefore not really tried, we are left with the luminously vivid Christian dogma that still maintains that "one good and happy man is an end in himself." And if we combine this dogma with that which would remind us that the Last Christian, who died on the Cross, came not for the just but for sinners, we can see that Chesterton's paradoxical sentences are exactly right.

Christianity does not purport to be easy, but it does claim to be true. It does give reasons for this claim. We would expect it to be difficult, because life itself is difficult. If the Last Christian died on the Cross, we might as easily conclude that therefore there is some ultimate truth connected with this particular death that could not be achieved by the death of anyone else. "One good and happy man" is an end in himself. This proposition applies to the Last Christian as well as to anyone else. "The lost causes are exactly those which might have saved the world." Because the Last Christian died on the Cross, His cause was not thereby disproved, but, in His own terms, proved—"for this I came into the world. . . ."

And what about this paradoxical situation when the rejected dogma remains true but difficult? Does this mean that the dogmas are not worth believing or trying because they are difficult? In other words, what are the effects on daily life of difficult doctrines? In the first chapter of the last part of *What's Wrong with the World*, Chesterton, referring to George Bernard Shaw, whom Chesterton with both playfulness and humor calls a Calvinist, explained just why he (Chesterton) is not a Calvinist, not someone, in other words, who believes in determinist predestination.

"The difference between Puritanism and Catholicism," Chesterton wrote,

> is not about whether some priestly word or gesture is significant or sacred. It is about whether any word or gesture is significant or sacred. To the Catholic every other daily act is a dramatic dedication to the service of good or evil. To the Calvinist no act can have that sort of solemnity, because the person doing it has been dedicated from eternity, and is merely filling up his time until the crack of doom.[4]

Anyone who has read John Paul II's *Crossing the Threshold of Hope* will recognize the truth of this Chestertonian passage about the essence of Catholicism. The death of the Last Christian on the Cross did have to do with the abiding significance of "the one good and happy man" who is "an end in himself." Every other daily act of those of us who find Christianity difficult but try it nonetheless is "a dramatic dedication to the service of good and evil."

This is why there is, as Chesterton remarked, such high drama in each human life and why the intellectual efforts to minimize or eliminate this significance result not in a happy man but in no man at all, in man with no meaning or significance because he cannot, by himself, do either good or evil even to the crack of doom. To do either good or evil we must presuppose the good that already is, the good that we did not create but was given to us. We act in a good and noble world in the light of our freedom. How we choose is our glory or our damnation. God so loved the world that He took the risk that good could and would attract us to something other than ourselves and our own definitions of good and evil.

On the Alternatives to Right and Wrong

Thinking of November, I casually looked up what Chesterton was writing about in this month. On November 24, 1906, in the *Illustrated London News*, for example, Chesterton wrote a column entitled "On Wicked Actions." By any philosophic standards, this title looked promising.[1]

Chesterton began by pointing out the difference between international aggression and dramatic raids. He gave no support to the former but he did have a certain "dark and wild sympathy" with aggression when it was manifestly absurd. Sudden raids are of no use as practical politics. They are rather like practical jokes. The French were given to useless raids as they were given to epics. In fact, that is the only good raids were capable of accomplishing: they easily turn into poetry, into epics.

What caused these reflections in Chesterton was an item datelined Geneva that he happened to come across. It seems that an English schoolboy by the name of Allen was arrested in the railroad station in Lausanne. His crime was that in the town of Payenne, he painted the statue of a certain General Jomini red. After he paid a fine of twenty-four pounds, the boy was let go. The boy, Allen, on release, went to Germany "where," according to the newspaper account, "he will continue his studies." Meantime, the locals in Payenne were angry at the insult and wanted to put Allen in jail for a few days.

When he came across this delightful account in the London press, Chesterton acknowledged the disorder of his own feelings. He "freely confessed" that, on reading this account, he could not help but having emotions of "profound and elemental pleasure." The reaction of the Swiss locals Chesterton acknowledged to be right. He also admitted that a few days in the clink for Allen would not have been all bad. "Still, I think the immense act has something about it human and excusable." The essence of Chesterton's reaction was not that the schoolboy's action was bold or successful but that it was simply "useless to everybody," including to Allen himself, who, by painting the statue red, "accomplished nothing but an epic."

Next, with obvious amusement, Chesterton took up the logic of the notice that Allen, on paying the fine, proceeded "into Germany to continue his studies." Just what sort of "studies," Chesterton asked, was this English schoolboy, Allen, engaged in that he was again about to pursue? Allen in fact did not "seem to be the kind of boy to be so absolutely immersed in his ordinary scholastic studies as to forget everything else in the world."

In short, if this Allen continued his "studies" in Germany, then we might expect soon to read in the German press accounts of a certain English schoolboy next being arrested in Berlin for painting the statue of General von Moltke "a bright pea-green." And in Coblenz locals would wake to find the statue of Wilhelm I painted "a bright blue with pink spots." Then the Rhinemaiden at Rudesheim would suddenly develop a red nose. In brief, Allen would continue the very "studies" he had pursued in Switzerland with General Jomini. Sending him across the border would accomplish nothing unless there was something wrong with what Allen did.

This reflection brought Chesterton to the language of morals —a prophetic discussion, really, as we shall see. "The morals of a matter like this are exactly like the morals of anything else; they are concerned with mutual contract, or with the rights of independent human lives." Thus, Chesterton himself has "no right to paint the statue of Lord Salisbury in London red."

But modern man and especially modern journalism, Chesterton thought, could not bring itself to state this essential principle, that certain acts were simply wrong. "The whole modern Press has a perpetual and consuming terror of plain morals. Men always attempt to avoid condemning a thing upon merely moral grounds."[2] If they did this condemning, it would imply they recognized some objective basis for their indignation.

What, we might ask, was Chesterton driving at here? He was admitting that there was a kind of useless nobility in Allen's prank. No one could avoid the daring and the wit of Allen in his delightful painting of General Jomini, a man he had no doubt never heard of. But still, it is wrong to destroy another person's property. Allen was sent off to Germany to continue his studies without ever any acknowledgment by Allen or by the Swiss about why what he did was wrong. We are only left with Allen being amused and the Swiss being angry.

Chesterton gave a splendid example of what he was trying to get at. Supposing he beat his grandmother to death in the middle of Battersea Park. What would the Press say of his action? It would avoid condemning him on "merely moral grounds." That is to say, he might be called "mad," though perfectly sane; he might be called bestial, vulgar, or idiotic. The one thing that would not be said of his act was that it was "sinful," which is the only word that comes close to touching its essential moral meaning. There is a terror of plain morals, of that by which we identify certain acts as simply wrong on some clear principle.

Going back to Allen and the painted statue, Chesterton remarked that such an action of an English schoolboy might be called in the Press "a senseless joke." However, that misses the point. "Every joke is a senseless joke. A joke is by nature a protest against sense. It is no good attacking nonsense for being successfully nonsensical."[3] To paint a celebrated Italian general red is nonsensical but also quite funny. But in calling the painting either nonsensical or funny, we do not state what the action itself is.

Thus, if you say of this action of the schoolboy Allen that it is "nonsensical" and you think thereby that you have come to the moral essence of his actual action, you are quite mistaken. With the modern Press, you are avoiding the duty of saying exactly what happened in moral terms. "But the real answer to the affair is not to say that it is nonsensical or even to say that it is not funny, but to point out that it is wrong to spoil statues which belong to other people."

Chesterton next stated the long-range consequences involved when we do not call a thing by its exact moral character, but refer to the action as merely mad, or bestial, or vulgar, or idiotic. None of these adjectives imply that the act of killing the grandmother in Battersea Park was wrong. Each avoids the moral issue.

> If the modern world will not insist on having some sharp and definite moral law, capable of resisting the counter-attraction of art and humour, the modern world will simply be given over as a spoil to anybody who can manage to do a nasty thing in a nice way. Every murderer who can murder entertainingly will be allowed to murder. Every burglar who burgles in really humorous attitudes will burgle as much as he likes.[4]

This passage was written in 1906, at the beginning of this century. At the end of this century, our television and film do in fact murder entertainingly and burgle humorously. We do manage to speak of say abortion in a nice, even, alas, in a humorous way, not to mention the other vices mentioned by the Commandments.

Chesterton, to make his point clearer, added another quaint phrase—why do we call a political assassination a "dastardly outrage"? There is, of course, nothing dastardly or cowardly at all in an assassination, which takes in fact a rather high degree of a perverted courage even to attempt. The modern assassin exposes himself to the risk of being torn apart by a mob.

What is wrong with his action is not that it is dastardly or cowardly, which it is not, but that it is a killing. "The man who does [the assassination] is very infamous and very brave. But, again, the explanation is that our modern Press would rather appeal to physical arrogance, or to anything, rather than appeal to right and wrong."[5]

By any standards, this is a remarkably perceptive analysis, one that makes us realize that, in a way, very little new has happened in the twentieth century but a drawing to their logical conclusions principles that were already there when the century began. Eric Voegelin said something like this in a chat he had in Montreal in 1980, when he remarked that there is very little new in the twentieth century. Chesterton had already sensed this intellectual climate at the turn of the century. All jokes are by definition senseless. The essence of an accurate description of our actions is in terms of right and wrong, terms which we do anything but properly use about our "wicked actions."

The Spirit of Christmas

Chesterton's Christmas essay for 1926 was entitled, in the *Collected Works* edition (Vol. XXXIV), "The Old Christmas Carols," while the essay for 1927 was called "The Rituals of Christmas." In one sense, of course, carols and rituals make Christmas. The essence of Christmas is the Nativity, the Birth of Jesus Christ, the Son of God, into this world. The Word was made flesh and dwelt amongst us.

Carols and rituals arise from our human attempts to say to ourselves what this Birth means. That is, we acknowledge that whatever else this glory of God on High is, we did not cause it. It is not ours to bring into existence, but it is ours to praise and worship.

Chesterton wondered why "old Christmas carols are so good when most modern Christian hymns are so bad?" Remember that this query was written in 1926! When at Christmas I get out some old tapes of Christmas music, I am always struck by the mood and the sentiment that these Christmas songs and hymns stir in my soul. I have often wondered why they have this charm and enchantment.

Songs like "White Christmas" or "Blue, Blue Christmas" which are neither Christian nor pious in sentiment nevertheless carry with them much of the ritual and mood that we associate with Christmas. Meanwhile "Silent Night" itself is not two centuries old. *Fides quaerens pulchrum.*

Chesterton began his 1926 essay by noting that medieval Christmas plays dressed King Herod, for example, as a medieval king. To suggest this practice to be anachronistic is beside the point, Chesterton thought. This choice of costume was not rooted in ignorance. "It was sometimes rather a profound and philosophical indifference. They [the medieval writers and designers] instinctively insisted on the brotherhood of men across the ages."[1] Herods still exist in our time.

The brotherhood of man across the ages reminds me of Chesterton's thesis about the democracy of the dead, that we cannot be complete if we forget the actual experience of those who have gone before us. We are, if we are medievals, more likely to understand the sort of king Herod actually was if he is dressed in contemporary garb of the time than if we dress him "in the costume of an Idumean prince under the suzerainty of Caesar Augustus."

The poets, the story-tellers, and the writers of carols can tell us the truth even if they have images and words that are less than historically accurate in accent or garb. The Madonnas with Child painted amidst Roman ruins or medieval villas did not miss the point of what the Nativity was about simply because they were not depicted as Bethlehem in the beginning of our era.

Chesterton wondered about the reason for the boisterous shouts and good cheer that are found in medieval Christmas carols. "I should be inclined to suggest," he wrote, "that some part of it may have been due to men really believing that there was something to shout about."[2] Chesterton was quite sure that "the spirit of Christmas is in these songs more than in any other literature that has been produced." I like that notion, I must confess, of shouting because there is something worth shouting about.

In 1927, Chesterton began his essay with this striking sentence:

> Christmas, with its Christmas candles and its hundred shapes and patterns of fire, from the old legend of the log to the blue flames of Snapdragon and the sacred oblation of burning brandy [in the true tradition of sacrifice, which is the destruction of the most precious thing for the glory of the divine powers] has rather irrationally thrown my thoughts back to the flames of a torchlight procession which I saw on the last great ceremonial festival in this city.[3]

This festival was the celebration in London of the Armistice of World War I.

What Chesterton was driving at here was the natural symbolism of things, burning things, associated with Christmas. He thought it a bit incongruous to substitute a burning log with an electric one. I saw a candle in a garage window the other day over off Connecticut Avenue. It was of course an electric light and not Christmas-tide. It looked like something permanent. The problem is akin to the sanctuary candle or votive candles. These same candles made of electric lights designed, presumably, for the same purpose, are not able to carry the same symbolism.

"If we are to have ceremonial, Armistice Day [November 11] has a great deal to learn from Christmas Day, and especially from the days when the Christmas ritual was created." Chesterton thinks that with modern lighting, all towns are already lighted with signs about pills and smoking and catsup, toothpaste and chewing gum, so that the symbol of light, the light coming from the darkness, is lost.

"All ceremony depends on symbols." The quality of our symbols will indicate the depth of our ceremony. And the symbols themselves are valid only insofar as they reach mystery and the truth of things. The Word was made flesh, so that Christmas carols and paintings of Madonnas reach back to *what is*.

Chesterton recalled:

> [I] was standing in the very heart of this holy town, opposite the Abbey, and within a stone's-throw of the Thames, when I saw the [Armistice] torchlight procession turn the corner and take the road towards the Cenotaph. Now, a torchlight procession is one of the most magnificent of all those instinctive and imaginative institutions by which men have sought to express deep democratic passions of praise or triumph, or lamentation, since the morning of the world.[4]

Such processions, Chesterton thought, should take place at night, if we can find night.

I can still recall as children that the greatness of the Christmas tree was precisely that the other lights were turned out. Nothing is more annoying than not to play Christmas music on Christmas Eve. To fail to surround ourselves with the symbols makes us neglect that toward which they point.

"Our streets are in a permanent dazzle, and our minds in a permanent darkness." Chesterton continued.

> It would be an intelligible process to abolish all ceremonies, as the Puritans did. But it is not intelligible to keep ceremonies and spoil them; and nothing in the literature of lunacy is weaker and wilder than the appearance of this wavering sort of lunatic, holding a lighted candle at noon.[5]

The ceremonies were planned so that the symbol riveted our attention on the truth around which they stood.

Chesterton recalled an old Christmas carol about St. Stephen. Evidently, according to the carol, St. Stephen was an important official in the court of King Herod. Chesterton does not think this occupation of St. Stephen is necessarily verified by "recent excavations in Palestine nor by the Higher Criticism." It is legend and poetry. To understand these things, "the first necessity is to have a certain affection for anachronism. It is right in all religious art that times should be telescoped together. Anachronism is only the pedantic word for eternity."[6]

If the Incarnation and Nativity of the Son of God happened, it happened in time and in the now. The affection for anachronism is the affection for eternity, in which all times and places and peoples are before the Lord, Born and Risen. We should praise God in carols, yes, as Chesterton called them, "lusty" and "boisterous" carols. They should be boisterous and lusty for us who really believe in what we sing and shout about midst the dancing fires of the Christmas candles and burning Yule logs.

Second Thoughts on Detective Stories

The May 1993 issue of *The Chesterton Review* contains an essay of Professor John Wren-Lewis at the University of Sydney entitled, "Adam, Eve, and Agatha Christie." Professor Wren-Lewis as a young man in London happened to be present when Agatha Christie's *The Mousetrap* was first performed in London some forty years ago. As that famous play is still going strong, Wren-Lewis began to wonder just why such a thing as a perfect detective story might prove so popular and enduring.

Wren-Lewis's reflections took him back to the account of the Fall, to modern man's need to account for evil. The detective represents a kind of savior figure. In *The Mousetrap*, the detective turns out to be the murderer. "And here I find a clear echo of a theme expressed in different ways in many of the world's ancient stories about the Fall," Wren-Lewis wrote,

> but most clearly in the one which, more than any other, has exercised emotional appeal across many different cultures, the biblical story in which the loss of Eden comes about because of a "snaky" temptation to assume a divine role of moral guardianship, "knowing good and evil."[1]

One should note here that not all stories of the Fall are the same. Indeed, the story of the Fall itself was designed to counteract another story in which the origin of good and evil was located in a god of good and a god of evil. The Genesis story was designed to deny that proposition. There was no god of evil. All creation was good. Therefore, evil is located in what is good but not God.

Wren-Lewis tells us that he "interprets" this account to mean that the responsibility for humanity's unnatural destructiveness lies within the very element of the psyche that purports to aim at harmony, the moral impulse—not that it is too weak, as conventional society wisdom assumes, but that it usurps power and tries to control all other impulses by judging and repressing.[2]

Again, though pride is the great vice, I am bothered by locating the disorder in an element of "the human psyche." The source of evil is essentially located in the human (or angelic) free will. The whole point is that human nature in all its parts, including the will, remains good as created even with the Fall. If the problem is located in the "human psyche" and this does not implicitly mean free will, as I am not at all sure it does here, then there is a confusion. As such the "human psyche" is good.

But what bothered me most in Wren-Lewis's account was what followed. He refers to William Blake as someone who sheds further light on this topic. The "essence of Christianity," for Blake, was that "the punisher alone is the criminal of Providence." I find this a very strange "essence of Christianity." In classical thought, punishment is something with a moral justification. It is redemptive. It restores justice. But notice that the subject here is Christianity, not Plato.

Wren-Lewis explains his position by referring to the findings of psychology and sociology. According to these scholarly gentlemen, "behind all really violent and destructive human behavior . . . there lies a screaming protest on the part of some much more limited desire that has been repressed by an overweening morality."[3] Destructive behavior comes from morality somehow, albeit "overweening." If these are the "findings" of psychology and sociology, I worry about these disciplines.

This passage appears to maintain that the cause of the horrible things we do to one another lies in this "overweening morality" against which some limited, but also good, desire protests. This situation becomes worse by righteous indignation on the part of morality. The Inquisition is brought up as an example. So are nuclear war and holy war. These dire things are said to result from a mentality of "better dead than red" or better to "have nuclear holocaust than to submit to the Great Satan of American Capitalism."[4]

It was this passage, I confess, that first raised my eyebrows, for it reminded me of the cant of the 60s and 70s. We have here, I fear, a radical underestimation of evil. We have evidently found a method, perhaps unnoticed, grounded ultimately in Hobbes, to justify our compromises with evil. If we are given a choice between fear of violent death and what the Leviathan wants, we choose the Leviathan. Even our democratic Leviathans are now busily assuming this power to decide what is good and what is evil. When we reject the validity of Socrates' refusal to cooperate with evil, the very foundation of our civilization is gone.

Wren-Lewis then proceeds to Bunyan's Satan who is really an angel of light gone wrong—the plot of the detective story, even in *The Mousetrap.* The true conscience is supposed only "to serve life." Again, in the classics, the choice to stay alive is worthy, but to stay alive at any cost, that is the very definition of incivility. Civilization is defined by what we are willing to die for, not by what someone will do or give up to stay alive at any price.

In Blake, Satan takes the place of godly things by becoming a repressive moralizer, not concerned with salvation. Jesus, we are told, died as a transgressor, because He saw this self-righteousness and urged instead "mutual forgiveness" for vice. Christ's message is ultimately taken over by the moralizers.

Again, I would remark that forgiveness is designed to uphold, not replace, the order of justice. The disorder is not in the one who punishes but in the one who does wrong. Forgiveness deals with the consequences of our evil acts. They remain what they are. Forgiveness does not change them. Forgiveness is not designed to change the absolute prohibition against something intrinsically wrong. The punisher alone is *not* the criminal of Providence.

The Mousetrap does not proceed to these depths, but Chesterton did, in Wren-Lewis's view. Father Brown unmasked the villains, but "only to redeem them." Blake's version was "to have pity on the Punisher and to restore the moral sense to its proper role as a servant of life, by subordinating its judgment to forgiveness."[5] If I read this correctly, this means that forgiveness serves life, that is, better not dead and red. In this theory, the "evil" empire becomes the moral alternative when true virtue is pursued. We then find out that if we expose this "satanic judgmentalism within the psyche," we will have a direct experience of "eternity" even midst this world's conflicts. For Blake this doctrine was "the everlasting Gospel of Jesus." Blake insisted also that, prior to Satanic perversion, "all religions are One."

Currently, this remarkable doctrine that combines all religions and the Gospel is also that of Krishnamurti, who "stood apart from formal religion." Krishnamurti, it seems, "urged the regular practice of 'non-judgmental choiceless awareness' as a way of opening to the eternal."[6] I cannot imagine anything more un-Chestertonian or un-Christian, for that matter, than "non-judgmental choiceless awareness."

The true essence of Christianity includes precisely judgment. Judgment distinguishes between good and evil as objectively distinct realities. We did not constitute them. In this judgment, we choose one or the other. We are not allowed to remain "choiceless," the very denial of the human essence. Nor can we have choices without objects. The "right to choose" as such is a contradiction in terms.

Wren-Lewis suggests that the unmasking of the villain at the end of a detective story is anti-climatic. Evil becomes something of a joke when seen. Evil, however, remains evil when seen. Thus this position of evil as a kind of joke is finally linked by Wren-

Lewis with Chesterton's remark from someplace that if the human race were struck with a sense of humor, we would "automatically" find ourselves "fulfilling the Sermon on the Mount." This position is finally related to Umberto Eco's thesis in *The Name of the Rose* about the monastic suppression of Aristotle's book on comedy because it is dangerous for mankind, who are too weak to bear humor.

Chesterton actually remarked in *Orthodoxy* that it was God's, not man's, mirth that was *not* revealed to us because we could not bear it. The human race in fact has a sense of humor. I cannot imagine Chesterton saying that we could "automatically" fulfill the Sermon on the Mount unless he meant that we freely choose it because we choose the delight of things.

In any case, to conclude, I was perplexed by this essay of Professor Wren-Lewis. I recalled that in *The Defendant*, that wonderful book that John Peterson once gave me for Christmas, Chesterton had an essay precisely on detective stories. But I would suggest that the Chesterton of *The Defendant* would not be pleased with his association with Blake or Krishnamurti as seen in this essay about Adam and Eve.

Far from this talk of forgiving punishment, Chesterton was on the side of the police.

> There is, however, another good work that is done by detective stories. While it is the constant tendency of the Old Adam to rebel against so universal and automatic a thing as civilization, to preach departure and rebellion, the romance of police activity keeps in some sense before the mind the fact that civilization itself is the most sensational of departures and the most romantic of rebellions. By dealing with the unsleeping sentinels who guard the outposts of society, it tends to remind us that we live in an armed camp, making war with a chaotic world, and that the criminals, the children of chaos, are nothing but the traitors within the gates. . . . The romance of the police force is thus the whole romance of man. It is based on the fact that morality is the most dark and daring of conspiracies.[7]

Here we have Adam and the "Old Adam" together. This is not vapid "non-judgmental choiceless awareness." The romantic rebellion of civilization is against evil. We live in an armed camp. We are to serve justice and honor at the cost of our lives. "Morality is the most dark and daring of conspiracies."

In concluding his essay, Professor Wren-Lewis suggests that when in London, we go to see *The Mousetrap*, even after forty years, because it is "fun" even if we know the ending. He suggested this in the context of his citing Chesterton's remark that if we had a sense of humor, we would automatically observe the tenets of the Sermon on the Mount. I think, however, this "humor" becomes much more enigmatic if we recall the lesson of Chesterton's detective stories—that is, "we live in an armed camp." God's mirth remains veiled.

On the Inability to Blaspheme

The first pages of *Heretics* (1905) are entitled "Introductory Remarks on the Importance of Orthodoxy." These remarks were written about five years after the turn of the twentieth century, just as these present remarks are written some five years before its ending. Were it not apt to make me sound out-of-date, I am inclined to think nothing much has changed. That is to say, the permanent things remain permanent and we are among the permanent things, even in our death.

I have always been struck by these particular introductory remarks. They say in their own way what John Paul II said recently, in *Veritatis Splendor*, that freedom needs truth, that things are not relative, that the most important fact to know about a man is what is his philosophy and whether it is true or not. We like to be nice and to be tolerant without ever wondering whether there are some things we ought not to be nice about or whether we ought to tolerate what will destroy us.

Chesterton began his remarks with a reflection on the strange fate of the word "orthodoxy," a word we have come to associate with Chesterton himself. Orthodoxy means literally right thinking or right thought. It implies, thus, that there is a wrong thought or thinking, that it is possible, indeed, incumbent, to distinguish one from the other. For someone who thinks contrary to the standard of truth, we traditionally use the word "heretic." The heretic is someone who deviates on some or all points from the "orthodox."

A new mood came in during Chesterton's time about the word "heretic." Formerly, the heretic never maintained he was a heretic. Rather, he maintained that he was orthodox and that everyone else who disagreed with him was heretical. He took the truth of his heresy seriously. The heretic wanted to be right, thought he was right, and fought for his rightness. This zeal does not mean that he was not still in principle a heretic, but the heretic belonged to the same world as the orthodox, to the single world in which truth was one and demanded the attention of every mind, demanded the test of truth for every doctrine and every position opposed to it.

What Chesterton noticed was that the "heretic" had suddenly ceased to claim he was right. He was looking for "applause" at the novelty of his views just because they were his. "Heretical" came to mean being "clear-headed," while the word "orthodoxy" came to be identified practically with "being wrong." The conclusion Chesterton drew from this situation was insightful: "It means that people care less for whether they are philosophically right. For obviously a man ought to confess himself crazy before he confesses himself heretical."[1] The heretic "boasts" of his heresy and does not worry about the implied craziness.

Of course, it is "foolish" for one philosopher to set another philosopher on fire simply "because they do not agree in their theory of the universe." This method was tried in the "last decadence of the Middle Ages" and found impractical. But at least the effort of one philosopher to set another of opposing views on fire attested to the seriousness of their mutual enterprise. What is objectively more absurd than this mutual burning is to suggest that the solution for the inflamed passions of the philosophers is to pronounce that ideas have no consequences and are unimportant.

The twentieth century arrived with this opinion that "philosophy does not matter." All general theories were deflated. The rights of man are as heretical as the fall of man. Shaw's famous dictum that "the golden rule is that there is no golden rule" was the lowest form of intellectual disorder to which we could descend. The fact that we have no general theory in which we validate all things means that we try to say that our ideas on particular things are significant but our theories on all things are insignificant. "A man's opinion on tramcars matters; his opinion on Botticelli matters; his opinion on all things does not matter."[2] After examining all particular things, modern man cannot claim to have found the cosmos, to have found some order. "Everything matters—except everything."

Thus, we pretend to think that it makes no difference to what philosophic system a man belongs. If a man seriously holds that all property should be in common, we should protect our silverware or wonder why he does not follow his philosophy. If a man says "life is not worth living," we think his ideas empty with no effect on the world. Logically, if his proposition were true, "murderers would be given medals for saving men from life."

We do not take ideas seriously because "we are convinced that theories do not matter." The older liberals, "who introduced the idea of freedom," however, did not maintain this unimportance of their own ideas. For them, philosophic and religious ideas might be better made in freedom, but there were ideas that ought to be tested. "Their view was that cosmic truth was so important that everyone ought to bear independent testimony." What happened is that this theory of freedom has come to mean its opposite. "The modern idea is that cosmic truth is so unimportant that it cannot matter what anyone says."

The result is that the very discussion of the highest things has to all intents and purposes disappeared.

> Never has there been so little discussion about the nature of man as now, when, for the first time, any one can discuss it. The old restriction meant that only the orthodox were allowed to discuss religion. Modern liberty means that nobody is allowed to discuss it. Good taste, the last and vilest of human superstitions, has succeeded in silencing us where all the rest have failed.[3]

I asked a class the other day to state accurately and briefly what the doctrines of the Trinity and the Incarnation were. I did not ask whether they held them, just what they were. Few could do so. If we are allowed in academia to talk of religion at all, it is as a kind of abstract analysis. We are never allowed to ask whether it, or anything else, is true.

What is the most practical thing we can know about someone? It is not his weight, his nationality, his work, or his age. "The most practical and important thing about a man is still his view of the universe." Here is, of course, one of Chesterton's greatest and most recurring paradoxes, that what we hold about the universe is, in the end, what most matters about us. We cannot be friends if we do not live in the same universe, that is, if we do not explain the universe in the same way.

"We think that for a landlady considering a lodger, it is important to know his income, but it is still more important to know his philosophy," Chesterton continued. It is the philosophy of the lodger that decides whether he thinks paying his rent is a valid contract, just as it is important for the lodger to know that the landlady does not hold mercy killing to be a kindly way to aid sick lodgers. To sum up this principle, in his most memorable way, Chesterton concluded that "we think the question is not whether the theory of the cosmos affects matters, but whether, in the long run, anything else affects them."

Chesterton thought that the doctrine of efficiency, the doctrine that results when no cosmic ideas are valid, gutted the enthusiasm that we need to carry out anything worthwhile. Moreover, even the most profound vices, such as blasphemy, require a theory of the cosmos. If the cosmos has no meaning, surely it is impossible to oppose it or defy it as if it does. Milton's Satan was a much more artistic figure than any thing that might have displaced it, because of Milton's theory of the cosmos. "Blasphemy is an artistic effect, because blasphemy depends upon a philosophical conviction. Blasphemy depends on belief and is fading with it."[4]

If we have no coherent understanding of the world, or if this understanding, however coherent, is not itself subject to the test of truth, of *what is,* then our actions will have no long-range purpose, no end toward which they strive. "I perceive," Chesterton concluded, "that it is far more practical to begin at the beginning and discuss theories." This practicalness is, ultimately, the purpose of education, of education that knows that questions of the profoundest import must first be asked—what is good? what is evil? what is virtue? what is man? what is our end? what is God? Thus Chesterton wanted to go back to "fundamentals." It was important to state clearly just what a man held, his idea, and to state one's relation to it in terms of what is right.

This was, if you will, the scholastic method of St. Thomas. It remains fundamental.

> I am not concerned with Mr. Bernard Shaw as one of the most brilliant and one of the most honest men alive; I am concerned with him as a Heretic—that is to say, a man whose philosophy is quite solid, quite coherent, and quite wrong. I revert to the doctrinal methods of the thirteenth century, inspired by the general hope of getting something done.[5]

That is, to get something done, one must believe the world exists, that it is good, that it can be changed, that we know what it can be changed into, that what we know is what we can put into the world. The most impractical man, in this sense, in Chesterton's sense, is thus the most practical. That is, our inability to blaspheme is the result of our failure to take the world and ourselves seriously enough to know that the cosmos is an order we did not make and redemption is a gift that we did not give ourselves. And when we know these latter orthodox truths, there is no need to blaspheme, only need to praise and rejoice.

"I Say As Do All Christian Men . . ."

A friend in Berkeley Springs had mentioned a new edition of Chesterton's *Ballad of the White Horse*. Though I naturally coveted this book, I never made any effort to buy, borrow, or steal it. Such are the designs of gods and men, however, that for Christmas, John Peterson, as is his kindly wont, sent me a present. I received it before Christmas. But as I am loathe to open presents before Christmas, I waited till after my California visit with the family to unwrap it. Yes, to my delight, it was this very book—edited by Sister Bernadette Sheridan and published in Detroit by the Marygrove College Press in 1993.

The illustrations in this edition are by Robert Austin. I was immediately struck by the first woodcut, which shows a mounted King Alfred of England riding behind his spear-carrying troops. Beneath this engraving are these mighty words: "I say as do all Christian men, that it is a divine purpose that rules, and not fate." We defy all philosophical pessimism with this one cry.

This passage is said to be King Alfred's addition to Boethius— and Boethius is a very great man—the last of the philosophical Romans, the first of the philosophical Christians in the very late Empire. But Albert's addition is the most important thing that can be said, yes, even to men of our time. We are ruled by a divine purpose, not by fate.

As I read this text, not recalling that I had ever read it before, I kept coming across passages I well knew. Indeed, I saw a couple of book titles, books I had on my shelves. *Joy Without a Cause*, by Christopher Derrick, *The Wise Men Know What Wicked Things Are Written on the Sky*, by Russell Kirk.[1]

I went back and read some Derrick; his first essay was an effort to compare *The Ballad of the White Horse* with the meaning and movement of World War II. And Kirk tells us that what Chesterton really had in mind was "those people in the twentieth century who declare that our culture is doomed for destruction." Here is the recurring problem of Eastern fatalism and Christian hope. We are doomed for glory, but, in the divine purpose, we must choose it.

Nor could I help wondering, furthermore, if there were any relation between Chesterton's phrase on joy and C. S. Lewis's *Surprised by Joy*. Do I not recall that one of the petitions in the Litany of Loretto is *"causa nostrae laetitiae,"* the cause of our joy? So what is this joy without a cause? this being surprised by joy?

I also have C. S. Lewis's *Surprised by Joy*. I had not read it for some time. Looking through my shelf, I found in this book some notes I had taken when I read an earlier edition from a library. Someplace, in the meantime, I had acquired, but not reread, the Harvest edition of *Surprised by Joy*. Looking at my notes, I saw that Lewis did talk about Chesterton. Lewis did reflect much on this curious nature of joy, of its being somehow more than we might expect.

Lewis tells of first coming across a book of Chesterton, a man at the time he had never heard of. On reading him, Lewis could not understand why he made such an impression on him. The book was a book of essays, not *The Ballad of a White Horse*.[2] As he thought it over, Lewis became very protective, almost, of Chesterton. "For critics who think Chesterton frivolous or 'paradoxical', I have to work hard to feel even pity; sympathy is out of the question."[3] Chesterton's humor, like Aristotle's definition of pleasure, to which Lewis actually refers, arose out of the reality of the thing he was dealing with.

Lewis concluded of Chesterton that, "strange as it may seem, I liked him for his goodness." This is a remarkably right statement about Chesterton, I think. Lewis then warned young men, potential philosophers, to be very wary of Chesterton: "In reading Chesterton, as in reading George MacDonald, I did not know what I was letting myself in for. A young man who wishes to remain a sound Atheist cannot be too careful of his reading."[4] Indeed.

What are we? In few places can we find more graphically an account of our lot, of our joy and, yes, of our doom, than in *The Ballad of the White Horse.* What are we?

> When God put man in a garden
> He girt him with a sword,
> And sent him forth a free knight
> That might betray his Lord . . .[5]

We are not gods, but we are of God, and we are free. This is the bravery of God, if you will. The free knights that we are can betray our Lord. If we do not know this, we do not know what we are.

In a passage reminiscent of Plato, and midst the theme of the essential sadness of the pagan world, we again hear of joy:

> For Rome was given to rule the world,
>   And got of it little joy—
> But we, we shall enjoy the world,
>   The whole huge world a toy.[6]

Plato had said that we are God's puppets and that this was the best thing about us. We can enjoy the world because we know that it is for us, yet that it is not God. "We shall enjoy the world."

What is this "joy without a cause"? Is there such a thing? The stanza in which this line appears is spoken to King Alfred by Mary. It contains a vision of things to come, dire things often, wicked things written in the sky.

> "I tell you naught for your comfort,
>   Yea, naught for your desire,
> Save that the sky grows darker yet
>   And the sea rises higher.

"Night shall be thrice night over you,
And heaven an iron cope.
Do you have joy without a cause,
Yea, faith without a hope?"[7]

As I read these lines now, I think that the answer to these questions is—"No, we do not have joy without a cause, nor do we
have faith without a hope." And yet, the joy is not rooted in any
merely earthly thing. All of our joy—and it is real and sometimes
immense—is unsettling, if only because it portends a joy whose
dimensions we do not yet know.

And yet, there is something about joy that seems almost
causeless, even though we know that God is the cause of all, of
joy itself. St. Ignatius, in his *Spiritual Exercises*, spoke of spiritual
consolation coming almost causeless, from nowhere. Lewis is
"surprised" by joy. What a wonderful phrase that is.

The finest passages on joy are probably St. Thomas's discussion
on joy (II–II, q 28) and Josef Pieper's little essay "Joy as a By-
Product" in his wonderful *Anthology*.[8] We do not set out to have
joy. Joy is the result of pursing what is right and true, of having
what we want when what we want is right. Aristotle had already
intimated that pleasure is not what we set out to seek. We seek
some good or object. Pleasure is a kind of "bloom" on this activ-
ity, as if somehow added to the act.

But I am distracted from the *Ballad*. It is a tract for the twentieth century, now closing, and beyond.

I have a vision, and I know
The heathen shall return.
They shall not come with warships,
They shall not waste with brands,
But books be all their eating
And ink be on their hands.[9]

What does confuse us is precisely ideas—scribes, professors, intellectuals. The tractate on pride is too much neglected in our time.

Our souls thirst for the truth and we are too lethargic to know it, to want it when it is before our eyes. The Holy Father called his encyclical *Veritatis Splendor,* and we have that sloth of soul not to be thrilled. The splendor of truth.

Joy without a cause—St. Thomas remarked that "the joy of the blessed is perfectly full, and even '*superplenum*' because they obtain more than is sufficient for their desires" (II–II, q 25, a 3). Our books and our ink do not tell us this. We live among the heathen. We are reluctant to acknowledge either our company or our lot.

"I say as do all Christian men, that it is a divine purpose that rules, and not fate." The splendor of truth—where are the other Christian men who say this? The heathen have returned. Still, it is a divine purpose that rules, not fate. We are doomed for glory but, in the divine purpose, we must still choose it.

Causa Nostrae Laetitiae. Our culture is only "doomed" to destruction if we choose it. What is not sure in our time, if we read our philosophers, is that we are not so choosing. This is why we might read again *The Ballad of the White Horse,* lest we too choose it.

"The Way the World Is Going"

At the beginning of *The Well and the Shallows* (1935), Chesterton writes six essays on his conversion after his conversion. These essays were written in response to the question of whether he ever regretted his conversion. Chesterton wrote in the days in which he did not have to, for ecumenical reasons, apologize to those from whom he was converted, lest it embarrass them or the Church to which he was converted. Chesterton wrote in the days, in other words, in which it was still possible to acknowledge that there were objective reasons to join the Catholic Church and to explain why there were deficiencies of major proportions in what one was being converted from.

The official reason for the conversion of the Duchess of Kent—"for personal reasons"—made it sound indeed that the good Duchess had no objective reasons worthy of mention to pass from Anglicanism to Catholicism.[1] I must confess I think rather more of the Duchess of Kent than of the Anglican and Catholic prelates who were unwilling to acknowledge some definitive reason, the truth of which any honest person could acknowledge as a reasonable, not a purely personal, argument.

Chesterton's six essays spelled out six reasons that had to do with things that happened to him after his conversion. These reasons, he pointed out, were sufficient to have made him convert even if he had not already done so. What I am interested in here is his second reason, which is contained in an essay called "When the World Turned Back."[2] I find this essay of particular interest because of an essay of Leo Strauss called "Progress or Return?"[3] Strauss's essay is strikingly similar to Chesterton's in many ways. This is one of Strauss's great statements about the relation of rea-

son and revelation, of his problem with "progress" as it is understood in modern intellectual history, of his own understanding of
the Bible.[4]

Chesterton's essay began with the citation from Matthew
Arnold that I have used as the title of this essay—"the way the
world is going." Chesterton pointed out that for the past hundred years, it was thought that things were necessarily improving
in almost every way, no matter what men did. Progress came to
be, as Strauss indicated, the substitute for the distinction of good
and evil. Reactionary, that is the past, was evil; what came about,
progress or future, was good. But that there was a criterion that
applied to any age, any place, this was denied. Things were simply
better because they were later.

Since Chesterton was writing during the Fascist and Nazi
eras, he had no trouble suggesting that the appearance of these
movements did directly challenge the theories of progress and
therefore their criterion to judge reality itself. Suddenly it appeared that the way the world, contrary to all theoretical expec-
tations, was going was distinctly not in a happy direction.

On observing this change of attitude during his time, Chesterton remarked that

> what a man knows, now, is that the whole march of mankind can
> turn and tramp backwards in its tracks; that progress can start pro-
> gressing, or feeling as if it were progressing, in precisely the contrary
> course from that which had been called progress for centuries.[5]

Obviously something must be wrong with the original analysis if
things that were considered bad can return again in the future.

And in what does this wrong analysis consist? The fact is that
the world, by itself, is not going any place. In a typically quaint
phrase, Chesterton observed, "The world is what the saints and
the prophets saw it was; it is not merely getting better or merely
getting worse; there is one thing that the world does; it wob-
bles."[6] What does Chesterton mean by this amusing and "wob-

bling" world? He means that the world is open to man's influence. What we mean by its getting better or worse depends on what we do with and in it. We must relate it to standards that we did not make ourselves. "Left to itself, it [the world] does not get anywhere."

Now Chesterton found that this wobbliness corresponds with what the Church has always said about man and the world. The idea of progress could not compare with the idea of human freedom exercised for better or worse in the world. "The Church never said that wrongs could not or should not be righted." We can, if we will, perhaps improve commonwealths or aid the economy or reduce cruelties. What the Church did say, however, was that these laudable improvements would not just "happen" because of progress or history or necessity or the future.

Here is how Chesterton put the right doctrine, the second of his great reasons for being converted were he not already converted. (If I recall *Orthodoxy* correctly, what probably converted Chesterton in the first place was that the world was a place in which we could be grateful, grateful for the sun coming up in the morning, grateful that there was someone to love.) On the question of progress and world improvement, even when we later realized that things could and were getting worse, the Church said

> we must not count on the certainty even of comforts becoming more common or cruelties more rare; as if this were an inevitable social trend towards a sinless humanity; instead of being as it was a mood of man, and perhaps a better mood, possibly to be followed by a worse one. We must not hate humanity, or despise humanity, or refuse to help humanity; but we must not trust humanity; in the sense of trusting a trend in human nature which cannot turn back to bad things.[7]

Here are reminders of the doctrine of original sin, of the fact that our lot is ever precarious because we can choose the good and turn right around and reject it. We cannot trust humanity because we cannot trust ourselves. And the fact that we do not know this, if we do not, makes us the most dangerous of the species.

Suddenly in the middle 1930s everything that was supposedly going right went wrong. And whence came this standard by which we noticed that we had "progressed," or better, "regressed," into evil things? Surely it was not from progress itself.

If we cannot go to the theorists of progress, where shall we go to explain these things? In Strauss's terms, is there some place to which we ought to "return"—a word in Hebrew that also means to repent. In this same context, Chesterton cited the phrase of Belloc, "faith is the only beacon in this night, if beacon there be." Again there is somehow a hidden theme here, in Belloc's remark, that even reason needs the beacon of faith. Strauss was wont to find the divergence of reason and revelation to be the cause of the vitality in the West, as indeed it was—and Christopher Dawson also pointed this out. Chesterton and Belloc, both coming close to pure mind, realized that it was faith that saved the reason and that reason alerted us to what we did not fully know.

Chesterton's summary conclusion is remarkable, I think:

> In the heart of Christendom, in the head of the Church, in the centre of the civilisation called Catholic, there and in no movement and in no future, is found that crystalisation of common sense and true tradition and rational reforms, for which the modern man mistakenly looked to the whole trend of the modern age. From this will come the reminders that mercy is being neglected or memory cast away, and not from the men who happen to make the next batch of rulers on this restless and distracted earth.[8]

Here we have Strauss's "modern project" already anticipated, the notion, which Strauss himself rejected so firmly, that we create our own nature and our own world from our own wills. What is more, we have here anticipated a Pope who writes an encyclical on mercy (*Dives in Misericordia*), who guides the *Catechism* so that we do not forget what is revealed. The Pope writes on morals so that the philosophers and theologians who influence the rulers do not forget the commandments in this restless and distracted earth.

Of this classic and revelational view of the world, of the realization that the world could progress or regress, but in either case, only because of our own choosing the good or because of our own untrustworthiness, Chesterton said that this reason was not the first in time but it was the "first in importance" among the reasons why he would become a Catholic, were he not one already.

The added pertinence to these reflections on progress or return, I think, has to do with the conflict at the heart of our time, our free, democratic time. Marxism is mostly dead. We had hoped for advance, progress beyond it. We are chagrined at people like John Paul II and Solzhenitsyn for not simply accepting that what is newest is the way of history. We find them suggesting that there is a fundamental disorder in the great democracies perhaps as serious as that in the former Marxist states. And the reason they find this situation in the democracies so serious is the same one Chesterton saw in the 1930s and seems to be based on the same reasons, namely, that we can choose to regress by our own wills.

The worry today is about the democracies, about their choosing, in the end, to allow no standard but their own wills, that their future is right simply because they chose it. This leads them to reject the great standard of rightness and wrongness found in Jerusalem and Athens, as Strauss put it. The philosophers who guide our rulers and our rulers who accept their guidance refuse to accept that, in ultimate things, there is "no movement," no future, that substitutes for *what is*, for what is right. Memory is not to be cast away. Progress means nothing without an end and a right end. Return means first repentance. And repentance means to acknowledge what is true, what is right.

On the Winning of World Wars I and II

Allan Bloom, in *The Closing of the American Mind*, argued that in fact the Germans won World War II. He meant by this provocative observation that the ideas that have come to undermine our morals and institutions were of German philosophical origin, dating back to Kant, Hegel, Feuerbach, Marx, and especially to Nietzsche, Heidegger, and Max Weber. Bloom recognizes also a French component in this conquest, one that must include Rousseau and the more recent deconstructionists.

Aristotle remarks in a famous phrase in *The Politics* that a small error in the beginning can lead to an enormous error in the end. The thesis of Bloom is that the disorder of soul found in our society arises primarily through the academy, through the teachings in the universities. Furthermore, he suggests that for various reasons these teachings were of German philosophical origin, particularly those that have been so destructive to life, love, family, morality, and human purpose. Bloom, as a student of Plato, was aware, of course, that many of these ideas were themselves already present in some form or another in Greek philosophy, where they were pondered and put into some kind of order. It is no accident that the great German philosophers also knew their Greek and Latin.

I bring all this up in the context of Chesterton in part to note Robert Royal's recent thesis[1] at Catholic University on the relation of Chesterton and Péguy to post-modernism, but mainly because I happened one morning to have been reading some of Chesterton's columns in the *Illustrated London News* on World War I.[2] Royal's thesis is that many of the things that post-modernism thinks it has suddenly come upon were already pondered and sorted out by Chesterton in his own way in the early part of this century.

During World War I (June 5, 1915), Chesterton wrote an essay entitled "What We Are Fighting For." To understand the import of his argument, I think, it is well to recall a controversy about Machiavelli, to go behind Hegel, Kant, and Spinoza. Machiavelli had wanted to be rid of the limits that classical philosophy and religion had placed on the Prince. Machiavelli wanted to advise the Prince on how to rule. He wanted to be the teacher of princes. Indeed, he became the teacher of many princes, especially of German princes, not to mention the teacher of many professors. The essence of Machiavelli's teaching was that the distinction between right and wrong as it had been understood in the tradition had to be subordinated to the distinction between successful and unsuccessful.

The good prince was a successful prince. The successful prince was one who retained power, however he retained it. Should the prince lose power because he refused to do something classically considered as "evil," he was, in Machiavelli's view, a "bad" prince. The "freedom" of the prince was the freedom over good and evil. Later on, in the nineteenth century, Nietzsche was to write a book called *Beyond Good and Evil*, in which he accused the Europeans, who had lost their faith and their philosophy, of not having the nerve to carry out the consequences of their practical acceptance that "God was dead" and that therefore the distinction of good and evil was in their own hands.

On first reading, Chesterton always sounds very "anti-German." Obviously, he was an Englishman writing during the Great War itself about an enemy nation. He was especially concerned, however, about German philosophy and about "Prussianism," which is the peculiar form of German militarism. Chesterton was not by any means a pacifist; two weeks previously (May 29, 1915) he had spelled out the reasons for his opposition to pacifism.

This latter essay, incidently, is one of the best arguments I have ever seen about the dangers of a World State with concentrated military, police, and legal power.

Chesterton began his essay "What We Are Fighting For" by talking about the bad or improper use of words in this way: "If I were the Grand Inquisitor, I would try to burn out of the world not so much certain beliefs as certain phrases. I would argue with people about creeds but I would kill them for catchwords."[3] The main misuse of words Chesterton had in mind was the expression during the Great War that "we want not people who talk but people who do things." Chesterton pointed out, however, that it is indeed "within the humble capacities of human nature to talk sense." He thought that the best thing a civilian could do during the war was precisely that, "to talk sense." Wars are also lost because of ideas rather than guns. Even just wars need to be comprehended, that is, explained as exactly that, just. Bloom's thesis, to recall, was that even when guns win wars, ideas can cause the peace to be lost.

The notion that there are men of action and men of words divides the world unnaturally into two sections, the speakers and the actors. However, "there is not, and never has been, the smallest grain of evidence that the two capacities are incompatible." Great men have the capacity to act and to speak. This division leads to the amusing absurdity that "a man is supposed to be able to do everything merely because he cannot tell anybody what he is doing."

Another expression that Chesterton had great fun with was that "we should fight the Germans with their own weapons." Immediately, Chesterton quipped, in refutation of this view, that a man "does not bite a shark." Obviously, Chesterton is leading to the most important of principles about what we stand for. We do not imitate our enemies, we do not fight with their weapons, "out of respect for ourselves" and for our principles.[4]

Obviously, our talk is something that has to inform our deeds, or even more basically, our deeds flow from our thoughts, which we must also formulate in words. Deeds do not speak louder than words, contrary to the old adage, because we must know what our deeds mean.

> We [that is the English in the name of the whole Western tradition] are fighting for human self-respect: we cannot possibly lose what [principle] we are fighting for, even in order to fight better. The Prussian sticks at nothing in the pursuit of triumph because he understands nothing except triumph. Losing the battle is to him what losing his soul is to a *dévot*. . . . But we do not and cannot make our salvation consist solely in our success. We do not and cannot think of defeat as the worst thing possible, any more than we can think of war as the worst thing possible.[5]

Notice that this test of "success," which Chesterton rejects, is the Machiavellian test. He also rejects the idea that war is always and everywhere "the worst thing possible." There are things worse than war, things that we shall probably get if we renounce war in principle. Staying alive at any cost is the definition of cowardliness and implies the lack of any principle but self-preservation.

The virtue of courage, on the other hand, requires the other virtues, particularly the end for which all virtues exist, which includes the defense of what is right and honorable, not merely success. "That spirit cannot exist without other virtues besides the virtue of fortitude; it always has in it something that looks before and after, the memory and the promise of peace. . . . Healthy and military pride cannot stand alone or grow out of nothing: it must have something to defend, and something that is worth defending."[6] Chesterton thought that the war effort itself would be more serious if the English knew what they were fighting for, spoke it, said it. Without this articulateness, courage would dry up. "For we are not fighting for something before us, but for something behind us; not for Empire but for home."[7]

In his almost scathing chapter on the student disorders of the 1960s, Allan Bloom wrote of the professors:

Of course anyone who is a professional contemplative holding down a prestigious and well-paying job, and who also believes there is nothing to contemplate, finds himself in a difficult position with respect to himself and to the community. The imperative to promote equality, stamp out racism, sexism, and elitism (the peculiar crimes of our democratic society), as well as war, is overriding for a man who can define no other interest worthy of defending.[8]

Professors steeped in certain strands of German philosophy have no philosophic principles that would allow them to defend anything very real and very concrete. A World State might be imposed on all to eliminate evil in the name of carrying out ideological ends at the expense of the home of the family. These understandings are common to Chesterton and Bloom. I have often thought that Bloom's chapter on the dire consequences of divorce in *The Closing of the American Mind* has no real parallel outside of Chesterton's discussion in *What's Wrong with the World*.

Chesterton already sensed during the Great War that what was at stake was civilization itself and more especially the ideas on which it was based. The spelling out of how these ideas continue to work to undermine the civilization in which we live is the history of the years since 1915 when he wrote. Few are brave enough or frank enough or witty enough to be men of words which would recount how our most cherished ideas—words like value, commitment, life-style, rights, and the abstract sins of sexism, elitism, or racism—all are rooted in a philosophic system that denies the existence of a natural order, of anything superior to the human will.

In the twenty-first century, we will be a long time in sorting out the twentieth century, if we indeed have the time. But when we do, we will find that Chesterton, near the beginning, and Bloom, near the end, had their fingers on the main problem—the relativism based on a will grounded in nothing but its own wants. This relativism is thence elevated to a philosophic position and taught to all the young in the best universities as if it contained no intrinsic contradiction. The Winning of World War I and II remains an issue of the mind, a struggle between the souls that remember and the souls that have forgotten where home is and in what it consists. Deeds follow words; and as both Chesterton and Bloom have pointed out, it is the words that we have wrong.

Christmas and the Most Dangerous Toy

The last chapter of an obscure book I published in England was entitled "Of God's Jokes, Toys, and Christmas Trees."[1] I was reminded of this chapter when I came across Chesterton's 1921 Christmas column in the *Illustrated London News*.[2] What had occasioned my earlier reflections on Christmas and toys was an essay in the *Wall Street Journal* about the dubiousness of the idea that giving little boys toy guns for Christmas was somehow dangerous or immoral. I was delighted to see that Chesterton's 1921 column was entitled "On Dangerous Toys."

Already here, in 1921, we find Chesterton concerned by the tendency to locate the problem of evil in things and not in wills, even in the case of children. In many ways, modern culture and society have almost completed the closed net by which individual human actions have no significance of their own or source in the individual person. The individual is not viewed as a being able to control his action by responsible choice or self-discipline, even if that discipline takes time and we can often err. The State is now in charge of our errors and seeks to counter them by its own policies and authority. Why we do wrong is not because we choose to do so, but because of our class, race, or gender or some other external cause. Things are out of our control, but they are in control of the State and those who manipulate its ideas about what can or cannot be expected of a human person.

Chesterton, it seems, had been in a toy shop talking with the proprietor. He was told that not too many toy bows and arrows were made because bows and arrows were considered dangerous for little boys. To such a proposition, Chesterton remarked with considerable humor and not a little pointed criticism of a flawed ideology, that certainly toy bows and arrows might at times be considered mildly dangerous. But it was always "dangerous to have little boys." We will not stop the possible dangerous use of any toy by banning the toy. We can only eliminate this dangerous use by abolishing all "little boys." Here, Chesterton found yet another classic example of modern mind's inability to distinguish between "the means and the end, between the organ and the disease, between the use and abuse."

To examine this question further, Chesterton proposed scrutinizing this question of "the dangerous toy." It turns out, of course, that just about everything a little boy runs into is potentially dangerous. In fact, "the most dangerous toy" is about the "least dangerous thing a little boy is likely to run into." Thus, there is hardly a domestic utensil that is not more dangerous than a little bow and arrow—tea kettles, carving knives, or fireplaces; almost anything about the house that can be broken is more dangerous than a toy. Any little boy could do much more damage with a stone he picks up in the garden than with a toy bow and arrow.

What is the cure for the danger that any little boy might find with a toy bow and arrow or the stone? Surely, the answer is not to empower the State to ban such toys, but rather to "trust your private relation with the boy, and not your public relation with the stone." That is, if a boy does damage with a stone, the answer is not to abolish all stones. "If you can teach a child not to throw a stone, you can teach him where to shoot an arrow; if you cannot teach him anything, he will always have something to throw."[3]

These reflections are, no doubt, even more pertinent today than they were when Chesterton wrote them in 1921. We are empowering the all-caring State to take charge of us in everything. The State is eagerly seeking this power to enter our homes and our minds to instruct us about what is dangerous for us, as if we could not figure this out ourselves. "The notion that the child depends upon particular implements, labeled dangerous, in order to be a danger to himself and other people, is a notion so nonsensical that it is hard to see how any human mind can entertain it for a moment."

Yet, such nonsense today enters quite a few minds, itself a sign of tremendous cultural change. If we ask, but how is it then that human minds do entertain such radical ideas that would relocate the whole problem of evil and will? The answer seems to be that we have internalized an image of the person, little boys included, in which free acts do not exist and good habits cannot be formed. Since all little boys are dangerous to themselves because they too have wills, we will make it impossible for them to be little boys, in which condition they normally learn to act responsibly because they can so be taught and guided by their parents. Since all parents fail, the State becomes the large parent. "The truth is that all sorts of faddism, both official and theoretical, have broken down the natural authority of the domestic institution." The documents proposed at the U.N. Beijing Conference, among other places, were little else but extreme applications of these ideas that Chesterton already perceived in the 1920s as those that would most undermine human worth.

"So the modern spirit has descended to the indescribable mental degradation of trying to abolish the abuse of things by abolishing the things themselves. . . . Thus, we have all heard of savages who try a tomahawk for murder. . . . To such intellectual levels may the world return."[4] Chesterton thought that there was something even lower than this effort to abolish evil by abolishing things or by trying tomahawks for murder. The example he discovered to make his point came, not surprisingly, from America. Chesterton, it seems, ran across a story according to which some American proposed that the reason why the little boy should give up bows and arrows or toy Christmas cannons was "to assist the disarmament of the world." Chesterton actually hoped that some little boy and not his elders thought of this silly principle. Yet, the proposition to abolish war by abolishing toy cannons was proposed in a "reverential spirit." This was in fact another step not in progress but in "cerebral decay."

We could see the absurdity of this logic of abolishing war by abolishing toy cannons by carrying the principle out to its logical conclusion. That is, we should not only abolish the toy cannon to achieve world peace but also photos of cannons or spears or bows and arrows. We would have to clear out most art galleries, of course, and even more all the great libraries of the world where we could read about wars and rumors of war. When we finally had abolished all toy bows and arrows, all photos of bows and arrows, and all stories of bows and arrows, it would finally begin to dawn on what rational being was still left among us that there must be "something wrong with the moral principle" by which such things were abolished. We could abolish all weapons and toys and still have wars with sticks and stones.

"What is wrong with their moral principle is that it is immoral. Arms, like every other adventure or art of man, have two sides according as they are invoked for the infliction or the defiance of wrong." The little boy with the bow and the arrow is playing out in a bloodless way this serious realization that some things need defending and that it is wrong not to defend them. What the little boy needs to learn is precisely the difference between good and evil, so that he can use those things that defend the one and defeat the others in the right way. He does not learn this by abolishing his games with toy guns or bows and arrows.

The danger, again, is not in the bow and arrow, but in the boy. The whole purpose of religion, education, and morals is to teach the good use of material things by beings who can admittedly use them ill because of their free wills. The purpose of little boys is to be little boys growing up to be good or bad men now using real bows and arrows. The purpose of the State is not itself to impose its own rule on every act of life so that nothing can to be done by anyone because any possibility of our acting dangerously—that is, morally—is taken away from us. This theory of taking away dangerous toys means that State power alone decides what is or what is not to be taken away. The State is left with full free play to command what it wants. The now grown-up little boys have been both physically and morally disarmed. They have been taught to believe that the cause of evil is in things and not in themselves. The State now has all the bows and arrows in its unlimited hands, the use of which is defined only by itself.

Chesterton was already right in 1921. The most dangerous Christmas toy was in fact the little boy endowed with free will and able to use anything for his purposes. Ultimately, we will be "safe" only if we are not "free," that is to say, we will be "safe" only if the kinds of beings we are, are denied existence. But if we are free and we do exist, then what will save us is not the State but the Incarnation. When God risked creating little boys, He risked Himself. Such is the meaning of the most dangerous toy in the season of Christmas.

Babies

A memorable essay in *The Well and the Shallows* (1935) is entitled "Babies and Distributism."[1] It may well be the most defiantly counter-cultural essay of our times, to be matched only by Flannery O'Connor's remark that the Church's pronouncement on birth control is the most spiritual doctrine of the Church. Neither Chesterton nor Flannery O'Connor had children of their own. Both wrote in disdain of the intellectuals, secular and ecclesiastical, of their era who advocated this practice. Both wrote knowing that their position would be rejected. Both understood that the Church's position had something profoundly right about it, something at the heart of human reality. Pius XI's encyclical *Casti Connubii* ("On Christian Marriage") had appeared on the last day of December, 1930, some four years before Chesterton wrote this essay.

Chesterton knew the bitterness of opposition to what the Pope maintained. Chesterton's essay today reads almost like direct revelation. The whole of our time, so it thought, "knew" the Church was wrong. Chesterton knew the Church was right, even before the issue really developed in the convoluted manner we know it today. Intellectual reputations were made, much publicity was gained, by openly opposing what the Church taught. All sorts of devious theories have had to be invented in order to justify this opposition. Almost every day, even yet, theologians and professors will be quoted to the effect that the Church will, must, ought to change its views.

In the meantime, John Paul II, as did his predecessors before him, repeats, clarifies, and demonstrates both why the Church will not change this position and what it is defending—human life and human love. Moreover, our times carry out in the lives of those who will not accept the Church's teaching what it means to defy what is the truth in these matters. The destruction of the family is in the news every day, but we choose not to make too many connections. It is too much to bear to think that the Church, even on empirical grounds, has been right all along, as it has been.

What is remarkable about Chesterton's short essay, I think, is not only his clear insight into what would happen if we denied the truth of the Church's position, which is the position of reason, but also his own personal reaction to the public policy of birth control. Chesterton was a mild and gentle man. He rarely was annoyed. Indeed, in this essay, he recounted this very serene quality of his own soul. Atheists did not particularly annoy him, as he could understand the narrow logic by which they limited themselves. Even Bolsheviks were people with the same narrow minds, but they at least were against something that needed to be corrected. But for the proponents of birth control, clearly Chesterton had only, as he tells us, "contempt."

When Chesterton had "contempt" for something, we can be sure that something was radically wrong with the position. He was one of those men who could both explain what was wrong and even sense it, feel it. A good man can often uncannily recognize the face of something that is really evil; he can see its evil because he can see where it leads and what it prevents, something close to the heart of God. We should never forget that human babies, from the moment of their conceptions, are very near the heart of God. Their angels look on His very face.

Chesterton gave three reasons for his "personal contempt" about this issue. He lived before the days in which those who proposed eliminating babies in wombs called themselves advocates of "choice" instead of killers of human lives, which is what they objectively are. Choice is a verb and must have an object.

"To choose" cannot be understood without its object. To be "pro-choice" does not mean in practice to be "for free will"—as if it referred to some sort of theoretical dissertation on the human faculty. It means, in context, always being willing to allow the killing of an incipient human life at some stage of its already-begun development. This current abuse of the language would have driven this gentle man into a rage, I am sure.

But Chesterton had something of the same language problem already in 1935. His first reason for opposing it had to do with the very phrase "birth control." Chesterton could not stand lying with words. He would not have minded it so much had its advocates called it "birth prevention," for that is what it was; but to call it "birth control" was simply a gross abuse of language. "I despise Birth-Control," he wrote,

> first because it is a weak and wobbly and cowardly word. It is also an entirely meaningless word, and is used so as to curry favor even with those who would at first recoil from its real meaning. The proceeding these quack doctors recommend does not *control* any birth. It only makes sure that there shall never be any birth to control. . . . Normal people can only act so as to produce birth; and these people can only act so as to prevent birth.[2]

What "birth control" means, to use the language precisely, is "birth prevention." Chesterton thought the very word was a lie and was intended to be a lie.

The second reason Chesterton had personal contempt for "birth control" was because of the thing itself. Chesterton is very blunt and frank here. He saw "birth control" to lack the courage of its convictions which even the eugenicists have. At least the consistent eugenicist would follow the example of dealing with animals where we let all the off-spring be born then choose which ones we want to keep. This would be a better position, Chesterton thought, than the "birth prevention" system which prevents or kills all birth.

In a reflection that may have something to do with the reason why many western countries have to rely on foreign labor, Chesterton wrote,

> By the weak compromise of Birth-Prevention, we are very probably sacrificing the fit and only producing the unfit. The births we prevent may be the births of the best and the most beautiful children; those we allow, the weakest or worst. Indeed, it is probable; for the habit discourages the early parentage of young and vigorous people; and lets them put off the experience to later years, mostly for mercenary motives.[3]

Chesterton thought that the "birth prevention" and eugenic movements were hiding their real program. They treat human beings in principle as we treat the animals, that is, we keep or kill only what we want for our own ideological or mercenary motives.

The most important reason the birth-control mentality bothered Chesterton was as follows: "My contempt boils over into bad behavior when I hear the common suggestion that a birth is avoided because people want to be 'free' to go to the cinema or buy a gramophone or a loud-speaker. What makes me want to walk over such people like door-mats is that they use the word 'free'." When human babies are not preferred to material possessions, this preference is a sign not of freedom but of servitude. Material possessions are not signs of freedom; children are.

Chesterton put the issue with much eloquence, by establishing what is first and what is second, what is important and what is its cause. "A child is the very sign and sacrament of personal freedom," Chesterton wrote.

> He is a fresh free will added to the wills of the world; he is something that his parents have freely chosen to produce and which they freely agree to protect. They can feel that any amusement he gives (which is often considerable) really comes from him and from them, and from nobody else. He has been born without the intervention of any master or lord. He is a creation and a contribution; he is their own creative contribution to creation.[4]

Chesterton here clearly reminded us of our priorities, of what is essential, of what is merely a means.

Chesterton in the 1930s already saw how words and ideas would be abused to further anti-human priorities and realities. At the heart of reality is the child, the baby. This is the sign of freedom. The child is a new will in the world. What we have forgotten is precisely the wonder of this will when it is protected and wanted by its parents against the world, if necessary. No state or authority may morally interfere with this parental freedom to establish its own family in which its babies are to be born.

The child is the parents' contribution to creation. The new free will and mind in the world represent that potential innovative force by which the material possessions needed to support us can be invented and come into being in the first place. The ultimate wealth is the human mind and will as it refreshingly comes to be in each new human birth. Human beings do not want to be free from children, their children. Babies teach us what stands at the heart of reality—"the sign and sacrament of personal freedom."

On the Dullness of Chaos

The other day I received from New York a copy of the 1986 British Penguin edition of *The Man Who Was Thursday*. A young friend spotted it in a book store and figured I would like it. How do you give thanks for such unexpected gifts?

What interests me here is the first chapter of *The Man Who Was Thursday* (1908). The book began with a poem dedicated to Edmund Clerihew Bentley, Chesterton's lifetime friend. Chesterton explained that out of all the arguments and mysteries of their youth and in spite of the fantastically wrong theories of our intellectuals—"Science announced nonentity / And art admired decay"—it was now possible to talk calmly of ordinary things, their wonder and their mystery. The poem ended:

> Yes, there is strength in striking root,
> And good in growing old.
> We have found common things at last,
> And marriage and a creed,
> And I may safely write it now,
> And you may safely read.[1]

But these are exactly the things that are not safe at last, the common things, marriage and the Creed, though they are the things that we most want and whose wonder most needs explanation to us.

The plot began in an extraordinary ordinary suburb of London called Saffron Park. Already here is Chesterton's theme, that the most extraordinary things in existence are the ordinary human beings we meet every day in the ordinary places in which they dwell. We mostly do not notice how extraordinary it is, just to be. "A man who stepped into its social atmosphere felt as if he had stepped into a written comedy."

The story began with a kind of sunset that was so unusual that everyone remembered it. "It looked like the end of the world." The colors were so fantastic and varied that they covered up the sun "like something too good to be seen." The clouds and light cast a glow over Saffron Park that made it seem mysterious. "It expressed that splendid smallness which is the soul of local patriotism."[2] All of this took place in an ordinary suburb on a day that might have been any day.

In this suburb lived a radical anarchist poet who believed, "with a certain impudent freshness," the old cant "of the lawlessness of art and the art of lawlessness." Into this suburb improbably came another poet, a poet of "order." The poet of revolt had a following of "vaguely emancipated women" who had some protest against "the male supremacy." But these were clearly not ordinary women. "These new women would always pay to a man the extravagant compliment which no ordinary woman ever pays to him, that of listening while he is talking."

The anarchistic poet had a sister, Rosamund, who was much taken with the poet of order, so different he seemed from her brother. "Mr. Syme," she said to the poet of order, "do the people who talk like you and my brother often mean what they say? Do you mean what you say now?" To which Syme responded, "Do you?"

The heart of the initial encounter between the poet of anarchy and the poet of order had to do with the remark of Lucian Gregory, the anarchic poet, that "an artist disregards all governments, abolishes all conventions. The poet delights in disorder only. If it were not so, the most poetical thing in the world would be the Underground Railway."[3]

The Underground Railway is, of course, the London subway. And true to form, the poet of order thought that in fact that the

London subway was the most poetical thing in the world. Gregory, the anarchist, thought the world would be more romantic if the next stop after Sloane Square would not be Victoria, as it was, but say Baker Street or Baghdad. Whether we know it or not, we are involved here in St. Thomas's proof for God's existence, the one from order, about why things do reach their ends.

Syme, the poet of order, was sure that it was more wondrous if the subway actually went to where it said it was going than if it just went anywhere. "Chaos is dull," he continued, "because in chaos the train might indeed go anywhere, to Baker Street, or to Baghdad. But man is a magician, and his whole magic is in this, that he does say Victoria, and lo! it is Victoria. No, take your books of mere poetry and prose, let me read a time-table, with tears of pride."[4] The opposite of chaos is order. We do not want to go just anywhere, but to somewhere. Syme felt that coming to Victoria was not unlike that "hairbreadth escape" from a world of chaos in which nothing gets anywhere, in which men have not the will or capacity to order their world because they do not love the smallness that made it the extraordinary place it is.

But Gregory, the anarchist, thought that man would be unhappy to learn that the New Jerusalem looked just like Victoria Station. "The poet will be discontented even in the streets of heaven. The poet is always in revolt." To this, Syme retorted, "Being sick is a revolt." And he explained, "It is things going right, that is poetical! Our digestion, for instance, going sacredly and silently right, that is the foundation of all poetry. Yes, the most poetical thing, more poetical than the flowers, more poetical than the stars—the most poetical thing in the world is not being sick."[5] The anarchist, of course, could hardly comprehend the poetical wonder of the fact that in us things go right and we do not even notice it. It is not merely how the Underground Railway gets from Sloane Square to Victoria, but how our blood gets from our heart to our toes.

Rosamund was watching Syme, who was discussing whether he or the anarchist or she was "sincere" in their questions. "She was looking at him [Syme] from under level brows; her face was grave and open, and there had fallen upon it the shadow of that unreasoning responsibility which is at the bottom of the most frivolous woman, the maternal watch which is as old as the world."[6] The maternal unreasoning responsibility protects *what is* simply because it is, the fierceness for being and life.

Not unmindful of Chesterton's own endless youthful all-night discussions with Bentley and his friends when they, as all young men should, were trying to figure out what dogmas were true, Syme is described walking with Rosamund in the garden. "For he [Syme] was a sincere man, and in spite of his superficial airs and graces, at root a humble one. And it is always the humble man who talks too much; the proud man watches himself too closely." The proud man watches himself too closely—whether this is the ultimate defense of loquaciousness, I do not know. But it is the defense of Chesterton's long conversations to find the truth, which required the humility of watching *what is*, of watching the Underground from Sloane Square actually rumble into Victoria, of knowing that his digestion worked best when he did not notice that it worked at all, of knowing that the New Jerusalem will not be a chaotic thing in which nothing in particular matters, but it will be a particular place to where our aims have always been directed.

Chaos is dull. "The rare, strange thing is to hit the mark; the gross, obvious thing is to miss it." This is what St. Thomas said. We will not be bored in the Streets of Heaven if we are delighted when the train from Sloane Square arrives at Victoria and not at Baghdad.

The Invisible Man

John Peterson, in generous exchange for my old paperbound Chesterton anthology of Father Brown stories printed during World War II (a volume he had never seen), kindly sent me *The Father Brown Omnibus: Every Father Brown Story Ever Written.* This is the Dodd, Mead edition of 1951, listing copyrights going back to 1910. I have not in fact read many Father Brown stories. I tell myself that I do not like detective stories, though I like them well enough when I get into them.

What first struck my eye in the index was the story entitled "The Invisible Man." I vaguely recall that I read this short detective story at one time or another. I am going to reread it again for this essay, but I believe I can recall the general plot of this short mystery story. The "invisible man" is the most obvious man, the man we do not see because we see him too easily, like the postman.

The original "invisible man" story, or at least the first one I know of, is in the Second Book of Plato's *Republic.* In its Platonic context, this story is designed to show that most people do not practice justice for its own sake. It has philosophic purpose as a story. It is designed to prove a common opinion, that we are just or virtuous only because of another reason, namely fear of the laws. The story recounts a shepherd who finds a corpse. On this corpse, he notices a marvelous ring, which he promptly pockets.

The shepherd next begins to examine the ring. A small node is found on the ring which he begins to turn back and forth. He discovers that when he turns the node to a certain angle, he becomes invisible; when he turns it back, he becomes visible. This quality of the magic ring gives the shepherd new power and temptation. What does he do with this new ring? He makes himself invisible. He goes into the palace. He kills the king and seduces the queen. Suddenly, he is in full command of the kingdom. The moral of the story is that the only reason we do not kill the king is because we fear punishment of the law. We would be unjust if we could. Thus, this story is designed to demonstrate that all of us are unjust by preference but just by force or coercion.

Chesterton's story is of an entirely different slant, though perhaps I can find a strange relationship. The plot of "The Invisible Man" is cast in the form of a love story. A young Scotsman, John Turnbull Angus, is in love with Laura Hope, who is a lovely young lady, a waitress in a pastry shop. Angus, in true Chestertonian fashion, is a disinherited artist. It seems that his uncle, an admiral, cut off Angus's inheritance "for Socialism." At first you expect the young man to have been the Socialist, but rather it is his uncle who learns that Angus "had delivered" a lecture "against that economic theory."

Angus tries awkwardly to propose to Laura over a halfpenny bun and a small cup of coffee. Though she is interested, she is not to be rushed. "'You don't give me any time to think,' she said. 'I'm not such a fool,' he answered; 'that's my Christian humility.'"[1] I have puzzled what this might mean. Christian humility prevents us from being fools by allowing us no time to think. I take it that in matters of the heart, such as this, humility is truth. We should not allow ourselves to get caught up in a lot of reasonings that do not explain the already evident fact of a mutual love.

Laura, in any case, came from a town called Ludbury in the eastern counties, where her father owned an inn called "The Red Fish," where she used to serve in the bar. The place was a simple inn for a few commercial travellers, "and for the rest, the most awful people you can see, only you've never seen them." Here already is the theme of the invisible man. Into this bar came two distinctly odd men, one a dwarf by the name of Isidore Smythe and a stranger man with "an appalling squint" by the name of James Welkin. Both gentlemen were somehow in love with Laura, but she could have nothing to do with them because "they were so impossibly ugly." Of course, she was too polite to give this as a reason, so she told them instead that she could never marry anyone who only had inherited wealth, who did not make his own way in the world.

Isidore Smythe, as a result, sets out to gain his fortune and does so by inventing a sort of mechanical robot to do house work, "Smythe's Silent Service." Laura tells Angus that she is now afraid that Smythe will turn up with his fortune, but she is more afraid somehow of Welkin. Suddenly she receives two letters from Smythe; almost at the same time she seems to hear Welkin's voice and his eerie laugh. She thinks there is something Satanic about it, or that she is going mad. Angus does not think she is mad. In a bit of classic Chestertonian doctrine on madness, he tells her, "If you really were mad, you would think you must be sane."

About this time the tiny Isidore Smythe appears in haste in his red roadster at the pastry shop. Someone has mysteriously placed some stamp paper on the window of the pastry shop on which are written the words, "If you [Laura] marry Smythe, he will die." This appears to be Welkin's handwriting. Angus, who recognizes Smythe as a rival, nevertheless goes to Smythe's apartment to help him. Angus knows Flambeau the detective and promises to go fetch him for Smythe.

In the meantime, on his way to Flambeau's, Angus tells the porter, a workman, a policeman, and a seller of chestnuts to keep their eyes on the flat in which Smythe is staying and not to let anyone else in. When Angus gets to Flambeau's nearby headquarters, Father Brown is also there. Angus tells the story of Smythe and his invisible enemy who has threatened his life. The three of them rush back to Smythe's apartment. They ask each of the four "guards" if anyone has entered into the flat. No one has seen anyone. It seems to be a late fall day, with snow just beginning to fall. Father Brown, however, wants to know why, if no one has seen anyone, are there footprints in the snow leading to the apartment? Again, the invisible man.

Flambeau and Angus burst into the apartment, find blood, but no Smythe. Now we have an invisible murderer and an invisible corpse. The two of them try to find the policeman, whom Father Brown, who has not gone into the flat, has sent to check the canal. The policeman comes back announcing that the body of Smythe was found in the water, but he was stabbed; he did not drown. Father Brown wants to know if anyone has found a "light brown sack"? Angus cannot make heads or tails of this question. So Father Brown explains the problem to him in his usual philosophic manner: "We always begin at the abstract end of things, and you can't begin this story anywhere else." Of course, we should expect him to begin precisely at the facts or concrete end of things, not at the theory end.

Father Brown begins his analysis in this manner: "Have you ever noticed this—that people never answer what you say? They answer what you mean—or what they think you mean."[2] He gives the example of someone going to a country house for the weekend and asking whether "anybody is staying there?" The answer is "no," even though the parlourmaid, the butler, the cook, and the handyman are there. "All language is used like that; you never get a question answered literally, even when you get it answered truly." Thus, when the four men—the porter, the policemen, the chestnut seller, and the workman—said that they did not see anyone enter the flat, they were not lying. They did not see anyone who looked like a murderer.

The real murderer, Father Brown implies to them, is "mental-ly" invisible. Father Brown explains the facts of the case in this light. If Laura heard Welkin laugh when the street was empty, but seconds later she received a letter from Smythe, then the street was not empty. The postman had to have been there, unless, he adds humorously, the letter was delivered by "carrier-pigeon." As Flambeau, Angus, and Father Brown discuss these philosophic points, it becomes clear that the most obvious man is invisible; because he is ordinary, we do not see him. The postman had walked by the lookouts, gone inside, killed the tiny Smythe, put him in the mail bag, and carried him out to the canal.

Now what is rather unclear to me is the ending of this story. Brown says to Angus, "You are not mad, only a little unobservant. You have not noticed such a man as this, for example." At this point Brown steps forward three paces and places his hand on the shoulder of an ordinary postman apparently just passing by unnoticed. Father Brown says, not unkindly, "Nobody ever notices postmen somehow; yet they have passions like other men, and even carry large bags where a small corpse can be stowed quite easily." It is not clear if Flambeau and Angus get the drift of this situation. At this point, the postman ducks against the garden fence, turns an alarmed face over his shoulder; apparently no one else but Brown notices him. He remains invisible to them. "All three men were fixed with an almost fiendish squint." So this is clearly Welkin, who has killed Smythe because he courted Laura, who, in her turn, was not in love with either Welkin or Smythe.

The last paragraph of this story tells us, not that Welkin was arrested, but that Flambeau went back to his office; Angus goes back "to the lady at the shop." "But Father Brown walked those snow-covered hills under the stars for many hours with a murderer, and what they said to each other will never be known."[3]

Now, I take it that neither Flambeau nor Angus nor the policeman nor the other three realized that Father Brown had solved the mystery of the invisible man, even though he had given them the principle on which to solve it. What does Father Brown do? Evidently, he goes back to find the postman by the garden fence. Welkin was said earlier to take long walks. Brown walks with the murderer for hours in the snow. The two talk to each other. Is Welkin mad? Evidently not. No, he is a man with "passions like other men." The fact that he thought Smythe, not Angus, was his rival with Laura made no difference. I would presume that, in the end, Welkin is redeemed. When Chesterton concluded that "what they said to each other will never be known," he had to be referring to the seal of Confession.

Wilde and Wilder

Readers have no doubt noticed that I have referred to Original Sin quite a bit of late. It is a fascinating topic, to be sure, the one subject about which Chesterton maintained we need no real proof. We just have to go out in the streets and open our eyes. Just how to describe or define Original Sin is always somewhat mystifying. I did come across a brief sentence, however, in Thornton Wilder's *The Matchmaker,* that comes pretty close.

The Matchmaker is of course *Hello, Dolly.* In it, Mr. Horace Vandergelder, the rich merchant from Yonkers, New York, has been talking to his clerk Malachi about Vandergelder's plans for a fateful trip to New York that eventually leads him to Mrs. Dolly Levi, a charmingly sentimental lady who thinks, not entirely without reason, that elegantly spending Vandergelder's considerable accumulation of cash is the cure to his, hers, and the world's problems. When Malachi also leaves for a New York errand, Vandergelder, who does not necessarily have a high opinion of clerks, turns to the audience to explain his views about the human condition. "Ninety-nine percent of the people in the world," he tells them, "are fools and the rest of us are in great danger of contagion."[1]

That wonderful statement is not exactly Original Sin, of course, but it hits amusingly close to our normal experience, especially of ourselves, according to which the doctrine of Original Sin is not entirely improbable. Undoubtedly, to recall the persistence of self-deception as a factor in human history, one hundred percent of the human race, like Vandergelder, think they belong to that one percent of the race that worries about the great danger of contagion even though they are not like the rest of men, already fools.

Liberty Fund in Indianapolis recently had a seminar on Thornton Wilder to which I was kindly invited. Out of curiosity, I wrote in advance to John Peterson inquiring about whether Chesterton ever had said anything on Wilder. John put a note in the *Midwest Chesterton News*, asking if anyone might have knowledge of such a reference. Promptly he received a note from Mr. Frank Laughlin, editor of the Chesterton *Newsletter* in England. It seems that there is at least one poetical reference to Wilder from the *G.K.'s Weekly* in 1929–30.

The reference is an eight-line poem entitled "An American Best Seller." The bestseller, of course, is Wilder's famous *The Bridge of San Luis Rey,* a novel we read in preparation for the seminar. Notice what Chesterton has to say in the poem about this book and about Wilder. The poem reads:

> The Decadents' bridges broke down in despair:
> It is something that someone could fling
> Some sort of Bridge over that dreary abyss
> In the name of Saint Louis the King:
> That Art may yet cross to the people, and purify
> Of the poisonous and slimes that defiles her;
> For when I was a child half the world had gone Wilde
> But now half the world have gone Wilder.

When I read this poem to the seminar, everyone laughed at the clever juxtaposition of Oscar *Wilde* and Thornton *Wilder*.

The poem was printed in Chesterton's own handwriting and was accompanied by an original Chesterton drawing showing, from the Peruvian abyss, St. Louis the King himself, shield in his left arm and right arm outstretched toward the broken bridge. What was St. Louis the King telling us?

On Friday noon, July 20, 1714, this famous, hundred-year-old Indian-built bridge between Lima and Cuzco collapsed, killing five people. The scene is watched by the Franciscan, Brother Juniper, who is exceedingly perplexed by the incident but looks upon it as an opportunity to prove the ways of God to men.

Brother Juniper sets out to see if he can explain just what it was in the lives of each of the five killed that might show that each died at exactly the right time, before God.

The famous last lines of this novel are always worth repeating:

> But soon we shall all die and all memory of those five will have left the earth, and we ourselves shall be loved for a while and forgotten. But the love will have been enough; all those impulses of love return to the love that made them. Even memory is not necessary for love. There is a land of the living and a land of the dead and the bridge is love, the only survival, the only meaning.

At first sight, this seems almost Christian. Much of Wilder seems almost Christian. Yet, love seems here a kind of abstraction from the five, from we ourselves. It is not the "impulses" of love that, hopefully, return to "the love that made them." Rather it is we ourselves who love and are loved. The only survival is we ourselves. The Bridge is not love, an abstraction, but Resurrection, something concrete.

What does Chesterton's poem mean in this light? Chesterton is writing between the Wars, though he does not know the between. He writes after the Great War. The result of progress, of the philosophy of the Decadents is precisely "despair." Chesterton compliments Wilder for tossing up "some sort of a bridge" across this dreary abyss of despair. Clearly, Chesterton does not see clarity in Wilder himself, but he recognizes that *The Bridge of San Luis Rey* does ask the right sort of questions about the meaning of providence, about the relation of life to death. Life is not despair, even when it lacks clarity. The Bridge bears in the name of Saint Louis the King, so it is not rooted in doubt.

Chesterton sees that what may yet save the common man from this decadent despair might well be "art," novels. Intellectual poisons and slimes defile both art and the people. They need to see that this despair is not right. Brother Juniper and the five who fall into the abyss between Lima and Cuzco in 1714 on a

Friday noon in July begin to ask the right questions. When Chesterton was a child, late in the nineteenth century, half the world followed Oscar Wilde and the Decadents. Forty years later, however, Thornton Wilder presented a more hopeful case in his art. The American bestseller obviously was addressed to something important, to something that responded to the Decadents in the direction of providence and the meaning of each human life.

Chesterton, no doubt, could not resist the juxtaposition of Wilde and Wilder. Both names seem utterly symbolic of what he was driving at. That the Decadents should even be considered was for Chesterton simply "wild." Once we have gone to the extreme of doubting all and living without a sense of order or providence, the most radical position we can take is to begin to suspect, even on the scientific and experimental grounds that Brother Juniper first proposed, that what is beyond "Wilde" is something intellectually even "wilder." For what is more astonishing, more "wild": to doubt all, or to begin to wonder about why five certain folks were killed one noon walking over the most famous bridge in Peru?

Brother Juniper himself, in the novel, is executed by the Inquisition for even bringing up these theological topics. Some think the reason for this execution was in fact his effort to know for certain, by his own powers, what divine providence had planned for each of us. Brother Juniper, in the spirit of modern science, wanted to be God.

Wilder himself evidently does not quite know what to make of this result of his own novel. He hesitated to save actual souls, and so he saved only "love"; the impulses of love return to their source, a kind of pantheism found often in Wilder. That too is pretty "dreary," if you come to think on it. This sentimentality about "love" is, it strikes me, why Chesterton saw in Wilder only "some sort of bridge" across the abyss of nihilism. Wilder was closer to the mark than Wilde. Wilder's bridge between the land of the living and the land of the dead, though better than solecism, was itself an abstraction by comparison with what we really were promised and what we really wanted. But in comparison with the despair of the decadents of all ages, it was already arching over the slimes and the poisons that caused so much hurt to the people who deserved an art that did lead them out of the abyss of despair. Chesterton gave Wilder credit for his alerting half the world of his time to the something else besides hopelessness.

Perhaps I can leave the last lines to Dolly Levi, speaking in the final act to the audience of *The Matchmaker* about why she has decided to capture the stern heart of Horace Vandergelder, even though she still had great affection for her deceased husband, Ephraim Levi:

> Money! Money!—it's like the sun we walk under; it can kill or cure.—Mr. Vandergelder's money! Vandergelder's never tired of saying most of the people in the world are fools, and in a way, he's right, isn't he? Himself, Irene, Cornelius, myself! But there comes a moment in everybody's life when he must decide whether he'll live among human beings or not—a fool among fools or a fool alone.[2]

There can, I think, be no doubt which of these choices, being a fool among fools or a fool alone, Chesterton would have chosen. His whole concern with the ordinary man and what can save him is already here, halfway with "An American Best Seller," and surely most of the way with Dolly Levi's wonderful reflection, so reminiscent both of the Fall and of our individual redemption midst our universal foolishness, yes, in concrete love, in Resurrection. Only a fool would want it otherwise.

The Horror

We cannot help today but be conscious of the degree to which both law and ideological pressure impose on language, requiring us to say certain things in certain ways or forbidding us from saying them in other customary or normal ways. We have to utter the boring "happy holidays" because "Merry Christmas" hints that Christ is important. We have to affirm that active homosexuals live noble lifestyles. We have to pretend that we are all morally equal, no matter what we do, a position that puts vice and virtue on the same level and allows no moral discourse about whether there be virtue and vice in the first place. We are more and more dominated by a coerced public language totally out of harmony with what goes on in reality and with what we actually think. We all begin to lie about the important distinctions of right and wrong because we are allowed no other way of speaking about them. No public discourse will mean what it says.

Things that are perfectly intelligible and clear are, for political reasons, said to mean something else when they really don't. If I say, for instance, that "man is a rational animal; he laughs, he cries, he floats on his back in the river," I am said arbitrarily to exclude from this sentence the feminine half of the human race. Therefore, I must not say that "man is a rational animal; he laughs, he cries, he floats on his back in the river." Rather, I must say awkwardly, that "the human being is a rational animal; he/she laughs; she/he cries, he/she floats on her/his back in the river." Preposterous, really.

Of course, in my original sentence, as any fair-minded person knows, I have not either in logic, grammar, or intention excluded half of the human race. Nothing exists in that original sentence that would not include each member, male or female, adult or child, of the human race. In order to think that it does, one must have been educated out of the normal understanding of words and their relation to concepts. Words can have different meanings. We can understand them when they do. The word "man" can and does refer to a concept that prescinds from, without denying, the distinction of male and female. Every language for thousands of years has recognized this multiple meaning for words.

The standard English pronoun that refers to this concept, "man," is "he." The pronoun makes the same adjustment that the word "man" does, meaning either the generic human being— prescinding from the distinction of male and female—or the male. Neither word, man or he, when used for the abstract concept, in any meaningful sense to anyone who understands the language, excludes females, since it does not talk about males or females as such. Both words, "man" and "he," in context are designed to talk of human nature, without adverting to the sexual distinction, but without denying it either. We can do this easily and clearly and habitually. Not to have this mechanism at our disposal makes our speech stilted, silly even. University lectures and academic journals have become boring, unending repetitions of unnecessary and confusing hes/shes in all their splendid ideology.

Another variety of this same problem occurs when we use words to cover up what we are really doing or talking about. The most obvious candidate in this category is what is known, with incredible paradox, as the "choice" movement. Today, if I say that I am for "choice," it does not mean that I have some elaborate theory about free will. It means rather, to put it clearly, that I think it all right to kill babies in wombs. The word "choice," by itself, does not tell us what is going on, except when we come to know how it is used. "To choose" never stands by itself. I always have to choose something, this or that. Simply having the power to choose, which all rational creatures have by their nature, tells us nothing at all about what individuals will do with their wills.

The "pro-choice" movement, thus, is not some debating club organized to combat radical determinism. It is rather a theoretical justification for killing certain human beings (euthanasia is also a part of this same movement) on the sole basis that we want to (choose to) do so. There is not the slightest scientific evidence that what we kill is not a human life in its initial form, already complete from the moment of conception.

Likewise, if I am opposed to the "pro-choice" movement," that does not mean that Schall is suddenly to be ranked with those philosophical systems that maintain that we *must* do what we do, that there is no freedom in the cosmos or in ourselves. In the "pro-choice" movement, choice does have a very particular, individual, tiny object that is impossible to separate from the power of choice itself in the act of its choosing. Every "to choose" of this type is to put an action in the world that kills a begun human life. The language cannot mean anything else in this usage. It cannot simply mean I am for "the power of choice," against which stand only theoretic determinists. If I am "for choice," it means both that I can justify the power of free will and that I understand that the object of choice determines whether choice is being used for good or evil. When what I choose is to terminate the life of another innocent human being, my choice is evil, even though the fact that I have this power remains good. If I try to hide from myself what I objectively do by some theory of privacy, I am in utter self-deception about myself, about what I do, about choice, about the world itself.

Recently, someone gave me a copy of Loyola University Press's sample collection from *G.K.'s Weekly*. I am not adept enough to figure out who wrote the unsigned editorials and columns in this remarkably quaint and fascinating journal. But

Chesterton did write a signed column or essay almost regularly. On October 17, 1931, he did a column called "The Horror." Needless to say, I was curious to find out just what this "horror" was. I thought at first it might be perhaps Hitler, or even some account of an English ghost or politician.

But the 1931 column turned out in fact to be about this very topic, the proper use of language, which has become so convoluted some sixty years later. The very first sentence of this essay reads: "Nearly all newspapers and public speakers are now entirely occupied with finding harmless words for a horrible thing."[1] What else is "pro-choice" but precisely "harmless words" designed to cover up "a horrible thing"? Political and polite society do not allow us to use the real words that give the true picture of what is happening.

Recently, however, I read *The Quotable Paul Johnson*, which George Marlin, Richard Rabatin, and Heather Richardson Higgins edited. In it, I read these absolutely clear words under the heading "Abortion Industry":

> The abortion industry has been given a green light to do, in effect, what it wills. A fully formed child can be ripped from its mother's womb, screaming and gasping for breath, and then coldly butchered on the waiting slab by men and women—"specialists"—whose sole job in life is performing such lawful operations.[2]

Here the language does not "find harmless words for a horrible thing." Rather, the language finds horrible words for a horrible thing. In other words, the language does what it is supposed to do. It tells the truth about what goes on by using appropriate and accurate words.

Chesterton, in his day, was dealing with prohibition. In 1931, we were prohibiting alcohol. Today we prohibit smoking, just as we, on the grounds of privacy, also prohibit parents from knowing when their daughters go to an abortion clinic. Thus, when we cannot hide the results of our choices, an impossibility in any case, we cover ourselves with the mantle of privacy, that is, we lie even to ourselves.

Here, then, we are interested in the use of words to lie to ourselves about what is going on. Chesterton himself had a kind of genius for seeing through the veneer of a language that deliberately lies to us about what it means. He could see the ironies to which this deliberately obscuring usage could lead us. "Everybody was taught to use the word 'temperance'," he remarked in the same essay, "to mean refusing to any man even the chance to be temperate. They talked about Birth Control when they meant preventing birth, just as they talked about Liquor Control when they meant forbidding liquor."[3]

"Birth control," that systematic blockage that especially liberal Catholics want to defend unto the death, was itself a most amusing phrase to Chesterton. He had quipped someplace else that "birth control," when examined for the actual meaning of the words, meant precisely "no birth" and "no control." This entertaining remark, no doubt, contains the essence of the papal position, that our actions and their consequences should be under our control, under our own wills. Contraceptives, abortions, RUD's, and all the myriads of similar paraphernalia simply do what Chesterton said they did: they prevent births without demanding any sort of control in the sexual act itself, which is where human relation and self-rule exist in this case.

The Liquor Control Commission evidently thought to solve a problem not by temperance, by allowing us to rule ourselves, but by forbidding that about which temperance usually exists, that is, drink. Again we find Chesterton protecting a philosophy by protecting words. He saw that words were being used to foster a new philosophy, one that retained on the surface words that sounded like the old morality but were in fact the new determinism disguised as choice or control. Abortion, after all, is often occasioned by a failure not only of control but even of the devices or the will to use them. The minute we place the problem in the wrong place, we will never solve it, or if we do solve it, we will have to use methods all out of proportion to the way human beings ought to rule themselves.

The "horror" that Chesterton already saw in 1931 is today a part of our very culture. We lie to ourselves in order not to have to admit to ourselves what we are actually doing. We then pass laws and enforce customs and language that prevent us from penetrating back to that reality which words are designed to indicate and describe. If we call abortion an "industry" protected by law, with highly paid practitioners who serve the law by their trade, we will begin to think we are dealing with something like General Motors or the restaurant industry. What we are doing, as Paul Johnson so graphically said, is butchering human beings for no other reason than because we choose to do so and it is legal. What would Chesterton have called such an "industry"? He would have called it what it is, a "horror."

Virtue and Duty

When I do a class on St. Thomas, I like the class to read with me during the semester Chesterton's book *St. Thomas Aquinas*. One rainy morning near the end of March, about eleven-thirty in the morning, by chance I read aloud to the class a short passage from the August 1995 *Chesterton Review*, a passage taken from an essay Chesterton wrote in 1911, "School Magazines," about his early writing at St. Paul's School. I guess I wanted to make the point to the class that almost any page of Chesterton can lead us to the most profound of topics.

Among the memorable lines in this essay were these: "Man always begins by owning the universe; it is only later in life that he learns to own a home. Men should always love virtue before they love duty; the reverse produces dried souls, incapable of joy."[1]

Now, I could (and eventually may, so be forewarned), write a column on the first of these two sentences, about owning the universe and finally owning one's home. Needless to say, Chesterton no doubt considered the latter ownership, of the home, to be more profound than the former, of the universe. Better, that the only sure way to learn to own the universe—which we do with our knowledge—is to own our own home wherein we can have the freedom and love that makes the more universal ownership flourish. But this essay is on the second sentence, the one about duty and virtue. Here is how it came about.

When I finished this passage, a young lady put up her hand. With a combination frown and inquisitive look on her face, she wanted to know why we could not have both duty and virtue? That was a good point, of course. Virtue is the habitual ruling ourselves to attain those goods to which our natural powers are ordered. Duty looks to our responsibility, not to the object to be attained. There is no reason at all that we cannot have both. So why would Chesterton separate them, or suggest the priority of virtue?

Let me attempt again to respond to this question, as I did to the student and class. In the modern world, there will always be something Kantian about the word "duty." It has the overtones of a philosophy that sees something wrong with pleasure and delight. To do our duty, of course, has something noble about it. When all else fails, duty may save us. Duty, while it does not entirely lose sight of the object of duty, emphasizes what we owe. It seems most distant from the object of duty itself: duty toward what?

Duty looks at things from our side. Duty refers to what *we* ought to do, what *we* must do. In a sense, duty looks at things insofar as we must do something about them whether we like it or not. Duty is designed to overcome our lethargy, our fear, our lack of certainty about what we ought to do. "To do your duty" implies that the rightness of the action is already decided. Duty at its best implies an orientation to what is good.

Chesterton contrasted virtue and duty. He said that man should always love virtue before he loves duty. If he does this, his duty will evidently be much easier. Thus, Chesterton does not deny that we can indeed love our duty. Yet, he says that right order implies that we love virtue first. "Why would this be?" we might asks ourselves. Why does loving virtue come first? The clue can be found first, perhaps, in the consequences of loving duty more. When we love duty more, Chesterton thought, we would produce in ourselves dried souls. We would be incapable, as a consequence, of joy.

Dried souls? Incapable of joy? Inspired or buoyant souls, souls capable of joy, must arise from virtue, or better, from that toward which virtue itself is directed. But how is this? Let us talk about loving our mothers. If we "obey" the Fourth Commandment, it tells us to "Honor thy father and mother." This is a command to us; it indicates a duty. When all else fails, we are still obliged to love our parents (or any one else we are obliged to love) because of our duty.

But it would be of little consolation to our mother if she thought that the only or primary reason that we loved her was because we were doing our duty, looking not at her but at what we "owed" her, what we were obliged to do. For that matter, she would not be happy either if she thought we were practicing virtue on her. Chesterton's point was rather that virtue directs to its object, to what it is about. We are to be virtuous virtuously, in Aristotle's tradition. That is, what is primary in virtue is not virtue, or duty, but what it is we love or do, the object of our love or duty.

Joy does not come to us because we go out to seek it. If we go forth to seek joy, we will never find it. If our mother gives us joy, it is not because we do our duty toward her, nor even act virtuously around her. Rather, we first love her, for herself. What will follow from this placing the object of our love first is precisely joy and the aliveness that comes from what is not ourselves. To be incapable of joy happens to us when we undermine in ourselves the grounds of joy. Joy is the possession of what we love. Both duty and virtue can and should lead us to concentrate not on ourselves but on what we love.

But if we so concentrate on either duty or virtue that it becomes our main concern, we will never get beyond ourselves to that toward which we are to look. When the Commandment implies that it is our duty to love our parents, it does not mean that we should not love them for themselves. That is what we are first to do, and if we do love and honor them first, we will do our duty to them in a very new light. The Commandment also means that, such is our condition, we may so allow our own desires, confusions, sins, or anger to come between us and that which we are to learn to love that the only thing that might save us is obedience or duty, which at least incites us to do the external acts of loving our parents. And after we do the acts of love, we may finally learn to love as we should in the first place. Joy follows from this, from what we love. Joy is not an object of our desire but a gift of loving what we ought, what is right for us to choose.

I am not at all sure what this good student thought of this explanation, which I more or less recount here. What strikes me now, as it often does, is that a single sentence in Chesterton, when we think about it, mull it over, can lead us to distinctions and reflections that carry us to the heart of things. Yes, virtue and duty do belong together, but in a certain order. What is important in thinking about them is not merely knowing what each is, but the order in which each is related to the other. Get this wrong, as Kant seems to have done, and everything else will go wrong. We will end up thinking that the duty of loving our mother is more noble than our mother and the gift of joy that she is.

Humanism

A gentleman in Ireland sent me a copy of *Humanism: The Wreck of Western Culture*, by the Australian philosopher John Carroll.[1] The thesis of this provocative book is simply that western humanism is dead, that its premises of complete human autonomy have proved to be impossible to maintain and dangerous to mankind. The major sign of this death is no doubt the contradiction that exists between our stated ideals and our practices. We cannot, say, abort millions of human beings a year and still maintain that all men are created equal with a right to life. Eventually, we come to affirm that not all of what is born of us is human. And if the simple fact of human existence does not suffice to create sufficient awe in us to guarantee our dignity, then we must look elsewhere for this guarantee—usually to the state that can continually redefine what it is willing to call and protect as human.

In a posthumously published essay, Russell Kirk remarked on his having run across a review that Flannery O'Connor did of his *Beyond the Dreams of Avarice*.[2] Kirk cited these words of Flannery O'Connor: "It [politics] is . . . a rethinking in the obedience to divine truth which must be the mainspring of any enlightened social thought." Though wholly orthodox, this blunt statement surprises us. We are wont to think that enlightened social thought needs no "obedience to divine truth." Yet, there is this record of modern social thought that has somehow slipped first into pure humanism and then into a kind of practical anti-humanism precisely within the culture in which humanism originally arose. Humanism itself is now pronounced to be precisely dead.

What are we to make of these remarks? In Chesterton's 1926 book, *The Thing: Why I Am a Catholic*, I happened to notice again the chapter entitled, "Is Humanism a Religion?"[3] The purpose of this chapter, of course, was to explain why true and elevated things that Chesterton had always believed eventually came to be denied in the movements that embodied them. The validity of these principles, however, remained central in the Catholic tradition. The question that Chesterton posed was whether humanism could "function as a religion."

Chesterton did not think that it could. "I do not believe that Humanism can be a complete substitute for Superhumanism." The reason for his position was one of experience. He had noticed the peculiar fact that modern movements were largely isolated segments of one or another central Christian truth, but now, since the Reformation, broken off and left to develop on their own. What Chesterton noticed was that after a generation or two, each of these break-off positions in turn either died or so radically changed its basic position that it was no longer recognizable in terms of the original reasons for its separation from the whole.

Chesterton's central theme was that the modern world was living "off its Catholic capital." This capital, including the capital that Christianity itself subsumed from the ancient cultures, is being used up. The example of this tendency that Chesterton proposes is his own memory of the democratic tradition, especially from Walt Whitman. In this tradition, "real men were greater than unreal gods. . . . A glory was to cling about men as men." Whitman even "adored Men. Every human face, every human feature, was a matter of mystical poetry."[4] However, by the end of the nineteenth century, this almost mystical memory of the dignity of each man was practically gone. Science in particular did not support this dignity.

Chesterton, to prove this exhaustion of the initial humanist, quotes from H. L. Mencken: "They [he means certain liberal or ex-liberal thinkers] have come to realize that the morons whom they sweated to save do not want to be saved, and are not worth saving." Gone is that premise of human dignity, of the visions of human camaraderie that we found in Whitman. Chesterton even wondered whether the conditions of modern science would not also have changed Whitman's idealism had he known of them.

What does Chesterton say to this death of the humanist ideal? Simply, "it is not dead in me." The reason it is not dead in Chesterton was that he did not hold the worth or dignity of each human person as a kind of sentiment, that can easily be eroded. Rather he held it as a "creed." Chesterton was still prepared to maintain that the worth and dignity of the most degraded and unfortunate of human beings was worthy of the highest destiny. He could recall paintings in which these very people were pictured with halos. This essential dignity of each human being no matter what his worldly condition was in fact the ancient orthodox position. "For the Catholic, it is a fundamental dogma of the Faith that all human beings, without any exception whatever, were specially made, were shaped and pointed like shining arrows for the end of hitting the mark of Beatitude."[5]

What Chesterton discovered was that humanism itself needed something more than humanism to retain its own ideals. This is, of course, Flannery O'Connor's "obedience to divine truth" necessary for any "enlightened social thought." It is again the strange paradox that in the modern era, humanism and pure reason cannot remain themselves by themselves. John Carroll argued that in fact the proud humanism that made man the autonomous, self-sufficient center of reality destroyed man. For Carroll, but not for Chesterton, free will itself, not its faulty use, was the one tenet of humanism that undermined it.

But why did the logic of the humanist ideal lead to the very opposite extreme of the dignity of each individual? Why did it start out with a mystical notion of human worth, only to isolate itself and cut itself off from the whole, and thus end by denying the humanity of many of these very human beings it sought to praise? The reason was largely because the older Catholic tradition was itself a whole and needed its whole coherence to enable its own mystical ideas to remain in place. Humanism was but one of its ideas separated from the balance of the whole, now interpreting everything else in its own narrow light.

Thus, as Chesterton pointed out, the "shining arrows" pointing to Beatitude were themselves "feathered with free will, and therefore throw the shadow of all tragic possibilities of free will." The Church, however, knew of this darker side, which independent movements are always rediscovering in isolation from the aim of Beatitude. The "gloriousness of the potential glory" is not minimized by the fact of free will's being used wrongly. Chesterton added, in a remarkable statement—itself mindful of the remark of Chesterton's grandfather that "he would thank God for existence even if he ended in hell"—that "in one aspect, it [free will] is even part of it [Beatitude]; since the freedom is itself a glory. In that sense they [those who used their wills wrongly] would still wear their haloes even in hell."[6] That is, the "good" of their being in which they were created in the first place remained even if they chose their own self-created or humanist good over that which was offered to them in revelation.

Chesterton deduced from this analysis that if we have a sound philosophic basis for believing that each person is created with an orientation to glory, a glory each person still must also choose, then we have a reason to see the mystical dignity of each human person, no matter what he might look like or appear to be. "That conviction does make every human face, every human feature, a matter of mystical poetry."[7] It was the truth of this poetry that Chesterton remembered from Whitman but whose basis he found intellectually defended only in Catholicism. Both modern science and modern poetry, Chesterton observed, have given this doctrine up, but Catholicism has not. It is in this sense that Catholicism is democratic. It is democratic not in the sense of being a "machinery for voting or a criticism of particular political privileges," but in the sense of placing itself firmly against Mencken's rejection of "morons," of ordinary folks who "do not want to save themselves and who are not worth saving."

Chesterton's conclusion is both ringing and amazingly contemporary. It is echoed in almost every talk of the Holy Father. It is rejected in almost every segment of the inheritors of modern humanism: "*There will be Diocletian persecutions, there will be Dominican crusades, there will be rending of all religious peace and compromise, or even the end of civilization and the world, before the Catholic Church will admit that one single moron, or one single man, 'is not worth saving.'*" Such, of course, is what is at issue in our day with the death of humanism. No other defender of the ordinary man in his transcendent dignity appears. No more haloes exist about anybody on other than supernatural grounds and, therefore, we are all vulnerable, especially to a state that makes the laws exclusively in the image of autonomous humanism.

Indeed, we do have free will with our darker and sinful side; we can in fact reject Beatitude. But even those who find themselves in hell, having so rejected glory, will nonetheless bear the haloes of their own power of choice. Such is their doom. Humanism wanted man to be human without supernaturalism. It wanted him to be the cause of his own laws of right and wrong and to establish his own being. What it has instituted in fact was the truth of Genesis that we remain free enough to choose against ourselves.

To save ourselves we need not, as Carroll intimated, Luther's denial of free will, but Chesterton's idea that, though we have the freedom to reject Beatitude, we are the kind of beings, each of us, to whom alone it is offered. This is our dignity and that for which we were created. It could not be otherwise. The Catholic Church indeed will not admit that one single man is not worth saving, nor will it deny that this one single man can use this same free will to choose only himself.

On Not Wrecking Divine or Secular Things

The Chesterton Review (May 1992) reprinted a Chesterton essay entitled "The Roots of the World." The essay was originally published in The Daily News in London on August 17, 1907. This would be about the time Chesterton was writing Orthodoxy. The essay begins with a kind of narrative parable. Father Boyd in his little introduction remarked that this was a very famous essay and that Chesterton used such parables "as a way of teaching moral truths." I suspect that he used it also as a way to teach the metaphysical truths upon which moral truths are based.

Essentially, Chesterton argued that the whole universe is connected, the highest things with the lowest things and the lowest with the highest. What you cannot do is change God, but you may just change yourself or the world if you try to change God into something other than He is. That is to say, the logic of changing one thing will necessarily result in changing something in the world. If you think wrongly about God, you will think wrongly about man.

The story is a sort of re-telling of the Fall in Genesis. There is a garden in which is growing an odd star-shaped flower, that a little boy is commanded not to pull up by the roots. He may pick the flowers but not pull the plants up by the roots. Naturally, the little boy, shades of the young Augustine, wants nothing more in this world than to pull up the flower by its roots. The elders on the scene give him a number of not very good reasons for not pulling up the plant. But the boy has a very "silly" reason for wanting to pull up the plant, whatever the reasons for not doing so are. He explains that "the Truth demanded that he should pull the thing up by the roots to see how it was growing."[1]

The boy's parents and tutors never really gave him the full reason for the prohibition which was that pulling up the plant by its roots "would kill the plant, and that there is no more Truth about a dead plant than about a live one." In other words, it would have been helpful perhaps for the parents to have given the boy an accurate reason for the prohibition, but even if they did not do so, the prohibition stood. Since the dead plant will not reveal the truth about itself, the boy risked the punishment for violating the prohibition and risked losing the truth itself that could not be discovered by his method.

It seems that one dark night the boy slipped into the garden and started pulling up the plant by the roots. Suddenly strange things began to happen. First, the boy could not succeed in pulling up the plant, but as he pulled, the great chimney of his house collapsed. He pulled again and the stables fell down. Cries of agony began to be heard. The castle itself fell down. This chaos seemed to frighten the boy but he managed to say nothing about the strange incident of the flower. He still did not want to obey the prohibition.

The boy grew up and decided to try again to uproot the plant. He was a politician and ruler now. He surrounded himself with a group of strong men and announced, "Let us have done with the riddle of this irrational weed." So they all began to pull it out with great force. Suddenly, the Eiffel Tower fell, the Great Wall of China, the Statue of Liberty. "St. Paul's Cathedral killed all the journalists in Fleet-street." The ruler recalled his earlier experience in the garden.

In their efforts, these strong men had managed to pull down half of the buildings of their country, but they still could not pull up the roots. Finally, the man gave up his project in frustration but he called his pastors and masters. He blamed them for not telling him that he could not root up this plant and that if he tried, he would ruin everything else. All they had told him was not to do it. He now saw the results but would not admit his responsibility.

This parable, of course, is about Christianity and the efforts of secular men to rid themselves of it. In attacking religion, the secularists do not eliminate religion but they do manage to pull up the roots "of every man's ordinary vine and fig tree, of every man's garden." Somehow there is a connection between religion and ordinary life.

We are warned about this relationship and we are given some half-baked reason for it. If we think the reasons to be wrong or not what we would do, we go ahead and try to uproot religion, only to end up destroying the very core of civilized life in the effort. We do not intend this result, but this is what happens. "Secularists have not succeeded in wrecking divine things; but Secularists have succeeded in wrecking secular things."[2]

The "enemies of religion," Chesterton concluded, are like the little boy. They cannot leave it alone. It is a kind of forbidden fruit, a challenge to their autonomy. They see all the prohibitions merely as arbitrary, as "something wild," not as something reasonable. They cannot believe that disorder flows from tampering with the solemn prohibitions. "They laboriously attempt to smash religion. They cannot smash religion; but they do smash everything else."

But why cannot they smash religion? The secularists and opponents of religion cannot touch the axioms of religion, which are dogmas and intelligible. These dogmas remain as they are no matter what goes on in the world. In not holding the doctrines of the faith, the secularists necessarily are committed to other doctrines. To maintain that man is not made in the image of his Creator is as dogmatic as to maintain he is.

Chesterton gave two examples, the case of the pacifist and that of the evolutionist. The pacifist has a doctrine about coercion. This results in the "intolerable and ludicrous" alternative "that I must not blame a bully or praise the man who knocks him down." Evolutionary theory is based on the endless gradations in nature. On this basis alone we cannot be forced to "deny the personality of God, for a personal God might as well work by gradations as in any other way." So the theory stands. What the evolutionist does, if his theory be taken strictly, is not to deny the personality in God but the personality in Jones.

If evolution is true, Jones is within the scope of evolution. That is, he is himself being "rubbed away at the edges." He is at this very moment evolving into something else. If everything is evolving, including ourselves, including Jones, then in strict logic, we are not really ourselves. What must finally be denied is not personality in God but "the existence of a personal Mr. Jones."[3]

If we want Jones to exist as Jones, then he must not even slightly be in the process of becoming Mr. Smith, or some higher species. The old religion wants Jones to remain Jones. If we try to root out this doctrine of religion, we do not end by changing the theory that Jones is Jones and that Jones wants to be Jones. But we do force ourselves to look on him as becoming not-Jones. In this evolutionary case, in its logic, the world is full of things, including Jones, that are not really themselves.

So, we cannot really wreck divine things, but we can certainly wreck human things. If we see human and secular things being wrecked, we must begin to suspect that we are violating some prohibitions. If we root up a certain flower, we will root up the world. We should not forget too, that the prohibitions were also rooted in the truth that the boy was seeking. The truth was that he would not know the real truth of the flower if he killed it by uprooting it. The prohibition would have saved the world. Reason would have saved the flower.

At the roots of the world lies disturbingly the will that wants only its own truth. The prohibitions tell us that there is a world we want, we, Jones, even if it is not the world we make. The flower was already there. Jones was already Jones. The commandments, the prohibitions, are designed to keep them both. Even when we pull down the world, we will not find our truth, but only the truth. There is only one theory, as far as I know, that allows Jones to be Jones. That theory is still called Christianity. This is the meaning, I think, of Chesterton's parable about the roots of the world.

Belloc on Chesterton

Frank Petta, on reading of my brother-in-law's troubles in finding Belloc's little book on Chesterton, was kind enough to send me a copy of the obituary—it is entitled simply "Gilbert Keith Chesterton"—that Belloc published in *The Saturday Review of Literature* for July 4, 1936. Belloc had written evidently a number of things on Chesterton just after he died, but I had not known of this particular essay. On receiving it, I read it but put it aside. I chanced to come across it the other day, looking for something else. I re-read it. And I read it a second time, and a third. I suddenly was struck by the profundity of this essay of Belloc, of how he saw the essence of Chesterton.

Belloc began the essay by analyzing why the English aristocracy and press never acknowledged Chesterton's greatness. Even though Chesterton was "the most English of Englishmen," he stood on the Catholic side of culture. Belloc thought Chesterton's fame would increase, so that Belloc's children and grandchildren would have a better chance to understand Chesterton than his own generation had.

However, Belloc himself knew Chesterton. "I knew him I think as well as any man ever knew another." This friendship was based on long acquaintance—"close on forty years"—but it was especially based on the quality of its intellectual exchange. Belloc wrote, "So thoroughly did my mind jump with his, so fully did his answer meet the question my own soul was always asking, that his conclusions, the things he found and communicated, his solutions of the great riddles, his stamp of certitude, were soon part of myself."[1] The great riddles of life were asked, answers were forged. This sense of actual answers to riddles, as Chesterton showed in *Orthodoxy*, is especially characteristic of Christian friendship. Not just the questioning that is perhaps more Platonic, but the realization that answers are there when the proper questions are asked. The nobility of the human condition is not merely that it can ask questions, but that it can know when its questions are answered.

Belloc observed, furthermore, that they both came of the same "stock." Belloc's mother was English. "My mother derived directly from that English middle class of yeomen and liberal stock which in literature and the arts, in law and even in arms, in merchant enterprise, and, most of all, in metaphysical and religious speculation, has determined the character of England from the moment of the Puritan triumph three hundred years ago."[2] Chesterton's family was in the real estate business in London. Both Belloc's mother and Chesterton came into the Church from "sheer power of brain."

Belloc acknowledged that he had grown in his appreciation of what Chesterton stood for. Belloc next remarked something that puzzled me, something I always thought he denied. I had to look it up. On his "path" from Toul to Rome, Belloc in 1902 or perhaps in 1901, remarked in a passage I have often cited, with considerable consolation, I admit, that "it is a good thing not to have to return to the Faith."

Here in the Chesterton obituary, we find Belloc reflecting:

> I myself have gone through a pilgrimage of approach, to a beginning at least of understanding in the matter [of faith]; but it was never my good fortune to bear witness by the crossing of a frontier: a public act. Such good fortune was his [Chesterton's]. I was born within the walls of the City of God: he saw it, approached it, knew it, and entered. I know not which is for the run of men the better fate, but his was certainly of our two fates the better.[3]

I suppose these two things can be reconciled. Yet I cannot help but think that Chesterton himself would have been surprised at

Belloc here. Chesterton would have thought that Belloc was right in *The Path to Rome* and wrong in the obituary. Chesterton the convert would have agreed that it was indeed "a good thing not to have to return to the Faith."

Belloc, to be sure, was comparing a person returning to the faith after having lost it to a person who, never having had it, subsequently finds it. Belloc suggested that, for most men, it may be better to have been born in the faith. He himself had had a struggle to see the faith, to know it. Chesterton's path was, to Belloc, more noble and clearer. If the issue were only between Chesterton and Belloc, perhaps Chesterton's was the better path.

Still there is something to be said for the Belloc of *The Path to Rome*. We who were born "within the walls of the City of God," as Belloc put it, using a phrase from Augustine, no doubt, must still bear witness, cross frontiers, make our act public. We must see, approach, know, and stay within.

And yet, the best and most profound part of Belloc's reflections on Chesterton were not about his origins, his Englishness, or even his friendship with Belloc. Chesterton's life, in Belloc's mind, was not spent in "search for truth." This understanding is too abstract. Chesterton was "hungry for reality." It is one thing to have a vague or abstract sense of this hunger, but quite another to think of satisfying this hunger. "He [Chesterton] was hungry for reality. But what is much more, he could not conceive of himself except as satisfying that hunger; it was not possible to him to hesitate in the acceptation of each new parcel of the truth; it was not possible for him to hold anything worth holding that was not connected with the truth as a whole."[4] Chesterton's was a "strange consistency" that placed each new reality he hungered for within the satisfaction of the whole. He knew where things belonged.

In a passage reminiscent of St. Thomas's famous dictum *contemplata tradere* (to pass on what is first contemplated), Belloc noticed that Chesterton's passion for "*what is*," a passion that made him reject both confusion and falsehood, was "the driving power moving his spirit to disseminate what he knew." Chesterton was so struck by reality, by *what is*, in its infinity of forms and shapes, that he wanted to respond to it, explain it, appreciate it. In short, he delighted in it.

Belloc stressed this latter quality as it was easy to miss. Chesterton's love of fun, of jesting, his vitality, made us forget or overlook what Belloc called Chesterton's "power of proof." This power of proof was "not only the central thing, it was the whole meaning of his work." In a passage mindful of Josef Pieper, Belloc continued to explain what Chesterton was about. "The whole meaning of his life was the discovery, the appreciation, of reality." We have, of course, read Chesterton's book *St. Thomas Aquinas*, in which this very quality is so evident. Chesterton's work "was made up of bequeathing to others the treasure of knowledge and certitude upon which he had come."

What follows from this basis, I think, shows that Belloc really did understand Chesterton in the most profound of ways. And through him, if not also through his own experiences, he knew that Chesterton's love of reality was something that was not merely his own, even when it was his own. "Side by side with and a product of that immense exuberance in happiness not only of himself but of all around, of that vital rejoicing not only in man but in every other work of God and in God Himself, the most conspicuous fruit was generosity."[5] The affirmation of *what is* that it is, the rejoicing in *what is*, that it is, the affirmation that *all that is* is worthy of praise, not excluding oneself—this is what Belloc called in a felicitous phrase "that intense exuberance in happiness." These qualities of rejoicing and praise lead to generosity, to the realization that what we are and have do not exist of ourselves. They exist because they are given in an abundance that we can only receive in wonder and awe.

Chesterton could "write on all things because he was in the spirit of all things and from this central position he could explain, predicate, and give peace." To "give peace," I think, means to know that the riddles have answers.

We often wonder about Chesterton's frequent paradoxes. Some folks do not like them; others wait for them, so illuminating they are. Perhaps this is Belloc's comment on this topic: "He exaggerated in nothing save in emphasis of expression when rhetoric demanded. In statement of truth he did not and could not exaggerate because truth, which was his sole concern, is of its nature absolute." This is right, of course.

Today, anyone who suggests that the truth is "absolute," let alone that he might have discovered and passed it on, is looked on as some sort of danger to the republic. Belloc noted that all conversation today is advocacy. It is rooted in opinion and uncertainty, even in the "certainty" that truth cannot exist at all.

Chesterton, however, was not an "advocate." He was almost the only man in England who was not an advocate. "He does not advocate but tells." What a marvelous thing to say of Chesterton, something that explains the feeling we often get from reading him that he has discovered the truth, but he has not invented it. "In the midst of such a chaos Chesterton's voice and pen proclaimed not selected evidence but the thing that *was;* the thing that he saw and knew." He simply "told" us what he knew and saw and reflected on. He gave us peace of mind because he believed we did have minds—minds, as he often said, that are by their very nature made to come to conclusions, to formulate dogmas, to tell the truth.

Belloc saw what was at stake in modern philosophy. He saw it as Chesterton saw it, namely, that the social world can be constructed according to human will, that we can, in some sense, make come to be what we want to be and not only what ought to be. Whether we will to reverse our principles and foundations remains to be seen. The challenge of religion and classical philosophy ought to do precisely this reversal, were it not for the fact that both religion and philosophy have often sounded very much like the social world that has come to be from pure will.

> Now Gilbert Chesterton throughout his life was on the side of those who at so much risk determined to reverse if reversed it could be the current of the time. All around him was a society which had determined upon the opposite and fatal course—hiding its weakness—and of erecting an imaginary world that should satisfy foreign critics and lull its own confidence in security.[6]

Only today are we beginning to understand in what that "risk" of restoring order might consist. The opposite and fatal course seems, at bottom, not to have been communism, but the system that communism shared with modernity.

Would this reversal be possible? Belloc thought that wrong ideas and systems, once entered into, usually had to bear their own bitter fruit in social reality before they could intellectually be seen for what they were. Belloc thought that this seeing required not merely intelligence and knowing *what is*, but "repentance." Belloc felt some connection between a failure to repent and the death of Chesterton, the man who "told" the truth, who loved the variety of things, appreciated them, saw them in the light of God who made them. Men can refuse *what is*. It was Chesterton who could affirm it—who could, as a result, be generous, for what he had, what he knew, was not his.

The Only Virtue

Volume III of the *Collected Works* (1990) includes a book known as *The Well and the Shallows* (1935). The book ends with two short essays, one of which was a Letter Chesterton wrote to *The Catholic Herald* entitled "Why Protestants Prohibit." Chesterton had evidently been asked to give an address on the BBC in the context of a series on "Freedom." He was asked to speak on freedom as it related to Catholicism. (I do not know if this address still exists on tape somewhere).

Evidently Chesterton's talk produced a myriad of not always complimentary responses. I bring these essays up in the context of whether we can really speak the truth in this or any other republic. We are so much under the influence of the idea of tolerance, the one virtue, that we are not allowed to suggest that any idea or institution can be described in terms of truth. Needless to say, there is a problem of logic, of contradiction even, at work here. If tolerance itself is the only "truth," the only virtue, then the only vice is "intolerance." And what exactly is not to be tolerated in this context? It turns out to be the very claim to truth. When tolerance is elevated to a theoretic principle, we are left, in the political order, with the inability to call anything at all wrong or evil.

The logic of the "only virtue" was the background of Chesterton's responses to his critics who complained about his talk about liberty. Chesterton's fault against the only virtue, it seems, was his remark that the Protestant notion of freedom was "wrong." Such a remark on the BBC was by definition offensive and intolerable. Chesterton was not asked to prove his position, but to state it and explain it. He was not so much faulted on the truth of his position as on bringing it up in the first place. His view was not wrong, but it was uncivil. People do not like to hear that their view is considered wrong. No discourse at the level of soul-searching is therefore possible.

"If, indeed, in this free country where (I am assured) all views can be expressed," Chesterton justly reasoned, "it is unpardonable to suggest that the Protestant view of Freedom is wrong, some responsibility must be shared by those who ask the Catholic to explain why the Catholic view is right."[1] The only other alternative, the one more prevalent perhaps in this country, is never to have an objective position about a serious topic made in the first place in the public media.

I should not, moreover, fail to point out here the delicate subtlety of Chesterton's position. If a country really is "free," this should imply that one has the obligation to state what his position is as he holds it. But if, at the same time, the very stating it "offends" someone and this "offense" is grounds for prohibiting the speech, then we cannot have it both ways. The end of liberty and its discussion is no liberty. The end of tolerance is intolerance.

Chesterton confessed his personal difficulty in dealing with all of these views forthrightly: "For the peculiar diplomatic and tactful art of saying that Catholicism is true, without suggesting for one moment that anti-Catholicism is false, is an art which I am too old a Rationalist to learn at any time of life."[2] Again this sentence is worthwhile spelling out. It is not here a question of the truth of Catholicism, but the truth of logic, of the mind.

If one is invited to state his position and to affirm its truth, if this explication is the purpose of the discussion, then it is necessary, and by implication not at all "intolerant," to suggest that something at variance with this truth is false. Whatever one might think of Chesterton's exposition of Catholic liberty, which he was, in the name of freedom, invited to present, it is impossible not to recognize that positions opposed to it are not the same. This is not a question of religion but of thought. It has no alternative but the cessation of thought.

Chesterton had made this same point in *The Thing* (same volume of *Collected Works*), in an essay entitled "Some of Our Errors." Chesterton was discussing whether it was necessary and possible to restate in better language the old truths of the faith. "Now I do really believe that there is a need for the restatement of religious truth," he wrote; "but not (in the process of restatement) the statement of something quite different, which I do not believe to be true."[3]

Thus, a serious issue is at stake when a laudable and benign exercise to clarify doctrine is used instead as a tool to change doctrine itself. Thus, "when the Modernist says that we must free the human intellect from the medieval syllogism, it is as if he said we must free it from the multiplication table."[4] Whether the syllogism is a valid form of mental procedure has nothing at all to do with whether the mediaevals used it. If we free the mind from the way the mind works when it works, from the syllogism, we are not freeing it but enslaving it. We are asking it to work but denying it the very process by which it does work when it is being what it is.

In another essay in *The Thing*, actually entitled "The Slavery of the Mind," Chesterton wrote, "What I mean by the slavery of the mind is that state in which men do not know of the alternative."[5] He suggested that very often we are determinists in historical events and cannot even imagine that it might have been a good thing had Napoleon or the South won their wars. They did not in fact win, but just because one side wins does not mean in principle that the better side won. Chesterton here was not so much concerned with discussing the merits of these positions, but again he wanted to suggest that we are "slaves of mind" if we cannot even imagine the alternative.

In this context, Chesterton referred to St. Thomas, a man with whom he has much affinity.

> St. Thomas Aquinas begins his inquiry by saying in effect, "Is there a God? it would seem not, for the following reasons"; and the most criticized of recent Encyclicals [*Pascendi Dominici Gregis*?] always stated a view before condemning it. The thing I mean is man's inability to state his opponent's view; and often his inability even to state his own.[6]

Chesterton did not mind objections to his own Catholic view on liberty, provided that the objectors could state it and relate it to their own. Simply to object to it because it was not tolerable made any intellectual discussion impossible.

Chesterton's notion of liberty included the liberty to state the truth as well as the liberty to state why something might be at variance with it. Indeed, to know the truth, as St. Thomas had indicated, one needs to state how something is opposed to truth and why. Or, to follow St. Thomas's example, he needs to know how any error contains some truth that it is the duty of the knower to explain in relation to the whole truth. The very purpose of a discussion of liberty on the BBC, after all, must not be merely to fill up time or deal out equal proportions of opinions. It must in some sense have the purpose of finding the truth or the good in argument and of recognizing what things are opposed to it.

But Chesterton's problem about tolerance and liberty was not with the BBC, which he thought in the second essay in *The Well and the Shallows* had "a relatively sound sense of liberty." It did not seem unusual or unfair for the BBC to ask a Catholic what he thought of liberty; nor did it seem unfair to realize in the process that other positions would not agree with the Catholic position. There is nothing intolerant about stating what one holds, or in realizing and stating clearly its difference from other positions. Both of these positions have something to do with the very nature of the human mind and how it operates.

"Having asked me specially for what I thought about Catholicism," Chesterton continued, "I did certainly divulge the secret that I thought it was true; and that, therefore, even great cultures falling away from it, in any direction, had fallen into falsehood."[7] Needless to say, this view is not "politically correct" thinking. It would recognize that all cultures are describable; whether they are true or good needs argument, needs testing, even if this testing requires the intolerable conclusion that something is in fact in deviation from the universal measure and standard to which our minds are subject if they work as minds should work.

The Coming of Christ

In April 1932, during the height of the Depression, Chesterton published an essay entitled "If Christ Should Come" in, of all journals, *Good Housekeeping* (reprinted in *The Chesterton Review*, February 1984). Chesterton, of course, loved houses and good housekeeping, as his *What's Wrong with the World* shows.

But this particular essay evidently was supposed to answer the question "How would Christ solve modern problems if he were on earth today?" Notice that the question presupposes that Christ is *not* on the earth today and, more soberly, that modern problems are somehow intrinsically different from ancient ones. Christ's initial solutions, it is implied, were completely bound to His time. They do not apply to us moderns. When we have "post-modern problems," then, we will have to have Christ take a third try at these presumably even newer problems.

Needless to say, this topic of Christ coming to our earth is a worthy one at the Christmas season. Are we still convinced that Christ would have come as an infant in some out of the way place, like Bethlehem? Was this method of His dwelling amongst us really a good one, we might ask ourselves? We like to figure, in our more iconoclastic moments, that if Christ had done it right the first time, the world would not be in the mess it seems to be in.

Chesterton's own response in the *Good Housekeeping* essay is delightfully proper to the occasion and to the issue:

> For those of my faith there is only one answer [to this question]. Christ is on earth today; alive on a thousand altars; and He does solve people's problems exactly as He did when He was on earth in the more ordinary sense. That is, He solves the problems of the limited

number of people who choose of their own free will to listen to Him. He did not appear as an Eastern sultan or a Roman conqueror then; and He would not appear as a policeman or a Prohibition agent now.[1]

Again Chesterton saw that the real problem was the modern question, not the Christian teachings.

Chesterton's answer was, then, threefold: (1) Christ is in fact among us in the Eucharist. He does solve problems of those who freely appeal to Him. (2) Christ's initial coming was not a mistake. That He was thought to be Joseph the Carpenter's son, Mary's son, was not something that revealed a kind of inferior strategy on the part of the Holy Ghost about worldly affairs. (3) No matter what form of Incarnation might have been selected, the problem of human free will, its power to accept or reject, will remain.

The Incarnation, then, did not fail. Men can fail because they are free to choose wrongly or to choose well. If we want a universe in which there are precisely human beings, that possibility of the refusal of grace and goodness cannot change, no matter what form of Incarnation we might think of, no matter how Christ might have come into the world today.

On the other hand, we should not conclude from this observation of Chesterton either that there is something intrinsically wrong with being a sultan, a Roman emperor, a policeman, or, indeed, a Prohibition agent. We still have Prohibition agents today—only they deal mainly with smoking, drugs, high cholesterol foods we all like, dairy products, and yes, even alcohol. And there are not a few sultans, policemen, and emperors about, to say nothing of carpenters. If God is going to appear among men, He might conceivably take on any trade or occupation. He seems to have been the son of a carpenter, but Peter was a fisherman and Matthew a tax collector; Paul made tents, and Luke was called a physician.

Chesterton's Christmas essay of 1908 in the *Illustrated London News* was entitled "The Wrong Books at Christmas."[2] This title reminds me of the early days of my studies at Los Gatos and at Mt. St. Michael's in Spokane, when we were finally encouraged to read more or less as we chose, and not principally materials directly related to our studies.

There is, I confess, a certain pleasure in finding and reading a book during Christmas season, the days of Christmas, some book we would never otherwise have read because we have some leisure time. If I might dare such a paradox, often the "wrong" book to read at this time is the "right" book. Just as there is something to be said about reading the best, or most popular, or the great books, so there is something to be said for reading just any old book to see whether it is great or not. To find a good book, you really have to read a lot of bad ones, I have no doubt. Otherwise, you will not know the difference.

My friends Mike and Caron Jackson recently gave me Tim Parks's *Italian Neighbors: or A Lapsed Anglo-Saxon in Verona*. I have just gotten the English couple settled in their apartment and finding the bar with the best cappuccino in town, not to be drunk after 10:30 A.M., however. Previously, the Jacksons had given me Peter Mayle's *A Year in Provence*. Then they proceed to go there just to see if the food was as good as claimed. Evidently, it was.

Then Scott Walter gave me the Sherwood Sugden reprint of Belloc's *Miniatures of French History*. Thumbing through it, I came across Belloc's essay "The Death of Chateaubriand" (July 4, 1848). After I read it, I said to a friend, to whom I read it aloud, Belloc is the best essayist in the world, isn't he!

"As he [Chateaubriand] so lay [in Rue du Bac], awaiting her [Jeanne Françoise Récamier, his early love], there returned to his weakened mind a certain phrase of his own writing not so long before," Belloc wrote, where he [Chateaubriand] had spoken of human affection and had said of love that time changes our hearts as it does our complexion and our years. Nevertheless there is one exception amid all this infirmity of human things, for it does come about sometimes that in some strong soul one love lasts long enough to be transformed into a passionate friendship, to take on the qualities of duty, and almost those of virtue. Then does love lose the decadence of our nature and lives on, supported by an immortal principle.[3]

No one writes more beautifully or profoundly than this. The infirmity of human things, the decadence of our nature, immortal principle, passionate friendship—these all are related, in their own way, to the Incarnation, to the coming of Christ.

Chesterton, in 1908, was rather concerned with the abidingness of religion. "The nation that has no gods at all not only dies," he wrote, "but what is more, is bored to death."[4] The routine transforming of all feasts into mere vacation days, all appearing on Monday, is getting us nearer and nearer to this existential boredom in which nothing new can happen. Chesterton thought that perhaps Christmas would outlast the secularization instinct that replaces Christ with Santa Claus and then proceeds to make him illegal, which replaces all sacred signs with abstract forms and colors with no concreteness. Christmas is the feast of concreteness, or it is nothing.

If faith does come back, "the English celebration of Christmas" will remain, Chesterton observed. Somehow it is too traditional, too beautiful for even the most radical secularists to drive it out. He added, "There is nothing really wrong with the whole modern world except that it does not fit in with Christmas."[5] That is to say, that the criterion of what is human and of what is true is not "does it fit in with the modern world," but does the modern world fit in with the coming of Christ, with Christmas?

"The real basis of life is not scientific; the strongest basis of life is sentimental. People are not economically obliged to live. Anyone can die for nothing. People romantically desire to live—especially at Christmas," Chesterton concluded.[6] The "desire to live" is not scientific, it is "romantic." To die for nothing, to die of boredom, this is the obverse of refusing to know the meaning of choosing to live.

"He [Christ] solves the problems of the limited number of people who choose of their own free wills to listen to Him." The very word "romance," Chesterton said someplace, comes from "Rome." To choose is to choose something, to limit ourselves to what we really want. And as in the Incarnation, when we find what we really want, it is through this one romance that everything is returned to us.

Chesterton's friend Belloc had it right about romance, about the "one exception amid all this infirmity of human things." The Nativity and the Resurrection are in fact related. "In some strong soul one love lasts long enough to be transformed into a passionate friendship, to take on the qualities of duty, and almost those of virtue. Then does love lose the decadence of our nature and lives on, supported by an immortal principle."

"How would Christ solve modern problems if He appeared on earth today?"

The Mass for Christmas Day takes the *Prologue* of John for its text. It is there we read that "the Word was made flesh and dwelt amongst us." Nothing is less boring or more particular than this, nothing more romantic. "Anyone can die for nothing." Christ died for our sins. This is where the great romance of freedom meets the great liberty of God. Only bored souls can fail to see the newness that remains the same in all the time in which men are given to live, to live "romantically," to live, that is, as if something really is lovely and given to them to choose.

"The Divine Vulgarity of the Christian Religion"

Several years ago, at a book sale somewhere here in Washington, I bought for a nominal price, to wit, fifty cents, the Double-day Dolphin Edition (no date) of Oliver Wendell Holmes's *The Autocrat at the Breakfast Table*. This famous collection of chatter, humor, and reflection was written between 1831 and 1832 by the famous American physician and author. I have never really gotten into this book, but I have looked at it and read some of it a number of times.

John Peterson had, in the meantime, called my attention to the Methuen collection *G.K.C. as M.C.: Being a Collection of Thirty-Seven Introductions*. The other day I was looking again at this book, which I had found in the Lauinger Library here on campus. I noticed that Chesterton had written an Introduction to this famous Holmes book for the 1904 British edition (Red Letter Library, Messrs. Blackie & Son, Ltd.) of *The Autocrat at the Breakfast Table*.

In 1904 Chesterton's career was just beginning. It would be four years before *Orthodoxy* was published. Holmes, of course, who lived from 1809 to 1894, had comments on all sorts of things, from Cicero's essay *De Senectute* to "My Last Walk with the Schoolmistress," on which he finally proposed to the young lady in these charming words:

> It was on the Common that we were walking. The *mall*, or boulevard of our [Boston] Common, you know, has various branches leading from it in different directions. One of these runs down from opposite Joy Street southward across the whole length of the Common to Boylston Street. We called it the long path, and were fond of it.
>
> At last I got to the question,—Will you take the long path with me?—Certainly,—said the schoolmistress,—with much pleasure.—

> Think,—I said,—before you answer; if you take the long path with me now, I shall interpret it that we are to part no more!—The schoolmistress stepped back with a sudden movement, as if an arrow had struck her.
>
> One of the long granite blocks used as seats was hard by,—the one you may still see close by the Gingko-tree.—Pray, sit down,—I said.—No, no, she answered, softly,—I will walk the long *path* with you!
>
> —The old gentleman who sits opposite met us walking, arm in arm about the middle of the long path, and said, very charmingly,— "Good morning, my dears!"

Such a passage, I am sure, the very philosophic and very romantic young Chesterton must have loved reading.

In his essay on Holmes, Chesterton maintained that Holmes was the most "aristocratic" of all the American writers. Indeed, Chesterton felt that Holmes would be more at home in the South than in New England.

> In American literature, indeed, he may be said to be, not by actual birth or politics, but by spirit, the one literary voice of the South. He bears far more resemblance to the superb kingless aristocracy that hurled itself on the guns at Gettysburg or died round Stonewall Jackson, than to Hawthorne, who was a Puritan mystic, or Lowell, who was a Puritan pamphleteer, or Whitman, who was a Puritan suddenly converted to Christianity.[1]

Needless to say, the very theological acumen that could speak so amusingly, yes so paradoxically, of "converting" a Puritan to Christianity reveals much about the mind of Chesterton in formation in 1904 or 1905, when he must have written this Introduction.

Recalling a good deal of the discussion of the "gentleman" and his place in political and social life that we associate with Plato and Aristotle, Chesterton saw Holmes not as a democrat but as precisely a "gentleman," with a breakfast table at which all things might be discussed in a most genteel manner. He was pre-

cisely an "autocrat," a self-ruler, not a democrat, a point with theological implications as I shall point out later in this essay.

But Chesterton was initially concerned in his comments with
the fact that Holmes was both a physician and a writer. "A good
doctor is by the nature of things a man who needs only the
capricious gift of style to make him an amusing author. For a
doctor is almost the only man who combines a very great degree
of inevitable research and theoretic knowledge with a very great
degree of opportunism."[2] The point Chesterton was making was
a subtle one, the distinction between fancy and imagination.
"Physical science has everything in the world to do with fancy,
though not perhaps much in the highest sense to do with imagination."[3] Here we get an initial hint of Chesterton's extraordinary sense of the meaning and nature of modern science and its
presuppositions.[4]

Imagination is the capacity to put things into a harmonious
whole, things that clearly belong together. Fancy, on the other
hand, sees relationships not when things seem to fit together, but
when they do not. Reality is more like fancy than like imagination; its configuration is divine, not human. That is, an order to
reality exists, but it is one that is ordinarily not seen by the human mind logically to follow or consistently to hold together,
even though there is a logic and a holding together. Holmes,
Chesterton thought, had this latter capacity of fancy because of
his combination of medicine and literature.

How Holmes understood God also became a fascinating
question for Chesterton. Holmes was not a materialist, nor was
he an agnostic, nor did he "rise to a refuge in a luminous mysticism and cleanse deity of all materialistic notions, hanging it
alone in the heaven of metaphysics." God was rather like the Father of nature. "His God was practically merciful, but he was
mercilessly practical."

Holmes protested "against the cruelty of taking human freedom too seriously." And in a passage almost directly out of Plato's *Laws*, Holmes, in Chesterton's view, tossed "to the images of God the pardon which is due to puppets." That is, these images, these puppets really were not responsible for anything they did. They were not free.

"What was the problem here?" we might ask. Holmes poked fun at the churches. Yet, these same orthodox churches "were founded on a certain grand metaphysical idea which Holmes never quite justly appreciated, the idea of the dignity and danger of the *imago dei*." The dignity *and* danger of the images of God was that they were not just puppets, but puppets of God, as Plato had said.

Thus, the "images of God" themselves had to choose God. Consequently, He took a considerable risk in creating them. Human freedom might indeed be taken "too seriously," that is, we might in fact not want ourselves to be so free that there is any real risk of not choosing God. This position is what worried Chesterton about Holmes. But if we refuse the risk, we refuse to be human at all. The "autocrat," in Chesterton's view, does not see the universality of both the risk and the choice. This is the same thing as not wishing to be free at all.

Both the Christian religion and the Declaration of Independence recognized this risk that underlay all dealings with men. Both were democratic in this sense that they believed the drama of life and destiny belonged to everyone, not just to the gentlemen, to the oligarchs or aristocrats. "So good a gentleman as Holmes could not really understand *the divine vulgarity of the Christian religion*."[5]

Chesterton admired Holmes's breakfast table, with its brilliant wit and exchange of remarks. "At the breakfast-table there is something more important even than the amazing cleverness which is lavished upon it. There is a human atmosphere which alone makes conversation possible." The highest things exist in conversation. The *Word* was made flesh.

Yet, the spirit of Holmes was not democratic but aristocratic. Not understanding the "dignity and danger of the *imago dei*" in all its forms, Holmes did not grasp the "divine vulgarity of the Christian religion" which presumed that everyone was to take part in the ultimate conversation. "Holmes was the most large-hearted and humorous of philosophers, but he was not the democrat of 'the open road' [Whitman]. He was the Autocrat of the Breakfast-Table."[6]

The Christian religion, on the other hand, is for the *vulgus*, for the great multitude of people, for the men and women who would understand Holmes's own long path in the light of God's risk in inviting them to take it, to choose it. Once we understand the dignity and danger of the *imago dei*, we will, Chesterton thought, also begin to understand *"the divine vulgarity of the Christian religion,"* even at the breakfast table, even strolling along the paths on the Boston Common that lead from Joy Street southward to Boylston Street.

On Becoming Inhuman out of
Sheer Humanitarianism

In the summer of 1926 (July 3 and 10), Chesterton wrote two essays in the *Illustrated London News* on literature and novels.[1] He began with some advice that I recall my old professor Rudolf Allers had also given some years ago, namely, "read even bad novels." Allers's point was that you will likely find in lousy novels some rather accurate insight into how people are thinking or acting that you will not find in good literature or in your own experience. It is not easy to imagine all of the silly and wrong things that we might perpetrate on one another, yet we need to know this if only to save us from a certain naïveté or ethereal innocence.

Chesterton, with considerable amusement, put the case in this way: "I have always maintained that trash is a good aid to truth. I will venture to say that most of our historical ignorance, and even our literary ignorance, comes from our not having read enough of the trash of different times and places."[2] But it is often difficult to find the trash of other civilizations or times because that "terrible taste of mankind for preserving masterpieces has defeated us."

Neither Chesterton nor Allers, of course, was maintaining that trash was not trash, or that masterpieces were not masterpieces. The one helped to define the other and vice versa. The point was rather that we must indeed know what can go wrong in ourselves and in others. We do not know what is right without at the same time knowing what is wrong.

Plato had insisted that to know the good we had also to know the bad, not just the elegant bad of the sophisticated tyrant, but the ordinary bad of everyday life. Thus, Chesterton, for his part, maintained that "it would be very interesting to try to trace through popular stories some notion of the ideal of conduct which now prevails." In such an effort, Chesterton thought, we would find out better which part of traditional morality remained and which part did not.

In some sense, Chesterton had his friend Bernard Shaw in mind. In the popular tales, Chesterton observed, we will find that "it does not matter very much whether you are divorced. It does not matter very much whether you indulge in conduct calculated to produce a divorce."[3] What matters is that, like Shaw, we still behave in a certain gentlemanly manner, that we do not "attribute any faults to a lady" even though the metaphysical or religious reasons for not doing so are no longer held.

What bothered Chesterton about this situation was that, if in rational principle there was nothing wrong with divorce or the acts that might cause it, we should not have to worry about the more general rules of conduct that were designed to support the vows of marriage. Shaw, for Chesterton, was a model of correct reasoning. "He would have said that, if the sexes were to be equal, the man would have as much right to blame the woman as the woman to blame the man." What happens is that we have retained the vague notion of manners but not the idea of vows upon which manners were premised.

The problem with divorce is not just that we are ignorant of its often dire results but that we do not discuss its alternative. The alternative to divorce is that a "dull, common-place fellow," that is, the ordinary man, can think "that the oath he swore before God really meant something in the way of loyalty to his wife."[4] Moreover, Chesterton thought, "Christianity did succeed in making [this] loyalty comprehensible to a large number of common people." The usefulness of the often trashy stories and novels that assume the opposite—that is, that vows mean little or nothing—is, in Chesterton's view, to describe accurately what such disloyalty might entail.

Chesterton then went on to discuss in the July 10th column "intellectual novelists." Already in 1926, he perceived the problem with compassion and sincerity theory that has become the instrument for overturning any conception of a stable and defensible morality.[5] Chesterton was fascinated with "the modern mind," with the way it can "almost destroy itself." Chesterton, then, was struck with "the way in which people have become inhuman out of sheer humanitarianism."

What did he mean by this humanitarian "inhumanness"? We cannot wholly neglect the Christian suspicion that one cannot be fully human by human means alone. Chesterton had already remarked in his *St. Francis of Assisi*, I believe, that whenever men set out to be purely natural, they end up being quite unnatural. Needless to say, this phenomenon is something we see every day in the streets of any of our cities or advocated in the halls of our legislatures or pages of our newspapers.

The process, Chesterton thought, could be traced quite easily:

> They [the humanitarians] begin by saying . . . that it is our duty to sympathise with everybody. They started sympathising, in an abnormally sensitive fashion, with abnormally sensitive people; and ended in actually sympathising with their lack of sympathy. First you were a Christian and were kind to the man whom all men hated. Then you were a Christian or humanitarian psychologist and sympathised with the man who hated all men. And then you practically ended up by being a misanthrope and hating all men yourself. At any rate, you ended up by having quite a disproportionate sympathy with the people who could not be sociable, and an entire lack of sympathy for people who were sociable.[6]

Needless to say, if we follow the modern moral history of divorce, homosexuality, euthanasia, abortion, and any number of other wrongs that have become "rights," we will see this peculiar pattern repeated over and over. We must marvel at Chesterton's understanding of its process.

Chesterton saw this process as what we might call today an essential aspect of the "culture wars." What amused him about the intellectual novelists who propagated this mentality was their utter lack of sympathy for those people who in fact tried to be sympathetic to others as a matter of ordinary living. "Why are we only to be humane to the unreasonable person, and never humane to the reasonable person?"

Just like the impoliteness of ever raising the problem of the unromantic nature of breaking vows by divorce—Chesterton thought that keeping vows was in fact the most romantic thing available to us, for it alone guaranteed the notion of love—so the unsocial nature of humanitarian sympathy with those who do odd and unnatural things reveals a certain anti-humanness. "Are we so to encourage human beings to be such very sensitive beings that they cannot be social beings? Are we always to insist on the clumsiness of conventional people and never on the callousness of unconventional people? . . . It never seems to occur to the highly intellectual novelist that people ought to be able to get on with one another, even if they do not understand each other, as nobody can understand except God."[7]

We have seen the notion of culture in our time turn into the notion of private rights. We are not asked to endure or pardon the faults and disorders of others. We are asked to approve them and adjust our lives to them, no matter what they do, lest we be unsympathetic. The culture wars are about those descriptions of human lives that are in some sense unnatural that we are politically required to acknowledge as "normal." Hatred is what the new "rights" promoters vent on those who are simply ordinary. We are to be sensitive to all sorts of disorder, and we are even required to praise them, lest we be accused of "verbal harassment." This means simply that we must keep the exterior form of politeness apart from any consideration of the moral basis on which it is to be rightly founded.

Chesterton had been discussing the case of a novel in which the normal wife was busy in the kitchen and her poet husband called her out to look at the beauty of the stars. She was accused of unsympathy for not dropping everything and rushing out to this supposedly unrivaled experience. Needless to say, Chesterton's sympathies were with the wife, not the modern poet. "The novelist and the critics yearn with sympathy of the tenderest sort over these sensibilities," Chesterton concluded.

> It seems to be admitted that nobody could be expected to endure such things from their fellow-creatures. It never seems to occur to anybody that people ought to be taught to endure their fellow-creatures. It never seems to strike them that the sane culture and training of a citizen ought to strengthen him to resist the shock of a loud sneeze or a large ear. Culture seems to mean the cultivation of disgust.[8]

What the ordinary people are now asked to do is to deny that any difference exists between one form of conduct and another. We are asked to endure what is in fact most disgusting and call it culture. What began as sympathy for the abnormal ended up as hatred for the normal. Chesterton wondered why the abnormal was so unsympathetic.

If we bring these two strands of Chesterton's thought together, that is, the way setting out to be human can end up with inhumanness and the fact that we should read trashy novels in order to know what things are praised, even if they be wrong and corrupting, we can see that he had already begun three quarters of a century ago to sense the direction our culture would take.

Our culture has come to accept the breaking of vows and to call it romance, when their keeping was the only romance worth having. Meanwhile, our culture set out to be human and seems to be ending up by sympathizing with all the disorders of our kind and calling them "rights." We are not to be in the slightest considerate, normal people, who see such things simply as what they are, trash. The callousness of unconventional people has set the tone of our time wherein we have, neglecting grace and logic itself, become "inhuman out of sheer humanitarianism."

"Woman and the Philosophers"

Quite by chance, I happened to pull out of my files the February 1985, issue of *The Chesterton Review* on the day after I had happened to see an amusing headline in *USA Today* (February 5, 1993). The headline read: *EQUALITY OF SEXES? GIVE IT 1,000 YEARS*. As it turned out, this headline was based on a report of the International Labor Organization, on a forty-one-nation survey about the "progress" of women.

Why the authors did not survey all one hundred and seventy nations in the world on this perplexing topic, I do not know. But given the lengthy time range, I guessed they would eventually get around to it. As Rex Harrison sang in "My Fair Lady," "Why can't a woman be more like a man?" According to this report, as I understand it, "progress" means when she does become more like a man, in a 1,000 years or so. Woman will be—a rather boring and startling prospect, no doubt, to most normal women and men—exactly equal to a man.

Apparently, this U.N.–sponsored research discovered that it would take women "another 1,000 years to match the political and economic clout of men." As there is not a woman alive who can wait that long, naturally this report was disturbing to me. I had an additional problem, as I did not happen to know any women who particularly wanted "to match the political and economic clout of men." Indeed, few thought that this goal was what being a woman was about or worth doing even if they could.

In any case, the report contained such horrendous statistics as these: It would take 500 years for women "to hold equal managerial posts of men" and 475 years for them to reach "equal political and economic status." Just what happened in the 25 years (500 minus 475) that would cause women to pass from equal political and economic status to equal managerial status was not made clear. I decided, however, it must be a cumulative statistic. That is, it would take 475 years to reach political and economic equality, and another 500 or so to become top managers. This must be where the 1,000 years came from.

Other shocking facts were reported: "Women make up 3.5% of Cabinet posts worldwide"; "Greece and Paraguay had a drop in female managers." "Women hold 40% of management posts in Australia and Canada; 8.3% in Japan and 4% in South Korea. Bangladesh ranks last with 1.4%." Conclusion? The richer you are, the more your women work?

The only comment in the article about this frightening information came from Eleanor Smeal, President of the Fund for the Feminist Majority. This too startled me, as I did not know feminists wanted to be a majority, nor that they needed a fund for it. Mrs. Smeal, however, pithily said it all: "It's a worldwide disgrace. Half the Earth's population is relegated to permanent under-status."

When I first came across this piece, I did not save it. To have my own copy—otherwise this perplexing essay would not exist!—I chanced to go out on a cold Sunday morning and luckily found a previous day's edition of *USA Today* in the old "Croissant Chaud" on N Street. I had been struck, however, on first cursorily reading the report, that the criteria of what it is to be a successful or equal women—that is, to be managers, politicians, or cabinet members—were exclusively economic and political ones, criteria often used to decide the success of men.

At first sight, it seemed that if you wanted to be a successful woman in 1,000 years and did not want to be part of a permanent "under-class," you would end up exactly like a man. It hardly seemed worth the wait to me. Surely there were other criteria for a good and successful woman? I find it difficult to believe that among the half the world's population that has ever lived on this planet up to this time, let alone in the next 1,000 years, that we have practically no examples of feminine success. I know a few myself, it seemed to me, but none of them were managers, politicians, or cabinet members.

It so happens that *The Chesterton Review* that I was looking at just after reading this ILO report had reprinted a review that Chesterton wrote in 1901, in *The Speaker*, of the English translation that the Rev. T. A. Seed made of the French of Alfred Fouillée's book, *Woman: A Scientific Study and Defense*. Chesterton's review is entitled, "Woman and the Philosophers." When I read Chesterton's review, I was truly sorry he did not have a copy of the ILO report and Mrs. Smeal's comment. But as I read his analysis, I realized that he did not need his own copy as the situation, contrary to what we might expect, had not much changed in the century between his review and the ILO report.

Chesterton began with this delightful introductory passage: "The title of the work before us is *Woman: A Scientific Study and Defense*. It never occurred to us before that woman stood in need of a defense of any kind; and what the women of our acquaintance would think of being made the subject of a 'scientific defense' we shudder to conceive."[1] On the crucial issue itself, Chesterton did not think that science had anything to say. "Whether woman is structurally different to man is a matter of physical science, whether she is superior or inferior or equal is not a matter of physical science; it is a question of what you happen to want."

The French author, it seems, to state the presumed scientific basis for the inferiority of women, had cited Herbert Spencer to the effect that "the interest of women is generally directed rather to persons than to ideas." Since men were said to come to abstract ideas last, this feminine predilection for persons was supposedly a sign of their inferiority.

Naturally, Chesterton had great fun with this evolutionary dogma holding that something that comes last is necessarily better. All concrete ideas of justice that a woman is likely to have are better than an abstract idea of justice, which a man is apt to have. Real justice is concrete, not abstract. The fact is that "to understand a man (as many women do) is to understand one of the most complex and untranslatable cryptograms conceivable, to understand a 'cause' is to understand the clumsiest thing created."[2] Besides, saying that a thing is better because it comes last is like arguing that "playing on a typewriter" is "superior to playing on the organ."

The next philosopher to be taken up in this discourse is Schopenhauer, who did not much like the human race, male or female. Evidently, Schopenhauer thought women inferior and therefore "the best guardians of children" because women themselves were "puerile, futile, limited." Chesterton obviously plunged into this argument with great zest. Evidently, the argument implies that women are the best guardians of children because women themselves are "puerile," though that seems like an odd adjective in context.

Chesterton immediately observed: "Now we know what women do for children; they nearly kill themselves over them with work and anxiety." To test the validity of Schopenhauer's thesis we should logically ask, "What do children do for children?" We do not find, however, little boys of seven killing themselves working for other little boys of seven. No indeed. "A [little boy's instincts] lead him to kick his [another little boy's] shins and to run away with his toys." This argument will never do. "In fact," Chesterton concluded, "the whole of Schopenhauer's theory of the childishness of women is capable of the shortest and simplest answer. If women are childish because they love children, it follows that men are womanish because they love women."[3]

Efforts to prove the superiority of anything by some sort of biological analysis are most dubious. The French book wanted to argue on a biological basis that from the very beginning "the two sexes have certain types and functions which may still be traced in their moral and mental attitudes." Chesterton thought there might be some truth in this view. "But while we suspend our judgment on the truth of the biological contention we are heartily in agreement with the moral contention, and cannot see that it requires any biological machinery at all. The divinity of woman is to be decided by what she is, not by how she was made."

The subject of the inferiority, equality, or superiority of women ought not to be seen as if there were nothing wondrous about the particular, diverse being of man or woman. The drive to make the criterion of whether a woman is "in a permanent under-status" is logically a drive not to see her at all. Even if we could prove "ten thousand times over (it has not yet been proved once) that woman laboured under eternal mental as well as physical disadvantages, it would not make us think less but rather more of that brilliant instinct of chivalry which saw in her peculiar possibilities and put her to highest uses."[4] That is to say, whatever the difference between woman and man, what it is to be woman has its own genius that need not be judged in terms of the proportionate number of prime ministers who happen to be female at a given time.

"The whole romance of life," Chesterton continued, "and all the romances of poetry lie in this motion of the utterly weak suddenly developing advantages over the strong. It is the curse of the modern philosophy of strength that it is ridden with the fallacy that there is only one kind of strength and one kind of weakness. It forgets that size is a weakness as well as littleness."

Just what form the dignity of woman was to take in the modern world, Chesterton remarked, was yet unclear at the beginning of the twentieth century as it will, no doubt, be at the beginning of the twenty-first. Chesterton was not "out of sympathy" with the effort to define this dignity. "We believe firmly in the equality of the sexes, and we agree, moreover, that to use woman merely as a wooden idol is as bad as to use her as a wooden broom."[5]

Yet, what might this equality really mean? Equality of pay? Equality of honors? "But in the interests of equality, we must say that we doubt whether the mere equalisation of sports and employment will bring us much further. *There is nothing so certain to lead to inequality as identity.*" Colleges must now spend an equal amount of money on men's and woman's sports. Sports pages must devote an equal amount of space. Or to quote again the *USA Today* article, "Women hold 41% of management jobs in the USA—11% high-ranking, 3% top-level." In the meantime, children are said to need mothers at home and mothers say they work because their husbands cannot support the family.

"A mere struggle between the sexes as to who will make the best tinkers, tailors, or soldiers, is very likely indeed to result in a subordination of women infinitely more gross and heartless than that which disgraced the world up to now. *What we really require is a revised and improved division of labour.*"[6]

That is to say, that Chesterton, in 1901, thought that the equality of sexes in 1,000 years, in which all jobs would be 50–50, was a scheme to dominate women. Chesterton put it bluntly: "Whatever solution may be best (we do not pretend for a moment to have decided) it must emphatically not be based upon any idea so paltry and small-minded as the idea that there is anything noble in professional work or anything degrading in domestic."

The elevation of woman ought not to be like "the elevation of the worst type of working man" in which the garb of work replaces her memories of hearth and home. If we do this, it will be an ironic twist, Chesterton thought. "For [the intellectual woman] will have toiled to reach the haughtiest eminence from which she can look down upon the housemaid, only to discover that the world has become sane and discovered that the house-maid is as good as she."[7]

Can we not but be amused that the two good ladies appointed to the Office of Attorney General (1993) were both shot down because they hired housemaids while they were away at work? Chesterton's point was not that the work in a cabinet was not worthy, nor even that a woman could not do it. He wanted to know whether what she did, if she did not do this public work, was not itself a more worthy vocation? This domestic work need not be compared with equality statistics of economic and political office holding.

We might suggest, to conclude, in the spirit of Chesterton, that women, "half the world's population," have never really been relegated to "permanent under-status." The discovery that the housemaid is as good as the woman cabinet member will send a shock through the world, but only if we remember that most housemaids, from Salvador or Mexico or wherever, are working because they want a home, because they know that somehow that is a better place than in a top managerial post or in a cabinet. In the end, the housemaids are smarter than the intellectual women who want to occupy cabinet posts, because the house-maids better understand that economic and political criteria are not the final definition of womanly success. This seems to be Chesterton's final word in 1901 on "woman and the philoso-phers."

On the Discovery of Things Whose Existence
Is Impossible to Deny

Somewhere along the line, I acquired Chesterton's little book on the English painter George Frederick Watts. This book was originally published in 1904. I have a 1906 Duckworth edition, printed in Edinburgh, a gift from John Peterson. One Saturday in March, I decided to read this book, only to find by the markings in the book that I had already read it. I vaguely recall thinking that this book did not contain many good Chestertonian insights, but on rereading it, I found it, not entirely to my surprise, full of very interesting and indeed wonderful things. Let me recount some of them.

The book starts off with a most contemporary issue, now that we have ended the twentieth century, about whether a century can be considered a philosophic statement as well as a mere arbitrary unit of time—"the mind of the eleventh century" sort of thing. Chesterton thought that perhaps the nineteenth century, which had just ended and during which Watts flourished, could be considered a kind of unit of thought.

Chesterton recalled that the nineteenth century was populated by agnostic intellectuals who, even in claiming that they could know little or nothing, still retained a passionate, if on principle illogical, interest in "caring" about whether they knew anything. "Men were in the main, agnostics: they said, 'We do not know'; but not one of them ever ventured to say, 'We do not care.'"[1] If they care, they must think implicitly that they know something that is important. Their actions contradict their words, their logic. After all, how could agnostics properly know enough about caring itself to care about it?

What struck me on the very first page of this book, however, was something that must almost be considered a heresy today, even though it is something as old as Plato. The modern heresy is that nothing exists unless it is political. Plato thought, on the contrary, that all political disorders originate in soul disorders, not the other way around. In our time, however, sin or evil must be located in some public place or institution, so that all reform is political or legal reform. Thus, personal sin or evil does not much exist or matter. Contrary to this position, however, Chesterton remarked that "the greatest political storm flutters only a fringe of humanity; poets, like bricklayers, work on through a century of wars, and Bewick's birds, to take an instance, have the air of persons unaffected by the French Revolution." No, I confess I do not know "Bewick's birds," though I assume that partridges survived the French Revolution just fine.

The elevation of politics to central importance is often accompanied by the idea that political heroes are the only heroes. I believe this view to be quite contrary to the New Testament. Ultimately every life, even those of poets, unknown bricklayers, and other ordinary folks, grounds the ultimate drama of humanity. "The desperate modern talk about dark days and reeling altars, and the end of Gods and angels, is the oldest talk in the world: lamentations over the growth of agnosticism can be found in the monkish sermons of the dark ages; horror at youthful impiety can be found in the *Iliad*."[2] This is but another way of saying that at all times we will find sufficient evil for the day, that daily life is where the drama of civilization exists, where ordinary people encounter it. The French or any other Revolution will not leave us free of our encounter with evil, with ourselves, our own souls before God.

As if to get at what he meant, Chesterton contrasted Watts, who was something of a stoic, with the Celt. In this comparison, Chesterton, I think, put his finger on the reason why we do not have to go to some Revolutionary Paris to find the true drama of human existence. "To the Celt, frivolity is most truly the most serious of things, since in the tangle of roses is always the old serpent who is wiser than the world."[3] Notice that this is not a criticism of frivolity, but a praise of it. The danger of ordinary things is a reflection of their intrinsic glory. The old serpent is indeed wiser than the world, but not wiser than what the world is ultimately about. The tangle of roses does not diminish the beauty of the rose, nor does the old serpent who tries to use it for his own purposes.

This little book contains some twenty black and white reproductions of various Watts paintings. Watts painted a good number of the great Englishmen of his time, such as Tennyson, Carlyle, Browning, Meredith, John Stuart Mill, Lord Lytton, William Morris, and Cardinal Manning. He has paintings entitled "Orpheus and Eurydice," "Hope," "Jonah," "The Habit Does Not Make the Monk," "Chaos," "The Court of Death," and "Good Luck to Your Fishing," which latter shows a little Cupid kneeling on the rocks of a shore, with a line in the stormy waters. I do not recall ever actually having seen a Watts painting, though there must be some in the National Gallery, which I shall certainly investigate the next time I am downtown.

Chesterton examined each of these paintings and the mood that created them. In the course of his analysis—the book was originally published for a series entitled "The Popular Library of Art"—we find him reporting to us a wonderful series of insights. Already in 1904, a year before *Heretics,* we can find him in full intellectual vigor. And already here is a theme that will be developed in *What's Wrong with the World:* the paradox that only the pure of heart who see God can be the ones who know the depths of human passion—"the great truth that purity is the only atmosphere for passion."[4] He calls this remark, be it noted, simply "a great truth."

The great mystery of human passion is that the Manicheans—who think that the body and all connected with it is evil—are wrong. We are not to be surprised at the serpent midst the roses here, but just because something can be abused, can go wrong, does not mean that it is evil or wrong. Chesterton noted how this difference in the evaluation of pleasure worked its way out in the case of pagan and Christian asceticism. "The essential difference between Christian and Pagan asceticism lies in the fact that Paganism in renouncing pleasure, gives up something which it does not think desirable; whereas Christianity in giving up pleasure gives up something which it thinks is very desirable indeed. There is a frenzy in Christian asceticism; its follies and renunciations are like those of first love."[5] Clearly, if pleasure is bad, we should give it up. But if it is good, it makes sense to give it up only if there is some higher good into which it is incorporated.

Notice the striking comparison that Chesterton used, that particularly Christian asceticism could lead to follies and renunciations of the kind that are typical of our experience of first love, when we are giving up many things to find one thing. Notice too that Chesterton uses the very strong word "frenzy" to describe the results of Christian asceticism, as if to say that we are immersed in a tangle of roses, an infinite multiplicity of good, but we know that only the first love, the great good, is what we want. Hence our follies, our renunciations, yes, our frenzy.

This principle leads Chesterton to one of his most remarkable definitions: "A man, I fancy, is after all only an animal that has noble preferences."[6] The only animal with precisely "noble" preferences—that is, when things are given up, it might very well be because something else, among so many good things, is preferred. Purity acknowledges that much is given up. But Chesterton implies that only when what must be given up *is* given up does the real context of what we want come into view, something we were seeking elsewhere but there where it really can be found.

"There is of course a certain tendency among all interesting and novel philosophers to talk as if they had discovered things which it is perfectly impossible that any human being could ever have denied; to shout that birds fly, and declare that in spite of persecution they will still assert that cows have four legs."[7] How amusing Chesterton can be! Here too we have his great theme in *Orthodoxy* that we set out around the world to find something really new and finally when we land on its shores, we are astonished to discover that it is our old home we have found, our first love; we have arrived there whence we started. Only philosophers could really think that they discovered as new something that everyone else already took for granted. That is to say, we do not see the ordinary things, we do not see the drama of every existence until someone denies what seems most obvious. In the end we discover something that is utterly impossible for anyone to deny. We now shout that birds fly and that we will not, even by persecution, deny that cows have four legs. There is no one who does not already know these things; and, yes, the very fact that there are birds flying and cows with four legs does seem worth shouting about.

The Campaign against the Ten Commandments

We have heard the complaint, no doubt, that religion, particularly the Christian religion, is so negative. It seems always to be telling us what we cannot do, not what we can do. We want a "positive" religion; we do not want to worry about *don'ts*. Just give us the *dos*. Having propounded this well-known thesis, we proudly content ourselves with our liberality, our progressivism in things to be done.

Such is a very common complaint, and yet, when examined, a very superficial one. When we sort it out, when we think of why the Ten Commandments "forbid," at least those that apply to us human beings and our relations to each other, we will realize that these negative dicta are the most positive things we could imagine. In the one positive Commandment, besides that of "keeping holy the Sabbath," we are told to "honor" our father and our mother. Now this positive command is rather more demanding than if we were simply told "Not to Dishonor Them." It is as if we were told—and the Greek philosophers do tell us this—that there is no way we can repay our parents for what they have given to us, that to honor them is an obligation that really never ends. The positive Commandment to "honor" our father and our mother is, in fact, the most difficult of things to do.

On the other hand, take the law of driving. The basic law of the State of California is simply "Drive Safely." This command is stated positively, but, as it stands, it is not really of much help. The laws—"STOP," "DRIVE SLOWLY," "SPEED LIMIT, 25 MPH"— give us the freedom and knowledge of what actually to do. Even these prohibiting commands always have to be interpreted in the light of "Drive Safely." The commands tell us what actually to do when we drive safely.

Now I bring up this consideration of law and Commandment because I purchased, at a reduced price, Volume XXXII of Ignatius Press's *Collected Works* of Chesterton (1989). These are the columns from *The Illustrated London News* from 1920 to 1922. The very first essay in this volume is dated January 3, 1920. Like so many of Chesterton's essays that I had never read before, on reading it, I just wanted to cheer, it is so well put.

This particular essay was given the title "Negative and Positive Morality." As the essay was written just after the Great War and during the time of New Year's resolutions, Chesterton noted that a "resolution" was a formal statement of hope. A resolution specifies what specifically we have to do to change ourselves, year after year. Thus, finding ourselves rather difficult suddenly to change, we will probably have to deal with our recurrent sins— "for the soul and its sins are in every sense a problem of eternity."[1]

Chesterton, referring to World War I, further remarked that, in being relieved and grateful for the end of the War, we should notice that our gratitude is greatest when our escape from evil is very narrow. Likewise, our resolutions of hope that we change ourselves, that we recognize our sins, indicate to us the narrowness of the gap that stands between ourselves and the evil we could do if we would, if we did not observe the Commandments.

We must further recognize that when we say "yes" to something, we at the same time say "no" to something else. Every "yes" is a "no." If we say "yes" to this, we say "no" to that; it cannot be otherwise. "The silliest sort of progressive complains of negative things," Chesterton continued. But that to which we say "no" defines in the simplest and most graphic way that to which we say "yes." When this "silly" progressivism becomes a "campaign against the Ten Commandments," it indicates that it does not understand what is going on when things are commanded not to be done. "The truth is, of course, that the curtness of the

Commandments is an evidence, not of the gloom and narrow-ness of religion, but, on the contrary, of its liberality and humani-ty."[2] Why is this so?

Why, in other words, are the Ten Commandments, mostly negative statements to be sure, rather signs of humanity and lib-erality than signs of gloom and narrowness as they are common-ly thought to be? This is the reason Chesterton gives us, in one of his finest sentences: "It is shorter to state the things forbidden than the things permitted, precisely because most things are per-mitted, and only a few things are forbidden."[3] The Lord did not list all the positive things that we should be doing because the list would never end and, besides, we are supposed to find out the positive things for ourselves. We are supposed to be surprised by the myriad of good things *that are*.

Thus, if we were to be commanded simply "Do good," instead of "Thou shalt not," we would never end with the good things that we should or could do, the most things that are permitted to us because the whole world is given to us. The natural law, in fact, already tells us "Do Good and Avoid Evil"; revelation adds what we need to know so that we will not be confused about the most essential things that we ought not to do.

Chesterton, by way of example, offered a marvelous list of good things we might possibly be commanded to do if, because we could not get the point otherwise, we insisted on having our Commandments stated positively: Thou shalt first "pick dande-lions on the common." Then the list would go on for a month with other things we might do before we come to, Thou shalt "throw pebbles into the sea, . . . sneeze, . . . make snowballs, blow bubbles, play marbles, make toy airplanes, travel on Tooting trains." The list would simply never come to an end before we come to consider the things we ought not to do, things that might make finding any ordered good in things impossible.

In comparison with what we might do and are permitted to

do, then, the Ten Commandments display "that brevity that is the soul of wit." Thus, "it is better to tell a man not to steal than to try to tell him the thousand things that he can enjoy without stealing." And if we insist that there are some things that we cannot enjoy unless we steal them, we at the same time deprive someone else of enjoying what we have stolen from him. Our "yes" is someone else's "no." By not observing the Commandment, we insist that what is not ours is ours. We give the same right to someone else to steal from us; we end up in a war of all against all because we do not observe the negative Commandment which lets everyone enjoy what is his.

Chesterton next, to clarify the point more graphically, takes up the problem of the positive side of the Fifth Commandment, "Thou Shalt Not Kill." Now the Commandment simply tells us not to kill anyone, including the mythical "Mr. Robinson" of Chesterton's example. What happens positively when we do not kill this Robinson? Well, basically, Robinson continues to live and do all those things for which Robinson is noted, things that we cannot imagine. Mrs. Robinson, no doubt, is delighted to have old Robinson still around. Robinson himself is delighted to be around, though he does not know the narrow escape he had by our observing the "Thou Shalt Not" of the Commandment.

Chesterton thought of the Great War in the same way as he did of Robinson, that, however destructive, it saved Western civilization, Christendom, from something worse, from nothingness. It was still around, though it might have been destroyed by Prussianism. "Nothing is negative except nothing; and it is not our rescue that was negative, but only the nothingness and annihilation from which we were rescued."[4] Thus, if the civilization is not destroyed, if Robinson is not killed, what results is civilization and Robinson, which, in both instances, is positive not negative.

Thus, if someone obeys the Commandment and does not get

rid of Robinson, the negative prohibition means that Robinson positively lives. "And to say it is not a positive good and glory to have saved him from strangling is to miss the whole meaning of human life. It is to forget every good as soon as we have saved it."[5] The point about the good we save is precisely the activities, the life, that continue in being. The important thing about not killing Robinson is not just the not killing him, but the things that good old Robinson does of which we probably have no idea.

Consequently, we are really to fear that good things can be lost or destroyed. The things *that are*, all that is good, we are permitted, provided in our pursuit and choice of them, we obey the Commandments, for these are the limits and guidelines by which we can really have, really enjoy what is good. We can have Robinson only if we do not kill him. We can have our property only if someone does not steal it. We can have our wife only if someone else does not covet her. All these "Shalt Not's" are resolutions by which we are free to enjoy the thousands of things that we are permitted to do, the end of which we shall never reach. This very experience indicates to us why we are, in the same revelation that gives us the Ten Commandments, given also the promise of eternal life.

But what is the most penetrating reflection that Chesterton gives to all these considerations of the positiveness of negative morality, of the reasons why the "campaign against the Ten Commandments" is so "silly"? That we can most appreciate what we nearly lost. We do not realize the wonder of an existing thing until we recognize that it might not exist, indeed, that it might not exist at our hands. The Ten Commandments are the other side of our realization of the wonder of existing things, the good things we let be and we choose because they are good. And this is Chesterton's great line: "We adorn things most when we love them most; and we love them most when we have nearly lost them."[6] This is what the Ten Commandments are really about.

The Commandments prevent us from losing things that we love most. We love them but we do not really see them as the goods they are until we nearly lose them. We can lose everything that is good if we do not observe the Commandments that are specifically designed to keep in being what is good. When we see that what we love is almost lost, we adorn it in thanksgiving; we respond to the beauty of *what is* with the added beauty of our own recognition of what is given to us, of what we almost lost because we did not observe the Commandments.

"An Awful Instance of the Instability of Human Greatness"

We have a public radio station here in Washington that plays what is rightly called "good music," that is, classical music. The only flaw in this station is that it also broadcasts National Public Radio "News." When you forget to turn this news off as quickly as you hear it come on, it forces you to go about the rest of the day annoyed at the unrelenting propaganda that passes for information on this station.

In any case, there is a program on this station called "Desert Island Discs," a program that consists in getting some congressman or other public figure to select the music he would take with him were he to be stranded on a desert island. This whole approach, of course, goes back to Stevenson and Robinson Crusoe and no doubt to a hundred other stories designed to force us to think about what we would need or want were we to find ourselves in a similar situation. Indeed, the whole exercise is to teach us to ascertain what is important in life.

I bring up this unlikely topic because John Peterson sent me a copy of a short collection he did that tried to give us some insight into what it might have been like actually to have heard Chesterton debate or speak. Peterson's essay is called, "And Now Mr. Chesterton Will Take a Few Questions from the Floor," from a book called *Crossings: A 'Liber Amicorum' for Denis Conlon*, published in Antwerp, Belgium, in 1992.

Evidently, Chesterton was once actually asked from the floor, "What single book would you choose if you were cast on a desert island?" Chesterton's response was as follows:

It would depend on the circumstances. If I were a politician who wanted to impress his constituents, I would take Plato or Aristotle. But the real test would be with the people who had no chance to show off before their friends or their constituents. In that case I feel certain that everyone would take *Thomas's Guide to Practical Shipbuilding.* . . . And then if they should be allowed to take a second book it would be the most exciting detective story within reach. But if I could only take one book to a desert isle and was not in a particular hurry to get off, I would without the slightest hesitation put *Pickwick Papers* in my handbag.

This list of Chesterton desert island books got me to thinking, I must say, not in the least because I have a half-read edition of *Pickwick Papers* on my shelf someplace. Chesterton in fact did an introductory essay to these very *Pickwick Papers*.[1]

The fact is that I myself would think that Plato or Aristotle would be exactly the right book to take to the desert isle. I cannot imagine any book, except the Bible which Chesterton did not choose either, that would save more civilization or teach more about life than Plato or Aristotle. I hope that does not necessarily make me a politician trying to impress my friends and constituents. I love Plato and Aristotle and we very much could use the solitude of the said desert isle to read them as quietly and as often as might be necessary really to understand them.

Unfortunately, Chesterton did not tell us what book he thought to be "the most exciting detective story in reach." I guess it might even have been Father Brown, but perhaps he did not care. My own problem with an exciting detective story, as opposed to Plato or Aristotle, is this: once you read the detective story, presumably for a time to distract you from the loneliness of the island, you would not have the same joy and marvel on reading it a second time (in case the boat did not come to find you) that comes from rereading Plato or Aristotle I don't know how many times.

This brings us to ponder why would Chesterton choose the

Pickwick Papers. Notice that the condition of choosing this famous Dickens volume would be that of leisure (another word familiar to Plato and Aristotle)—"and was not in a particular hurry." Mr. Pickwick, Sam Weller, Mr. Tupman, Mr. Winkle, and Mrs. Cluppins will delight us again and again every time we meet them at the "George and Vulture Tavern and Hotel, George Yard, Lombard Street" or at the "Marquis of Granby" in Dorking. Who, on a desert isle, could ever stop dreaming of being at such enthralling places!

Listen to what Chesterton thought the *Pickwick Papers* were, even from his own youth:

> "Pickwick," indeed, is not a good novel, but it is not a bad novel, for it is not a novel at all. In one sense, indeed, it is something nobler than a novel, for no novel with a plot and a proper termination could emit that sense of everlasting youth—a sense as of the gods gone wandering in England. This is not a novel, for all novels have an end; and "Pickwick," properly speaking, has no end—he is equal unto the angels. The point at which, as a fact, we find the printed matter terminates is not the end in any artistic sense of the word. Even as a boy I believed there were some more pages that were torn out of my copy, and I am looking for them still.[2]

Here, no doubt, is the metaphysical reason for taking *Pickwick* to the Desert Island. If we cannot dwell with men, we must prefer to dwell with angels. The really good things of existence have no end. This is the real mystery of revelation, caught here by Chesterton on a desert isle with the *Pickwick Papers*.

In Chapter XXV, Mr. Pickwick is brought before the Magistrate, Mr. Nupkins, whose wife and daughter are described as follows:

> Mrs. Nupkins was a majestic female in a pink gauze turban and a light brown wig. Miss Nupkins possessed all her mamma's haughtiness without the turban, and all her ill-nature without the wig; and whenever the exercise of these two amiable qualities involved mother and daughter in some unpleasant dilemma, as they not infrequent-

ly did, they both concurred in laying the blame on the shoulders of Mr. Nupkins.[3]

After that, who could help but like this improbable Nupkins!

Mr. Pickwick is falsely accused by a certain Mr. Grummer of preparing to fight a duel. In the course of the story, it turned out that Mr. Nupkins and family, especially the ladies, had been put upon by a certain Mr. Jingle, who pretended to be a charming Captain Fitz-Marshall. Mr. Pickwick's assurance in a private meeting with the Magistrate convinced him that Pickwick was indeed the subject of a fraud. This discovery, moreover, would be cause of endless embarrassed among the other distinguished members of the Dorking gentry, such as Mrs. Porkenham, because the Grummer ladies had introduced Fitz-Marshall, alias Jingle, as a man of quality.

When Mr. Grummer was asked to restate the charge against Mr. Pickwick, "he managed to get involved, in something under three minutes, in such a mass of entanglement and contradiction, that Mr. Nupkins at once declared he didn't believe him." Grummer was ordered out of the city. Here is the exalted conclusion of Dickens to this fall of the mighty: "An awful instance of the instability of human greatness, and the uncertain tenure of great men's favour."[4]

When this chapter ends, the scene changes to Sam Weller's visit to his father in Dorking. Evidently, Mr. Pickwick is also being sued for breach of promise by his landlady, Mrs. Bardell, with her shady law firm of Messrs. Dodson and Fogg. Weller is to see how the case looks to Mrs. Bardell and her friends Mrs. Cluppins and Mrs. Sanders.

This sequence again suggests Chesterton's thesis about Dickens that he could invent character after character, almost that there would be a never-ending series of events and characters whose drama and delight would take forever in the telling. This seems to be why the *Pickwick Papers* were chosen for the desert isle.

When Sam Weller arrives, Mrs. Bardell is preparing a snack for her two friends, one of whom is quite stout. Mrs. Bardell was preparing "a quiet cup of tea, and a little warm supper of a couple sets of pettitoes and some toasted cheese. The cheese was simmering and browning away, most delightfully, in a little Dutch oven before the fire; the pettitoes were getting on deliciously in a little tin saucepan on the hob."[5] The fat lady is concerned that Sam be invited to share the cheese and pettitoes, which would lessen her share.

Soon they take to drinking a little wine and commiserating with each other on the caddishness of Mr. Pickwick. "Then the ladies emptied their glasses in honour of the sentiment, and got very talkative directly." The more the ladies drink, the more Sam finds out. "The mere idea of Mrs. Bardell's failing in her action [against Mr. Pickwick], affected Mrs. Sanders so deeply, that she was under the necessity of refilling and re-emptying her glass immediately; feeling, as she said afterwards, that if she hadn't had the presence of mind to do so, she must have dropped."[6]

Now, in all of this goings-on with the pettitoes and the toasting cheese, the reader has a sense of never-ending delight. On a desert isle, who would want anything more than such pettitoes and cheese? Dodson and Fogg are crooks; Sam Weller can do anything.

Mr. Pickwick himself is noble and yet absurd. Mr. Pickwick announced to the Magistrate in terms worthy of the First Amendment:

> You may order your officers to do whatever they please, sir [Pickwick was ordered to hold his tongue in court]; and I have no doubt, from the specimen I have had of the subordination preserved amongst them, that whatever you order, they will execute, sir; but I shall take the liberty, sir, of claiming my right to be heard, until I am removed by force.

There is something right about Chesterton choosing for our leisurely sojourn on a desert isle a book of such delight.

The *Pickwick Papers* is a story that does not end, even though it has a final page. Chesterton contrasted this book he refused to call a novel, good or bad, with mythology. Novels, Chesterton said, were produced "by a small educated section of the society." Then he added, in a famous passage, "Fiction means the common things as seen by the uncommon people. Fairy tales mean the uncommon things as seen by the common people."[7]

But the nineteenth century wrote long novels. In the twentieth century, we have mostly short stories. Chesterton did not think this accidental. "It means that existence is only an impression, and perhaps only an illusion."

> The moderns, in a word, describe life in short stories because they are possessed with the sentiment that life itself is an uncommonly short story, and perhaps not a true one. But in this older literature, even in the comic literature (indeed, especially in the comic literature), the reverse is true. The characters are felt to be fixed things of which we have fleeting glimpses; that is, they are felt to be divine.[8]

In the end, to take the *Pickwick Papers* to our desert isle is to take with us the intimations of what we are, of our immortality before the admittedly "awful instances of the instability of human greatness" that we can find with so little difficulty and so much delight at the "Marquis of Granby" in Dorking or at "the George and Vulture Tavern and Hotel, George Yard, Lombard Street."

The Dogmas Are Not Dull

Chapter twenty-nine of Chesterton's *The Thing: Why I Am a Catholic* is entitled "What We Think About." It is a remarkable chapter because it states most clearly the reason Chesterton is not a modernist and what effect, by contrast, the Catholic dogmas have on our ability to think at all. Briefly, they free us to think because they do not exclude the most difficult things about which we might think. Not to be a modernist means that the human mind is open to ideas and realities that are not limited by a narrow notion of what modern man "can" believe, itself determined by a certain methodology that excludes the higher reaches of things.

If we should just look at that title, "What We Think About," we might respond that we think about ourselves or the world or our dreams. Chesterton's thesis is that what makes Catholicism different and worthy to be taken into consideration is that what is revealed to it is itself worth thinking about. Indeed, once we begin to think about what is revealed, we think more accurately and more clearly even about things not revealed, because what is given to us to think about—say, that Christ had two natures or that the world was created—somehow requires us to think more correctly than we would have had we not this doctrinal position to confront.

Chesterton had seen an essay about the British novelist Arnold Bennett that referred to Chesterton himself. The reference was not very flattering. It implied that what Chesterton said he held was not really what he held. Thus, we could not believe his own words. No one could possibly believe what Catholicism held. If someone actually held what Catholicism holds, he would be a fool. Chesterson was no fool. Therefore, the argument proceeds, he must have believed something other than what he said he held.

If we believe that Chesterton has some secret doctrine other than the one that he actually held, then we spend our time looking for the secret doctrine. We fail to notice the fertility of what Chesterton did in fact hold: the dogmas of Catholicism. "People who cannot possibly know anything about me except what I say, should for the sake of our general convenience believe what I say."[1] The modernist, since his philosophy prevented him from even considering revelation's possibility, could only assume that every other philosophy had to conform to his own.

Chesterton was exasperated by the modernist mentality that could not imagine that someone in the modern world would think that this world was not itself intellectually justified, as Chesterton did not so think. The problem, as Chesterton saw it, was that Catholicism really was different from anything else in the universe. Its doctrines, like the Trinity or Incarnation, did require a deepening of intellect itself in order to treat them fairly.

Chesterton was merely testifying to the fruitfulness of his then-recent conversion to Catholicism. "Conversion," he explained, far from dampening thought, "is the beginning of an active, fruitful, progressive and even adventurous life of the intellect." This position was quite the opposite of the way most moderns thought of Catholicism, for they could hardly allow themselves to entertain the possibility that Catholicism might just be true and therefore intellectually stimulating.

If one thinks about the Mass, for example, in terms of what Catholic dogma says it is, then this thinking about the Mass forces the intellect to think more clearly and more profoundly. But if we see the Mass as something merely like a hundred other pagan religious passages, we will fail to see why it is unique even in the order of intelligence.

Chesterton would not allow for a moment the idea that religion is somehow apart from its doctrines about itself. "If he [the modernist] would condescend to ask what the dogmas are, he would find out that it is the dogmas that are living, that are inspiring, that are intellectually interesting." What makes the Catholic interesting is precisely certain ideas that he holds about the cosmos.

The most "interesting of all the ideas are those which the newspapers dismiss as mere dogmas." The dual nature of Christ is what is interesting, not the monophysite thesis that He is either wholly God or wholly man, but not both. If we held that Christ is only God or only man, but not both, we would have an infinitely less challenging and less intellectually stimulating doctrine.

The intellectual stimulation of dogma is precisely its accurate statement, its realization that what it must hold to is what the tradition taught and not what is acceptable to modern thought or philosophy. The fact is that dogma is closer to science. Indeed, it may be the origin of science, which needs a stable series of secondary causes known only by investigation, something that Christianity alone has provided for.

We can thus possibly, in comparative literature, have myths about suffering gods. But in Christianity this is not a myth but a fact. The relationship of life and longing may be found in various ways in other religions; only in Catholicism are the longing and the life brought together. "A mind filled with the true conception of this Deity has plenty to think about."

What is remarkable about Catholicism is the particularity of the revelation—not how it is like other religions but how it is different. "Christ, as conceived by the Catholic Church, is himself a complex and a combination, not of two unreal things, but of two real ones." These two real things are man and God. Likewise, the thinking about the Madonna is quite distinct as a result of this teaching on the Incarnation.

"Dogmas are not dull," Chesterton concluded in a famous phrase.[2] Its paradox is almost too delightful precisely because it is true. "Theology does introduce us to the structure of ideas." Chesterton concluded that "I have plenty of things to think about" in the uniqueness of Catholicism, but not from that part of it that might seem similar to other religions.[3] It is the former, the uniqueness, that causes real thought.

The dogmas of Catholicism are not dull, because they arise from the effort of human intellect to fathom the Wordness of all reality, including the reality of God. We are, as Aristotle said, thinking beings, and we are to think what is thinkable. Dullness comes from those who would deny the dual natures of Christ, or the Trinity, or the Madonna, or the Creation. These are the modernists who think they can only think what moderns think, not what it was revealed to all men to think.

Conclusion

The columns from which these chapters were drawn began in 1989. As far as I can now tell, after we have read and reflected on the whole vast corpus of Chesterton, we will find as much there when we read him again as we found when we began. As Chesterton intimated in his reflections on St. Thomas, there is no limit to *what is*. And yet there is something definite that Chesterton adds to *what is*, namely, a word, an illumination about what it is we see, when we in fact do see. Reality is not complete until we speak it, both within our souls and to one another. Reality is, in a way, incomplete until it is spoken, understood.

These particular essays have been selected because they remind us of how Chesterton himself was content with nothing less than thinking about everything. Aristotle had already told us that our minds are made to know *all that is*. Christian revelation in this sense is Aristotelian, only with the added surprise that we are to know God, Who is. Chesterton certainly saw the big things, the higher things, but, uniquely, he saw them in whatever was around him, in the tiny things, the small things. In some proper sense, it is as much a wonder that a flower exists or that we exist, as that the universe exists. Chesterton never lets us forget that if we start with the flower, or with ourselves, we will eventually find all things, including why anything is at all.

The works of Chesterton are something like the universe itself. No matter where we start, we are started. We have taken the first step when we open the first page, no matter what it is. We might begin with a Father Brown story, or with an essay in *Tremendous Trifles*, or with the *Everlasting Man*. It does not much matter if we are alert to what we read. Chesterton is one of the few authors who command our attention before we realize what it is he is telling us. His charm is such that he will have us thinking about things, including the condition of our own souls, before we realize what exactly it is we are doing. Yet, Chesterton has that unusual and wonderful quality of allowing us to open ourselves to reality, even when we have chosen to cut ourselves off from it.

These concluding remarks are necessarily brief. This has been a book of essays, essays written because Chesterton wrote his own essays. Often we do not know where we will go when we begin to think of any thing. Chesterton seemed in his own way to be in almost direct contact with reality, and vividly aware that this same reality did not cause itself to be what it is. Chesterton too was most alert to what went on in the human heart. For a man who was as good and open as he was, we learn an amazing amount about evil when we read him. But we also laugh a lot in reading him. Chesterton knew about the Fall, but he also knew about the Redemption. This knowledge was the source of his delight about reality and about our place within it.

This book is a book about many things—poetry, philosophy, redemption, family, evil, blessedness, good humor, good will. Chesterton is someone who still teaches us, still delights us. These essays can teach us how to read him—carefully, prepared to encounter *all that is*. When I have read all that I have read of and about Chesterton, I am still aware that I have only begun, that what is worth reading once is worth reading often. Indeed, we will seldom grasp all there is in anything of Chesterton in a single reading. This is because he was himself aware of the relation of all things to one another. He was in fact surprised by existence, by his existence and by the existence of what all else is. This surprise, this wonder that we cannot help catching when we encounter Chesterton, is, I hope, the fruit of reading these essays, which he occasioned simply by being himself interested in and open to *what is*.

Epilogue: On the Enemies of the Man Who Had No Enemies

Chesterton (1874–1936), the great English essayist, journalist, and philosopher, was a man of singular good will, engaging charm, and broad interests. From all eyewitness reports about him, he never really had any enemies. He does not seem to have loved those who hated him, for the singular reason that no one hated him. Even those who most disagreed with him on a given issue still had great affection for him and enjoyed his company. To be bested by Chesterton in an argument was a sort of badge of honor—that someone of Chesterton's stature would take another's arguments seriously even if he proved them wrong. Chesterton was evidently difficult not to like. He was a man of great girth and of enormous wisdom, the two qualities that somehow seemed, in his case, naturally to go together, as the similar combination did in the lives of St. Thomas and of Samuel Johnson, both of whom Chesterton greatly admired. These three—St. Thomas, Johnson, and Chesterton—along with Aristotle were probably the "sanest" (a favorite word of Chesterton) men who ever lived.

Chesterton personified, in a remarkable degree, that very Christian and very delicate notion of hating the sin but loving the sinner. He did indeed hate sin; he sharply attacked error. We seem nowadays, by contrast, to be living in an age wherein loving the sinner, as a condition, explicitly involves approving the sin. We cannot, apparently, figure out how our actions and our ideas do not belong together. We end up defining wrong subjectively. We have an inalienable right to do whatever we will. Even less can we figure out how it is that what we will to put into effect may not be what ought to be put into effect. Our rights have come to be tied up with what we will, no matter it is what we will. Rights are will-rights, not reason-rights. We end up insisting that we be praised for what we ought not to do simply because we will to do it. Those who refuse to praise our deviant ways we charge with intolerance, with lack of compassion. We establish sin and moral disorder as just another "will-right" of the public order. We call it anything from multiculturalism, to progressivism, to liberalism, to tolerance, to compassion.

In a sense, what Chesterton has to teach us is precisely how to deal with with those whose ideas or actions are wrong in some objective sense. We do not, if we think about it, want to end up by approving what is wrong or evil in errant actions. Neither do we want to deny either the intrinsic dignity of the person in error or the fact that free people can do evil things that ought not to be done. It was characteristic of Chesterton, who loved controversy and debate, clearly to grasp the logic of ideas or passions that would, if uncorrected, lead a person or a society of persons into error or sin. In an almost uncanny way, he saw where ideas, if not attended to, would lead. As I read him today, I almost think Chesterton foresaw in thought and argument all the errors of the twentieth century before they happened in reality. But he always paid his opponent the compliment of taking his ideas seriously, even when he took them humorously. Sometimes, perhaps, the only way we can take an idea seriously is if we take it with some amusement. Chesterton had no doubt that the origin of all disorder was found in will, but he also knew that will referred back to and depended on intellect, on ideas, so that the work of thinking was in some sense prerequisite for right doing.

II

But if Chesterton had no "enemies," how can I boldly talk of the "enemies" of the man who had no "enemies?" In an *Illustrat-*

ed London News column from December 3, 1921, he wrote, "People are professing nowadays that it is perfectly easy to love their enemies, so long as they are not asked to be just even to their friends."[2] Not only does loving one's enemy include being just to him, Chesterton implies, but it likewise includes being just to one's friends. We are not, after all, to be indifferent or unjust to our friends solely that we might have the glory of loving our enemies. It is not a virtue to love our enemies but have no friends. The only way that "loving our enemy" can be "perfectly easy" is if we treat him as we treat those friends to whom we are unjust. Besides, the Christian tradition has never intimated that being just to our friends was not also quite difficult. And no one in his right mind ever really thought that loving his enemies could really be "easy." If it were, we would not need specific, revealed instruction on the matter. Neither was loving our enemy conceived as involving some naive downplaying of real hostility, as if enemies were figments of our imagination or a simple misunderstanding, easily corrected. It included, to be sure, the possibility of an action that sought grounds whereby enemies could be friends. It realized the possibility of suffering injustices.

The word "enemy," it would seem, always connotes a someone who opposes us for some, probably illegitimate, reason of his own (and let us not forget that, because of our willful acts, we ourselves can well be the cause of legitimate hatred in others). The very word "enemy" implies injustice and probably hatred. We speak of "enemies" of our country or of our faith or of our language. In this case, we are opposed not necessarily for anything we ourselves do personally but for what we are in our birth or heritage. We are thus taken as members of a collectivity of some sort. We bear a kind of corporate guilt because of what we are. Any culpability we bear in this regard is usually not directly due to something we actually did to someone else, as is usually the case in person-to-person hatreds. We can in this sense also

speak of codes of honor among enemies, among those who recognize a common basis of humanity or chivalry even in their
struggles. We think of Grant and Lee at Appomattox.

Many of history's saddest episodes are the results of enemies
fighting each other but for a public or collective cause—Romeo
and Juliet in a broad way fall into this category. The individual
soldier or citizen has nothing in particular against the individual
immediately fighting against him. In other circumstances, they
might well be friends. Chesterton himself, a man who lived
through the Great War and saw the early stages of World War II,
never showed much sympathy for the Prussians, their ways or
their ideas. He never considered that spelling out the dangers of
Prussianism might somehow be contrary to his Christian duty to
love his German foe or contrary to his intellectual duty to state
the truth. Indeed, he thought that his elaboration of what was
wrong with Prussianism was part of his Christian and intellectual duty, whereby we could arrive at an understanding of what
was right for both the English and the Germans.

Too, there is the more personal enemy, someone who seeks
vengeance against us in particular, someone who will, if given a
chance, destroy our reputation, work, family, or even life. Loving
this sort of enemy does not mean giving up all common sense
about self-protection or all sense of justice that ought to exist between any given individuals. Love of enemies does not imply ap-
proval of injustices; it implies the opposite. The love of enemies is
designed to uphold the truth, not to relativize it. Though he
talked a good deal of dueling, however, Chesterton himself was
never challenged to a duel. As much as he enjoyed a pint in a
raucous English pub, he was never known to end the evening in
fisticuffs. And of those whom he criticized or opposed in print,
his main profession, he always treated them fairly and with that
courtesy from the Middle Ages that he praised so much.

A happy laughter was thus never far from his pen. I have often recalled his famous remark in *Orthodoxy*, for example, at the beginning of "The Ethics of Elfland," that some things "we want a man to do, even if he does them badly."[3] He singles out dancing as one of these things. In *Heretics*, he added, "I should regard any civilization which was without a universal habit of uproarious dancing as being, from the full human point of view, a defective civilization."[4] To think of Chesterton is to think of gratitude and joy. "The test of all happiness is gratitude," he tells us in *Orthodoxy*, even when he is not sure to whom he should be grateful.[5] "Man is more himself, man is more manlike, when joy is the fundamental thing in him, and grief is superficial."[6] Clearly it is difficult not to love and admire a man who thinks these things.

III

So what do I mean by the "enemies" of the man who had no "enemies"? Chesterton, who seems to have been a very good and honorable man in his own personal life, was by no means so innocent that he did not know that there was plenty wrong in the world. It is one of the acute mysteries of the life of Chesterton that he knew so much about evil but did not himself learn this evil from practicing it. He learned of it from thinking about it. He does seem to have wrestled with evil and, like St. Thomas, to have understood its charm and reality quite well and written of it at length. We cannot help but have the impression that, whenever Chesterton spoke of evil, he knew that whereof he spoke. It takes a good man, to recall both Plato and Aristotle, to know both good and evil, to do the one and avoid the other.

Indeed, recalling his awareness of profound disorder in the world itself, Chesterton wrote a wonderful book in 1910. In retrospect, it was a very prophetic book about what did happen in the twentieth century. The book was entitled, exactly, *What's Wrong with the World*. The book's title does not have a question mark behind it, almost as if to say that Chesterton thought he had a pretty good idea about what is in fact wrong with the world. Anyone who does not think that there is anything wrong in the world, Chesterton thought, was simply not paying attention, even to himself.

This particular book, as we recall, was written, as so many of Chesterton's books were, as a result of a kind of dare or challenge. It seems that one of the London newspapers had advertised an essay contest. Readers were supposed to write in their answers to the rather grandiose question, "What's wrong with the world?" Chesterton, characteristically not being able to resist such a challenge, immediately sat down and wrote a two-sentence reply. It reads: "Dear Sir: 'What's wrong with the world?' I am. Signed, G. K. Chesterton." One is almost stunned to notice the profundity of this succinct response. It went to the heart of the matter. The disorder in the world is not to be located in some Rousseauian external reorganization of society or property, not in matter, not in someone else, but in our own wills and souls. If we do not know this location of evil's cause, then nothing much else that we do know will matter.

Chesterton could see the import of original sin in the very midst of popular journalism. Could it be that our main enemies are in fact to be found within ourselves? Are we our own enemies? Are we looking in the wrong direction when we seek to remedy what is wrong? Did Chesterton's own early mental struggle with evil prepare him for the dire results that appeared in the world as the result of the actions of those who did not successfully struggle with it, of those who positively chose it? But this conclusion is surely a Chestertonian paradox. We are not just sure what to make of it.

We are, for the most part, unused to the idea that we could choose against our very selves, as if our selves bore in them already some standard whereby we are called to be most ourselves.

We hesitate to imitate St. Paul, who, in a famous passage, acknowledged that the good that he would do, he did not. Yet, that very acknowledgement seems to be one of the core things we must do, if we are honest with ourselves. Chesterton's abiding enemy is the person who denies what seems obvious, namely original sin, the one Christian doctrine, so he thought, that need not be revealed to us. All we had to do was to go out in the streets and open our eyes.

IV

Yet, we need to be careful when we locate the blame of what is wrong with the world in ourselves. We can easily mislocate the source of the problem. Indeed, we oftentimes want to mislocate it, since it serves to keep us from facing our own responsibility for the things we do. It seems fitting here, at a college dedicated to St. Thomas, to recall Chesterton's famous biography, *St. Thomas Aquinas*, a book not to be missed. In it, Chesterton recalls that both St. Augustine and St. Thomas spent a good deal of intellectual energy in combatting the Manichees, combatting the idea that matter explains the existence of evil among us. Things are good, in this view, if they are spiritual; things are bad if they are material. Therefore, the spiritual means escaping from matter. Matter was necessary, so what happens had to happen. We are not responsible. Therefore, we are not responsible for the famous sins of the flesh. We need not blame ourselves.

Chesterton did not think, in fact, that St. Augustine was always careful enough in these matters. Thus, Chesterton, like Aquinas, is always found, not at the end of a process wherein great errors are visible to everyone, but at the beginning wherein their slight deviation from the good is barely noticed. But these initial deviations can be foreseen by a man of wisdom as they might work their way through the human condition. Augustine learned the errors of Manicheanism by being himself a Manichee for a time. He soon discovered that the thesis he used to justify himself and his own deviant ways did not in fact explain himself to himself. In the end, he was honest enough to recognize this fact. Aquinas figured this difficulty out intellectually, perhaps after having read Augustine, without the necessity of going through the latter's much-publicized sinful life.

Augustine himself has warned us about the relation of heresy and spirit, that the most dangerous heresies arise, not from being too worldly or too materialistic, but, paradoxically, from being too spiritual. The devil in his being, after all, is an angel of light, not a beast or a dragon. Here is how Chesterton saw the problem with Augustine and ultimately with Plato:

> Granted all the grandeur of Augustine's contribution to Christianity, there was in a sense a more subtle danger in Augustine the Platonist than even in Augustine the Manichee. There came from it a mood which unconsciously committed the heresy of dividing the substance of the Trinity. It thought of God too exclusively as a Spirit who purifies or a Saviour who redeems, and too little of a Creator who creates. This is why Aquinas thought it right to correct Plato by an appeal to Aristotle; Aristotle who took things as he found them, just as Aquinas accepted things as God created them. In all the work of St. Thomas the world of positive creation is perpetually present.[7]

Imagine calling attention to a heresy that "divided the substance of the Trinity" as if this division were the most dangerous thing in the world! But of course, the goodness of real things is in fact, certainly for us, the most vital thing in the world. To find God, we do not have to escape the world, or our very material bodies, even though God is not the world or our bodies. Thus one of Chesterton's main enemies is the idea that things as things are not good.

Compared to other thinkers, then, Chesterton thought St. Thomas was quite unique in his attention to things, to almost anything. Just as a thing was, just the fact it existed at all, this was the marvel. Chesterton was astonished at the existence of any thing at all and figured that God was astonished too or it would not exist. St. Thomas, Chesterton tells us, was "avid in his acceptance of Things; in his hunger and thirst for Things. It was his special spiritual thesis that there really are things; and not only the Thing; that the Many existed as well as the One."[8] Thus, reality as such is not our enemy. If something is wrong in our world, it is not reality itself; it is not *what is.*

V

Chesterton himself sometimes explained how he dealt with critics. In another column from the *Illustrated London News* (March 25, 1922), he distinguished between defending his "opinions" over against defending his "writings." "My opinions, as opinions," he explained, "are all quite correct. Any thinking person will see that to say this is only saying that these are my opinions. A man has not got a conviction if he is not convinced of it."[9] On the other hand, Chesterton pointed out, "my books, as books, are very far from being all correct; and I wonder that they are not more often corrected." What Chesterton puts in his books are his convictions for which he has arguments. He is not just explaining his opinions, which are simply what they are, namely, his views. He is setting down his reasons. Chesterton acknowledged that he often made errors of small fact. But everyone could see that the error was not deliberate. He called a nephew, for instance, what was in fact a brother-in-law. He has, he thinks, likewise, written books badly on subjects about which others might have written well.

Chesterton next proceeded to comment on the various critics of his book *Eugenics and Other Evils.*[10] Anyone who reads this book will still realize that the proponents of eugenics were then and would still be now Chesterton's enemies. He saw them as enemies of human nature as such. His book may have been a bad "book," Chesterton thinks, but he wants to criticize the critics of this book, not about being wrong about the book, but about their being wrong about "the subject of the book," that is, eugenics.

Indeed, Chesterton thought that perhaps in fifty years—*Eugenics and Other Evils* was published in 1922—the book would be unintelligible because people in the meantime would have seen the errors of the arguments for eugenics. Alas, this has not been the case. The errors that Chesterton saw in 1922 are far more popular and far more dangerous today than when he examined them. We actually practice many of them. Chesterton saw in eugenics, the effort to manage who is born by "scientific" and political methods, to be the sure path to tyranny in future years in which those judged not worthy of birth would be eliminated or prevented from being born. Needless to say, the prevention of birth is a growth industry today.

One of Chesterton's favorite adversaries and friends was Bernard Shaw. What Chesterton criticized, in this regard, was Shaw's having an "almost religious idea of evolution." Shaw will not see that this very idea of evolution—which Chesterton once remarked in another context, meant merely the survival of those who have in fact survived—leads to the empowerment of the state when what in fact is evolving is not to our liking. "The ignorant must be controlled so long as they are not controlled by the instructed." That is, the logic of eugenics leads to the political control of who is to be begotten or an intellectual instruction about what to do about life.

Another of Chesterton's critics on this issue was Dean Inge, who had accused Chesterton of wanting, in his *Eugenics* book, to bring back the Dark Ages. To this view, Chesterton replied that it seemed curious that Inge warns of Chesterton's bringing back the Dark Ages "when he himself [Inge] is always warning us of a

Dark Ages in the future; and has to trust the next generation with all the powers of tyranny, when he will not trust it with the rights of freedom." Those in favor of eugenics, in other words, think that normal begetting of human beings by human beings, those activities which result from the "rights of freedom," will lead in the future to some degeneracy of the race; to prevent that, we must grant tyrannical power to the state to decide who is or is not to be born or who is or is not to die. These proposals to deny the basic rights and dignities of the human family Chesterton genuinely hated.

What is to be noticed here is that Chesterton, much like St. Thomas, was able to understand what was implicit in ideas and arguments. He was not concerned with his own opinions, which were just that, opinions. He was concerned with the subject to be addressed. If he was accused of wanting to bring back the Dark Ages, he was quite clear that this unenlightened age is precisely what, in effect, his critic wanted to establish not in the past but in the future, an age in which the intelligent ruled the supposedly ignorant with an iron hand and could not tolerate anything other than what the intelligentsia themselves wanted. Chesterton, of course, hoped that by spelling out where ideas led, he could both prevent the tyranny implicit in them and make the proponent see what was implicit in the argument. Neither Shaw nor Inge was Chesterton's "enemy," though both held ideas that would, Chesterton pointed out, lead in their logic to a tyranny that placed the state in charge of all begetting, of all living and dying, because it could not trust the "rights of man" and his freedoms.

VI

Chesterton's hatred of eugenics was the reverse side of his love of marriage, of its romance, of its bindingness. Chesterton could see that the condition and reality of the child is the heart of both religion and of society. For him, the Incarnation was no mere accident, as if the stable at Bethlehem was merely an incidental event in the history of religion. Rather it was at the heart of religion that God becomes man, not as a philosopher or a banker, but as a child in an obscure part of the world. These are the places in which all the great romances and adventures begin and end. If someone had told Chesterton that, after he chose his wife, he was still free to choose another wife, he would have told them that they understood neither what a wife was nor what choice was. Chesterton genuinely hated those who made the things we really want impossible.

"I could never conceive or tolerate any Utopia which did not leave me liberty for which I chiefly cared," he declared in his chapter "The Eternal Revolution" in *Orthodoxy*, "the liberty to bind myself."[11] And he added, as an afterthought on the metaphysics of it all, "complete anarchy would not merely make it impossible to have any discipline or fidelity; it would also make it impossible to have any fun." Would it be too paradoxical to maintain that the enemies of Chesterton are those who do not allow us to have any fun?

Chesterton completes the essence of his argument in these memorable and beautiful lines about the meaning of romance and promises:

> For the purposes of even the wildest romance results must be real; results must be irrevocable. Christian marriage is the great example of a real and irrevocable result; and this is why it is the chief subject and center of all our romantic writings. And this is the last instance of the things that I should ask, and ask imperatively, of any social paradise; I should ask to be kept to my bargain, to have my oaths and engagements taken seriously; I should ask Utopia to avenge my honor to myself. All my modern Utopian friends look at each other doubtfully, for their ultimate hope is the dissolution of all special ties. But again I seem to hear, like a kind of echo, an answer from beyond

the world. "You will have real obligations, and therefore real adventures when you get to my Utopia. But the hardest obligation and the steepest adventure is to get there."[12]

Modern utopian friends whose promise for happiness lies in what is in effect the "dissolution of all ties" are Chesterton's enemies. He knows that what we want is not to be free of our own promises, but to be bound by them. No romance can begin without a commitment. This is why, for Chesterton, obligations alone can result in adventures. If we are free to break our promises, we will have no real adventures.

VII

One of Chesterton's earliest books (1905) was entitled precisely *Heretics*. This book made everyone sit up and take notice. The supreme irony of this wonderful title, *Heretics*, is, of course, that, in terms of modern thought, the heretics whom he treated— Wells, Shaw, Kipling, George Moore, Tolstoy, Nietzsche, Lowes Dickenson, Whistler—were quite the avant-garde of what everyone thought, or was about to think. The only real, genuine "heretic" around was, of course, Chesterton himself, who was "orthodox," as he stated in his next book, *Orthodoxy*, a book again written as a challenge to those who claimed that they knew what he was against but not what he was for. If a "heretic" was someone who said something different from everyone else in the neighborhood, then the only real heretic in England in the first third of the twentieth century, indeed in the whole century, was Chesterton himself. The "orthodox" Chesterton did not burn anyone at the stake, of course, but he did make many a standard argument look silly and its authors burn with a kind of embarrassment. But again, it was all both light-hearted and devastating.

Chesterton loved Francis of Assisi, but he was dubious of the

Franciscan insight when it was taken out of some higher context and was proposed for its own sake. In a sense, Chesterton was the enemy of simplicity. "One great complaint, I think, must stand against the modern upholders of the simple life in all its varied forms, from vegetarianism to the honourable consistencies of the Doukhobors," he wrote in *Heretics*. "This complaint against them stands, that they would make us simple in the unimportant things, but complex in the important things."[13] Things like "diet, costume, etiquette, and economic systems" are not where the drama of life exists. We can have simple garment, eat bread and water, say "yea" and "nay" all the time, and still miss the point of the human condition and where its problems lie. The real differences and problems lie in philosophy, not dress. Or as Chesterton put it most amusingly: "It does not very much matter whether a man eats a grilled tomato or a plain tomato; it does very much matter whether he eats a plain tomato with a grilled mind."

What is Chesterton getting at here? There is a simplicity that makes a difference, the "simplicity of heart, the simplicity which accepts and enjoys." After all, our whole problem with the world is that it is something we have been given; it is given precisely for our enjoyment. It is not at all clear to Chesterton that the convoluted system of the simple life is at all simple, is at all the best use of the world. "There is more simplicity in the man who eats caviar on impulse than in the man who eats grape-nuts on principle." It is well to recall that "grape-nuts" were themselves historically rooted in a kind of religious fervor to get rid of the breakfast of mush and beer. Thus, eating "grape-nuts" on principle told us much more about a very complicated view of the world than eating caviar because it was good.

Those leading the simple life will not be improved by what they affirm to be "high thinking and plain living," Chesterton thought. Again we have a touch of Manicheanism here, a refusal to believe how abundant the world really is. What those of the simple life lack is festivity, that highest act of our culture and of our appreciation of what we are. How remarkably clearly did Chesterton see that those who profess the simple things as a way to exalt and aid humanity miss its very essence. "A little high living . . . could teach them the force and meaning of human festivity, of the banquet that has gone on from the beginning of the world." What a wonderful sentence that is—the meaning of human festivity, the banquet from the beginning of the world. Chesterton saw these things, saw that what might at first sight be so attractive was in fact a narrowing of our vision and of our destiny.

Such proponents of the simple life, Chesterton thought, needed to learn that, in a very real way, "the artificial was older than the natural," that is to say, what is natural was given for us, to be our dominion. The natural is for us; we are not for it. "A little plain thinking would teach them how harsh and fanciful are the mass of their own ethics, how very civilized and very complicated must be the brain of the Tolstoyan who really believes it to be evil to love one's country and wicked to strike a blow." Chesterton understands that the love of one's country is a wholly proper thing and the refusal ever to strike a blow simply results in empowering the wicked in the name of a simplistic virtue. "Plain thinking will . . . decisively reject the idea of the inevitable sinfulness of war." There can be, given the complexity of human nature, as much sinfulness in not fighting as in fighting. The "man in sandals and simple raiment, with a raw tomato in his hand" who tells us that family affection and love of country are enemies of human love, in Chesterton's view, simply does not understand the particularity in which all love exists.

"Nothing is more materialistic than to despise a pleasure as purely material." In the classical writers, pleasure as such is not evil or wrong. It is rather what accompanies all of our activities. There are intellectual and material pleasures, all good. Pleasures can be used wrongly, but this is not the problem of pleasure itself, but of the will that seeks to direct them to ends in which they do not properly flourish. Nothing misunderstands matter itself more than to think that the difficulties we have with matter come from matter itself.

"Our conclusion is that it is a fundamental point of view, a philosophy or religion which is needed, and not any change of habit or social routine. The things we need most for practical purposes are all abstractions." This too is a remarkable sentence. Chesterton has just told us that we need to see that pleasures are good, that we need to be festive, that we need abundance and joy, and here he is telling us about our practical need for "abstractions." But of course he is right. The real enemies are those who do not have things in proper order, as St. Thomas says.

Somewhere Chesterton tells us that when something goes wrong with, say, our automobile, we may need a mechanic. But if the mechanic cannot figure out what is wrong, we may need the original engineer and designer. And if there are things he cannot handle, we may need the impractical scientist or philosopher, who cannot tie his own shoe laces. The "abstractions" we need tell us what we are and how we are to live, who God is and what the world is about, what is good and what is evil. We cannot live a "simple life," or any other kind of life, if we do not know what we are. If Chesterton finds in proponents of a simple life to be enemies of what is good—I suspect their current names are ecologists or environmentalists—it is because he can see that the world is made for something other than keeping itself in existence forever down the ages.

VIII

In conclusion, the last enemy that I want to point out that Chesterton, from a very early age, fought was the enemy of that power which made our vows and promises possible, namely, the enemies of free will, the determinists of whatever hue. Chesterton always maintained that he came to philosophy and theology not by directly studying them but indirectly, because of the contradictions that modern thinkers themselves displayed in their attacks on religion and human thought. In his *Autobiography*, Chesterton recalls something of his early arguments from 1905 with Robert Blatchford, whose ideas seem themselves to have come from the scientist Theodore Haeckel. Chesterton was not at first interested in divine election or the Trinity, but he was concerned with the idea of responsibility itself, that what we did and enjoyed was in fact ours.

Chesterton states his case graphically:

> It is not that I began by believing in supernatural things. It was that the unbelievers began by disbelieving in even normal things. It was the secularists who drove me to theological ethics, by themselves destroying any sane or rational possibility of secular ethics. I might myself have been a secularist, so long as it meant I could be merely responsible to secular society. It was the Determinist who told me, at the top of his voice, that I could not be responsible at all. And as I rather like being treated as a responsible being, and not as a lunatic let out for the day, I began to look around for some spiritual asylum that was not a lunatic asylum.[14]

The imagery of "the lunatic let out for the day" remains. Chesterton's enemies were those who by their abstract ideas made life impossible for those who, like Chesterton, rather liked being treated as "responsible beings." Chesterton liked a world in which those who made vows could also keep them.

In the end, the man who had no enemies knew that there are ideas and choices that make sane and normal human existence impossible. He knew we are not determined, that we are free, but that we can choose wrongly. He knew that matter and body are not evil. He knew that the world is not parsimonious, that festivity and joy are closer to its essence than fasting and poverty, though these too have their place. He understood how we could turn ourselves over to eugenists and forget what we really are. Chesterton, in short, knew what we really want. We want promises that will be kept, worlds that will be ordered, lives that will be chosen in the light of what we are first given. He knew that we should love the sinner but hate the sin, but he also knew that sin exists and that we can choose it.

The great freedom is the freedom to bind ourselves, to bind ourselves to the wonder and goodness of *all that is*, to all that is given to us, but especially to one another. For Chesterton, we are all like Grant Allen; he would rather know what God thinks of us than what we think of God. But if we do think of God, Chesterton knows that it is important to think rightly even about God, lest we think erroneously about ourselves. Only when we think rightly about God can we understand why festivity tells us more about ourselves than the simple life or indeed than the sinful life.

Notes

Notes to Preface

1. See William B. Furlong, *Shaw and Chesterton: The Metaphysical Jesters* (University Park, Pa.: The Pennsylvania State University Press, 1970).

2. See Michael Coren, *Gilbert: The Man Who Was Chesterton* (New York: Paragon House, 1990); Michael Ffinch, *G. K. Chesterton* (London: Weidenfeld & Nicolson, 1986); Maisie Ward, *Gilbert Keith Chesterton* (New York: Sheed & Ward, 1944); Joseph Pearce, *Wisdom and Innocence: A Life of G. K. Chesterton* (San Francisco: Ignatius Press, 1996); Robert Spaight, *The Life of Hilaire Belloc* (New York: Farrar, Straus & Cudahy, 1957); A. N. Wilson, *Hilaire Belloc: A Biography* (New York: Atheneum, 1984).

3. See James V. Schall, S.J., "On the Mystery of Teachers I Never Met," *Modern Age* 37 (Summer 1995), 366–73.

4. James V. Schall, *Idylls and Rambles: Lighter Christian Essays* (San Francisco: Ignatius Press, 1994).

5. Stanley L. Jaki, *Chesterton: A Seer of Science* (Urbana: University of Illinois Press, 1986).

Notes to Introduction

1. G. K. Chesterton, *The Autobiography in Collected Works* (San Francisco: Ignatius Press, 1988), XVI, 276. Henceforth, the *Collected Works* will be cited as *CW*, Volume, Page.

2. Peter Milward, "G. K. Chesterton's Faith and Journalism," *The Chesterton Review* VII (November 1981), 348.

3. G. K. Chesterton, "The Ignorance of the Newspapers," *The Illustrated London News, 1914–16*, in *CW*, XXX, 92.

4. *CW*, XVI, 176.   5. Ibid.

6. Ibid.   7. Ibid.

8. Ibid., 176–77.

9. Michael Ffinch, *G. K. Chesterton: A Biography* (London: Weidenfeld & Nicolson, 1986), 137.

10. *CW*, XVI, 276–77.   11. *CW*, XIX, 267.

12. Ibid., 265–66.   13. Ibid., 267.

14. Ibid., 269.

15. Larry Arnhart, *Aristotle on Political Reasoning* (DeKalb: Northern Illinois University Press, 1986), 7.

16. *CW,* XXVIII, 501.

17. Ibid., 237.

18. G. K. Chesterton, *Illustrated London News,* in *CW;* (1986) XXVII, 1905–1907; (1987) XXVIII, 1908–1910; (1987) XXIX, 1911–1913; (1988) XXX, 1914–1916; (1989) XXXII, 1920–1922; (1990) XXXIII, 1923–1925; (1991) XXXIV, 1916–1928; (1991) XXXV, 1929–1931.

19. W. H. Auden, "Chesterton's Non-Fictional Prose," in *G. K. Chesterton: A Half-Century of Views,* ed. D. J. Conlon (Oxford: Oxford University Press, 1987), 263.

20. *CW,* XXVII, 71.

21. Ibid., 72.

22. *CW,* XXVIII, 54.

23. Ibid., 55.

24. Ibid., 540.

25. *CW,* XXVII, 153.

26. Ibid., 512–13.

27. *CW,* XXVIII, 354.

28. Ibid., 357.

29. Ibid., 257.

30. Ibid., 257–58.

31. Ibid., 258.

32. Ibid., 377.

33. Ibid., 378.

34. *CW,* XXVII, 462.

35. Ibid.

36. Ibid., 463.

37. *CW,* XXIX, 162.

38. Ibid., 163.

39. Allan Massie, "The Master Writer beneath the Card," in *G. K. Chesterton: A Half Century of Views,* 365.

40. *CW,* XXVIII, 181–82.

41. Ibid., 530.

42. Ibid.

43. Ibid., 531.

44. Ibid.

45. *CW,* XXVII, 130.

46. Ibid., 131.

47. Ibid., 132.

48. *CW,* XXIX, 258.

49. Ibid., 259.

50. Ibid., 250.

51. "The Importance of Doing Nothing," *CW,* XXX, 243.

The Natural Home of the Human Spirit

1. *CW,* III, 61.

2. Ibid., 62.

3. Ibid., 63.

4. Ibid., 67.

5. Ibid., 68.

On the Nature of "Yes" in the State of Maine

1. *CW,* XXX, 62.

2. Ibid., 65–66.

The Philosopher with Two Thoughts

1. G. K. Chesterton, *The Victorian Age in English Literature* (New York: Holt, 1913), 43.

2. Ibid., 31.

3. Ibid., 32.
4. Ibid., 33.

The Traditional Scene of the Nativity

1. G. K. Chesterton, *The Spirit of Christmas* (New York: Dodd, Mead, 1985).

2. Ibid., 85.

3. Ibid., 34.

4. Ibid., 87.

5. Ibid., 49.

On the Qualified and Experienced

1. *Midwest Chesterton News,* August 1989.

2. Dean R. Rapp, "G. K. Chesterton's Criticism of Psychoanalysis," *The Chesterton Review* XV (August 1989), 341–54.

3. Ibid., 347, from *G. K.'s Weekly,* May 10, 1934.

4. Ibid., 345–46.

On Staring at the Picture of "Tuesday"

1. G. K. Chesterton, *Daylight and Nightmare* (New York: Dodd, Mead, 1986), 30.

The Real End and Final Holiday of Human Souls

1. *CW,* XXVII, 531.

2. Ibid., 533.

3. Ibid., 537.

A Definite, Defiant, and Quite Unmistakable Thing

1. James V. Schall, *Another Sort of Learning* (San Francisco: Ignatius Press, 1988). See also *A Student's Guide to Liberal Learning* (Wilmington, Del.: Intercollegiate Studies Institute, 1997).

2. Quoted in Robert Royal, "G. K. Chesterton and Charles Péguy: Post-Modern Paradigms." Ph.D. dissertation, The Catholic University of America, 1994.

3. *CW,* XXXIV, 463.

4. Ibid., 462–63.

5. Ibid., 461.

6. Ibid., 461–62.

On Looking Down at the Stars

1. G. K. Chesterton, *The Defendant* (London: Dent, 1914), 53.

2. Ibid., 54.

3. Ibid.

4. Ibid., 55.

5. Josef Cardinal Ratzinger, *"In the Beginning . . ."*:*A Catholic Understanding of the Story of Creation* (Huntington, Ind.: Our Sunday Visitor Press, 1990), 43–44.

6. Chesterton, *The Defendant,* 56.

7. Ibid., 58.

8. Ratzinger, *"In the Beginning . . . ,"* 68.

The Most Inexhaustible of Human Books

1. G. K. Chesterton, "Dr. Johnson," in *G.K.C. as M.C.,* ed. J. P. de Fonseka (London: Methuen, 1929), 65–66.

2. Ibid., 65,

3. Ibid., 74.

4. Ibid., 69.

5. Ibid., 75.

6. Ibid., 66.

7. Ibid., 67.

8. Ibid., 66.

9. Ibid., 68.

10. Ibid.

11. Ibid., 75.

On God's Making both Hell and Scotland

1. G. K. Chesterton, "Boswell," in *G.K.C. as M.C.,* ed. J. P. de Fonseka (London: Methuen, 1929), 3.

2. James Boswell, *London Journal: 1762–1763* (New York: McGraw-Hill, 1950), 221.

3. Ibid.

4. *G.K.C. as M.C.,* 3.

5. Boswell, *London Journal: 1762–1763,* 260.

6. Ibid.

7. *G.K.C. as M.C.,* 10.

8. *Boswell's Life of Johnson* (London: Oxford, 1931), Vol. I, 286–87. The parallel passage in the *London Journal: 1762–1763,* 302, reads: "He [Johnson] said he would not advise a plan of study, for he had never pursued one for two days.'And a man ought just to read as inclination leads him, for what he reads as a task will do him little good. Idleness is a disease which must be combated. A young man should read five hours a day, and so may acquire a great deal of knowledge.'

"He advised me when abroad to be as much as possible with men of learning, especially the professors in the universities, and the clergy. Indeed, I imagine myself that the clergy, especially the Jesuits, will be most instructive companions. I hope to learn from them, and to settle by degrees into a composed and a knowing man."

The Ten Thousand Reasons

1. *CW,* III, 127.

2. Ibid., 129.

3. Ibid., 127.

4. Ibid., 129.

5. Ibid., 130.
7. Ibid., 128.

6. Ibid., 132.
8. Ibid., 127.

Against Pride

1. G. K. Chesterton, "If I Had Only One Sermon to Preach," in *As I Was Saying,* ed. Robert Knille (Grand Rapids, Mich.: Eerdmans, 1985), 194.
2. Ibid., 190.
4. Ibid., 191.
6. Ibid.
8. Ibid.

3. Ibid., 188.
5. Ibid., 192.
7. Ibid., 193.

The Christian Ideal

1. *CW,* IV, 183.
3. Ibid., 35.

2. Ibid., 37.
4. Ibid., 129.

On the Alternatives to Right and Wrong

1. *CW,* XXVII, 331–36.
3. Ibid., 335.
5. Ibid., 335.

2. Ibid., 334.
4. Ibid., 336.

The Spirit of Christmas

1. *CW,* XXXIV, 224.
3. Ibid., 437.
5. Ibid., 439–40.

2. Ibid., 225–26.
4. Ibid., 439.
6. Ibid., 222.

Second Thoughts on Detective Stories

1. John Wren-Lewis, "Adam, Eve, and Agatha Christie," *The Chesterton Review* XIX (May 1993), 197.
2. Ibid.
4. Ibid.
6. Ibid.

3. Ibid., 198.
5. Ibid., 199.

7. G. K. Chesterton, "A Defense of Detective Stories," in *The Defendant* (London: Dent, 1914), 122–23.

On the Inability to Blaspheme

1. *CW,* I, 39.
3. Ibid., 41.
5. Ibid., 46.

2. Ibid., 40.
4. Ibid., 44.

"*I Say As Do All Christian Men . . .*"

1. Christopher Derrick, *Joy Without a Cause* (LaSalle, Ill.: Sherwood Sugden, 1979); Russell Kirk, *The Wise Men Know What Wicked Things Are Written on the Sky* (Washington: Regnery Gateway, 1987).

2. C. S. Lewis, *Surprised by Joy* (New York: Harvest, 1955), 190–91.

3. Ibid., 191.

4. Ibid.

5. G. K. Chesterton, *The Ballad of the White Horse,* ed. Sister Bernadette Sheridan (Detroit: Marygrove College Press, 1993), 58 (III, 303–6).

6. Ibid., 47 (III, 104–7).

7. Ibid., 16–17 (I, 254–61).

8. *Josef Pieper—An Anthology* (San Francisco: Ignatius Press, 1989), 32–39.

9. Chesterton, *Ballad,* 166 (VIII, 245–52).

"*The Way the World Is Going*"

1. *Catholic World Report,* February 1994, 18–19.

2. *CW,* III, 362–66.

3. Leo Strauss, "Progress or Return?" *The Rebirth of Classical Political Rationalism,* ed. Thomas Pangle (Chicago: University of Chicago Press, 1989), 227–70.

4. See Susan Orr, *Jerusalem and Athens: Reason and Revelation in the Works of Leo Strauss* (Lanham, Md.: Rowman & Littlefield, 1995).

5. *CW,* III, 363.   6. Ibid., 364.

7. Ibid.   8. Ibid., 366.

On the Winning of World Wars I and II

1. Robert Royal, "G. K. Chesterton and Charles Péguy: Post-Modern Paradigms," Ph.D. dissertation, The Catholic University of America, 1994.

2. *CW,* XXX.   3. Ibid., 219.

4. Ibid., 221.   5. Ibid.

6. Ibid., 222.   7. Ibid.

8. Allan Bloom, *The Closing of the American Mind* (New York: Simon and Schuster, 1987), 314.

Christmas and the Most Dangerous Toy

1. James V. Schall, *The Praise of "Sons of Bitches": On the Worship of God by Fallen Men* (Slough, England: St. Paul Publications, 1978), 177–86.

2. *CW,* XXVII, 301–4.

3. Ibid., 302–3.

4. Ibid., 303.

Babies

1. *CW,* III, 439–41.
2. Ibid., 439–40.
3. Ibid., 440.
4. Ibid., 441.

On the Dullness of Chaos

1. G. K. Chesterton, *The Man Who Was Thursday* (Harmondsworth, England: Penguin, [1908] 1986), 7.
2. Ibid., 11.
3. Ibid., 12.
4. Ibid., 13.
5. Ibid., 14.
6. Ibid., 15.

The Invisible Man

1. G. K. Chesterton, "The Invisible Man," *The Father Brown Omnibus: Every Father Brown Story Ever Written* (New York: Dodd, Mead, 1951), 84.
2. Ibid., 98.
3. Ibid., 100.

Wilde and Wilder

1. Thornton Wilder, "The Matchmaker," in *Three Plays* (New York: Harper Perennial, 1985), Act 1, 270.
2. Ibid., Act 3, 395.

The Horror

1. *G.K.'s Weekly: A Sampler* (Chicago: Loyola University Press, 1986), 325.
2. *The Portable Paul Johnson,* ed. George Marlin, Richard Rabatin, and Heather Richardson Higgins (New York: The Noonday Press, 1994), 3.
3. Ibid.

Virtue and Duty

1. G. K. Chesterton, "School Magazines," *The Chesterton Review,* XXI (August 1955), 293.

Humanism

1. John Carroll, *Humanism: The Wreck of Western Culture* (London: Fontana, 1993).
2. Russell Kirk, "Flannery O'Connor: Notes by Humpty Dumpty," *University Bookman* 35 (Summer 1995), 35–38. Also in Russell Kirk, *The Sword of the Imagination* (Grand Rapids, Mich.: Eerdmans, 1995), 180–84.

3. CW, III, 146–56.
5. Ibid., 150.
7. Ibid.

4. Ibid., 148.
6. Ibid.

On Not Wrecking Divine or Secular Things

1. G. K. Chesterton, "The Roots of the World," *The Chesterton Review* XVIII (May 1992), 161.
2. Ibid., 163.
3. Ibid.

Belloc on Chesterton

1. Hilaire Belloc, "Gilbert Keith Chesterton," *The Saturday Review of Literature* 10 (July 4, 1936), 4.
2. Ibid., 3.
4. Ibid.
6. Ibid., 14.

3. Ibid., 4.
5. Ibid.

The Only Virtue

1. *CW,* III, 520.
3. Ibid., 283.
5. Ibid., 289.
7. Ibid., 526–27.

2. Ibid.
4. Ibid., 282.
6. Ibid.

The Coming of Christ

1. G. K. Chesterton, "If Christ Should Come," *The Chesterton Review* X (February 1984), 9.
2. *CW,* XXVIII, 249–53.
3. Hilaire Belloc, "The Death of Chateaubriand," in *Miniatures of French History* (LaSalle, Ill.: Sherwood Sugden, 1990), 280.
4. Chesterton, "If Christ Should Come," 249.
5. Ibid., 251.
6. Ibid., 253.

"The Divine Vulgarity of the Christian Religion"

1. G. K. Chesterton, "Oliver Wendell Holmes," in *G.K.C. as M.C.,* ed. J. P. de Fonseka (London: Methuen, 1929), 16.
2. Ibid., 11.
3. Ibid., 13.
4. See Stanley L. Jaki, *Chesterton, A Seer of Science* (Normal: University of Illinois Press, 1986).

5. Chesterton, "Oliver Wendell Holmes," 17.
6. Ibid., 18.

On Becoming Inhuman out of Sheer Humanitarianism

1. *CW,* XXXIV, 117–25. 2. Ibid., 118.
3. Ibid., 119. 4. Ibid., 121.
5. See James V. Schall, "Sincerity, The Most Dangerous Virtue," in *The Praise of "Sons of Bitches": On the Worship of God by Fallen Men* (Slough, England: St. Paul Publications, 1978), 53–62.
6. *CW,* XXXIV, 122. 7. Ibid., 123.
8. Ibid., 124.

"Woman and the Philosophers"

1. G. K. Chesterton, "Woman and the Philosophers," *The Chesterton Review* XI (February 1985), 16. Originally appeared in *The Speaker,* January 26, 1901.
2. Ibid., 17. 3. Ibid., 18.
4. Ibid., 19. 5. Ibid., 20.
6. Ibid. 7. Ibid.

On the Discovery of Things Whose Existence Is Impossible to Deny

1. G. K. Chesterton, *George Frederick Watts* (London: Duckworth, 1904), 8.
2. Ibid., 101. 3. Ibid., 27.
4. Ibid., 40. 5. Ibid., 57–58.
6. Ibid., 65. 7. Ibid., 116.

The Campaign against the Ten Commandments

1. *CW,* XXXII, 17. 2. Ibid., 18.
3. Ibid. 4. Ibid., 19.
5. Ibid., 20. 6. Ibid.

"An Awful Instance of the Instability of Human Greatness"

1. *CW,* XV, 245–53.
2. Ibid., 83–84.
3. Charles Dickens, *The Pickwick Papers: The Posthumous Papers of the Pickwick Club* (New York: Washington Square, 1960), 370–71.
4. Ibid., 370. 5. Ibid., 383.
6. Ibid., 386. 7. *CW,* XV, 86.
8. Ibid., 87.

The Dogmas Are Not Dull

1. *CW,* III, 298.   2. Ibid., 303.
3. Ibid., 304.

Notes to the Epilogue

1. This Epilogue was originally given as an address to the American Chesterton Society, at the University of St. Thomas in St. Paul, Minnesota, June 12, 1998. It was subsequently published in *Vital Speeches,* LXIV (July 15, 1998), 590–95.

2. *CW,* XXXII, 278.   3. *CW,* I, 250.
4. Ibid., 166.   5. Ibid., 258.
6. Ibid., 364.   7. *CW,* II, 468.
8. Ibid., 505.   9. *CW,* XXXII, 343–44.
10. Ibid., IV.   11. *CW,* I, 328.
12. Ibid.   13. Ibid., 110.
14. *CW,* XVI, 172.

Bibliography

Chesterton Works Cited in Text

The Collected Works of G. K. Chesterton. San Francisco: Ignatius Press, 1986 to Present

The Autobiography, XVI, [1936] 1988.
The Catholic Church and Conversion, III, [1927] 1990.
Chaucer, XVIII, [1932], 1991.
Chesterton on Dickens, XV, [1906] 1989.
Eugenics and Other Evils, IV, [1922] 1987.
The Everlasting Man, II, [1925] 1986.
Heretics, I, [1905] 1986.
The Illustrated London News.
    1905–1907, XXVII, 1986.
    1908–1910, XXVIII, 1987.
    1911–1913, XXIX, 1988.
    1914–1916, XXX, 1988.
    1920–1922, XXXII, 1989.
    1923–1925, XXXIII, 1990.
    1926–1928, XXXIV, 1991.
    1929–1931, XXXV, 1991.
Leo Tolstoy, XVIII, [1903] 1991.
Orthodoxy, I, [1908] 1986.
The Outline of Sanity, V, [1926] 1993.
Robert Louis Stevenson, XVIII, [1927] 1991.
St. Francis of Assisi, II, [1923] 1986.
St. Thomas Aquinas, II, [1933] 1986.
The Thing: Why I Am a Catholic, III, [1929] 1990.
The Well and the Shallows, III, [1935] 1990.
Thomas Carlyle, XVIII, [1902] 1991.
What's Wrong with the World, IV, [1910] 1987.

Individual Books of G. K. Chesterton

The Ballad of the White Horse. Edited by Bernadette Sheridan. Detroit: Marygrove College Press, [1911] 1993.
The Defendant, London: Dent, [1905] 1914.

The Father Brown Omnibus. New York: Dodd, Mead, 1951.

G. F. Watts. London: Duckworth, 1904.

The Man Who Was Thursday. Harmondsworth, England: Penguin, [1908] 1986.

The Spirit of Christmas: Stories, Poems, Essays. Selected and Annotated by Marie Smith. New York: Dodd, Mead, 1985.

The Victorian Age in English Literature. New York: Holt, 1913.

Anthologies

As I Was Saying: A Chesterton Reader. Edited by Robert Knille. Grand Rapids, Mich.: Eerdmans, 1985.

A Chesterton Anthology. Selected and Edited by P. J. Kavanagh. San Francisco: Ignatius Press. [London: The Bodley Head, 1985].

The Common Man: Essays, Articles, and Introductions, 1901–1936. New York: Sheed & Ward, 1950.

Daylight and Nightmare: Uncollected Stories and Fables. Selected and Arranged by Marie Smith. New York: Dodd, Mead, 1986.

G.K.C. as M.C.: Being a Collection of Thirty-Seven Introductions. Selected and edited by J. P. de Fonseka. London: Methuen, 1928.

G. K. Chesterton: A Half Century of Views. Edited by D. J. Conlon. Oxford: Oxford University Press, 1987.

More Quotable Chesterton. Edited by George J. Marlin, Richard P. Rabatin, John L. Swan. San Francisco: Ignatius Press, 1988.

The Quotable Chesterton. Edited by George J. Marlin, Richard P. Rabatin, John L. Swan. San Francisco: Ignatius Press, 1986.

Secondary Sources

Arnhart, Larry. *Aristotle on Political Reasoning.* DeKalb: Northern Illinois University Press, 1986.

Auden, W. H. "Chesterton's Non-Fictional Prose." In *G. K. Chesterton: A Half-Century of Views,* edited by D. J. Conlon. Oxford: Oxford University Press, 1987.

Belloc, Hilaire. "Gilbert Keith Chesterton." *The Saturday Review of Literature* 10 (July 4, 1936): 3–4.

———. "The Death of Chateaubriand." *In Miniatures of French History.* LaSalle, Ill.: Sherwood Sugden, 1990.

Bloom, Allan. *The Closing of the American Mind.* New York: Simon and Schuster, 1987.

Boswell, James. *London Journal: 1762–1763.* New York: McGraw-Hill, 1950.

———. *Boswell's Life of Johnson.* Vol. I. London: Oxford University Press, 1931.

Carroll, John. *Humanism: The Wreck of Western Culture.* London: Fontana, 1993.

Catholic World Report (February 1994): 18–19.

Coren, Michael. *Gilbert: The Man Who Was Chesterton*. New York: Paragon House, 1990.

D'Arcy, Martin C. *Laughter and the Love of Friends: Reminiscences of the Distinguished English Priest and Philosopher, Martin Cyril D'Arcy.* Westminster, Md.: Christian Classics, 1991.

Derrick, Christopher. *Joy Without a Cause.* LaSalle, Ill.: Sherwood Sugden, 1979.

Dickens, Charles. *The Pickwick Papers: The Posthumous Papers of the Pickwick Club.* New York: Washington Square, 1960.

Dorsett, Lyle W., ed. *G.K.'s Weekly: A Sampler.* Chicago: Loyola University Press, 1986.

Ffinch, Michael. *G. K. Chesterton.* London: Weidenfeld & Nicolson, 1986.

Furlong, William B. *Shaw and Chesterton: The Metaphysical Jesters.* University Park: The Pennsylvania State University Press, 1970.

Jaki, Stanley L. *Chesterton: A Seer of Science.* Urbana and Chicago: University of Illinois Press, 1986.

Johnson, Paul. *The Portable Paul Johnson.* Edited by George Marlin, Richard Rabatin, and Heather Richardson Higgins. New York: The Noonday Press, 1994.

Kirk, Russell. *The Wise Men Know What Wicked Things Are Written on the Sky.* Washington: Regnery Gateway, 1987.

———. "Notes by Humpty Dumpty." *University Bookman* 35 (Summer 1995): 35–38.

Lewis, C. S. *Surprised by Joy.* New York: Harvest, 1955.

Massie, Allan. "The Master Writer beneath the Card." In *G. K. Chesterton: A Half Century of Views,* edited by D. J. Conlon. Oxford: Oxford University Press, 1987.

Midwest Chesterton News, vols. 1–9, 1989–97. Continues as *Gilbert!*

Milward, Peter. "G. K. Chesterton's Faith and Journalism." *The Chesterton Review* VII (1981): 348.

Orr, Susan. *Jerusalem and Athens: Reason and Revelation in the Works of Leo Strauss.* Lanham, Md.: Rowman & Littlefield, 1995.

Pearce, Joseph. *Wisdom and Innocence: A Life of G. K. Chesterton.* San Francisco: Ignatius Press, 1996.

Pieper, Josef. *Josef Pieper—An Anthology.* San Francisco: Ignatius Press, 1989.

Rapp, Dean R. "G. K. Chesterton's Criticism of Psychoanalysis." *The Chesterton Review* XV (August 1989): 341–54.

Ratzinger, Josef Cardinal. *"In the Beginning": A Catholic Understanding of the Story of Creation.* Huntington, Ind.: Our Sunday Visitor Press, 1990.

Schall, James V., S.J. *The Praise of "Sons of Bitches": On the Worship of God by Fallen Men.* Slough, England: St. Paul Publications, 1978.

———. *Another Sort of Learning.* San Francisco: Ignatius Press, 1988.

———. *Idylls and Rambles: Lighter Christian Essays.* San Francisco: Ignatius Press, 1994.

————. "On the Mystery of Teachers I Never Met." *Modern Age* 37 (1995): 366–73.

————. *A Student's Guide to Liberal Learning.* Wilmington, Del.: Intercollegiate Studies Institute, 1997.

Spaight, Robert. *The Life of Hilaire Belloc.* New York: Farrar, Straus & Cudahy, 1957.

Strauss, Leo. "Progress or Return?" In *The Rebirth of Classical Political Rationalism,* 227–70. Chicago: University of Chicago Press, 1989.

Ward, Maisie. *Gilbert Keith Chesterton.* New York: Sheed & Ward, 1944.

Wilder, Thornton. "The Matchmaker." *In Three Plays.* New York: Harper Perennial, 1985.

Wilson, A. N. *Hilaire Belloc: A Biography.* New York: Atheneum, 1984.

Wren-Lewis, John. "Adam, Eve, and Agatha Christie." *The Chesterton Review* XIX (May 1993): 193–200.

Index

Schall on Chesterton was designed and composed in Bembo by Kachergis Book Design of Pittsboro, North Carolina; and printed on 60-pound Writers Natural and bound by McNaughton & Gunn, Inc., Saline, Michigan.

BAKER & TAYLOR